CHINA'S SEARCH FOR PLENTY
The Economics of Mao Tse-tung

To Rose Yin-chee

Leo Goodstadt

China's Search for Plenty
The Economics of Mao Tse-tung

WEATHERHILL
New York & Tokyo

First edition, 1973

Published in the United States, Canada, and Japan by
John Weatherhill, Inc., 149 Madison Avenue,
New York, N.Y. 10016, with editorial offices at
7-6-13 Roppongi, Minato-ku, Tokyo 106;
by arrangement with Longman Group (Far East) Limited.

Printed in Hong Kong and bound in Japan.

LC 72-84112
ISBN 0-8348-0075-6

The Longman edition of this book
was published in 1972 under the title
Mao Tse-tung, The Search for Plenty.

Contents

Abbreviations

SW	*Selected Works of Mao Tse-tung* (1967 edition), Volumes I to IV.
SR	*Selected Readings from the Works of Mao Tse-tung* (1967).
MW	*Selected Military Writings of Mao Tse-tung* (1968).
SU	*Socialist Upsurge in China's Countryside* (1957).
PE	*Mao Tse-tung: Four Essays on Philosophy* (1968).
PW	*Mao Tse-tung: Speech at the Chinese Communist Party's National Conference on Propaganda Work* (1967).
AC	*Mao Tse-tung: On the Question of Agricultural Co-operation* (1966).
Quotations	*Quotations from Chairman Mao Tse-tung* (1966).
ID	*Important Documents on the Great Proletarian Cultural Revolution in China* (1970).
GSCR	*The Great Socialist Cultural Revolution in China* (1966), a series numbered (1), (2), etc.

(All the above published by the Foreign Languages Press, Peking.)

LL	"Long Live Mao Tse-tung Thought", *Current Background*, No. 891, 8 October 1969. (Translation modified.)
CS	"Collection of Statements by Mao Tse-tung (1956-1967)", *Current Background*, No. 892, 21 October 1969. (Translation modified.)
NCNA	*New China News Agency*.
PD	*People's Daily*.
KMD	*Kuang-ming Daily*.
TKP	*Ta-kung Pao*.
RF	*Hung Chi* (Red Flag Journal.)
ER	*Ching-chi Yen-chiu* (Economic Research.)

ABBREVIATIONS

RS   Radio Service: unless otherwise identified, refers to a report broadcast by the radio station of the province or city mentioned in the preceding sentence.

CC   *Communist China 1955-1959: Policy Documents with Analysis* (Harvard University Press: Cambridge, 1965).

Chinese Titles of Newspapers and Journals:

Ta-kung Pao	a Peking daily newspaper
Wen-hui Pao	a Shanghai daily newspaper
Che-hsueh Yen-chiu	Philosophical Research
Chiao-wu Pao	Overseas Chinese Affairs
Chiao Shih Pao	Teachers News
Chung-kuo Chin-jung	China Finance
Chung-kuo Ching-kung-yeh	China Light Industry
Chung-kuo Ching-nien	China Youth
Chung-kuo Ching-nien Pao	China Youth News
Chung-kuo Nung-pao	China Agricultural News
Hsin Chien-she	New Construction
Li-lun Hsueh-hsi	Theoretical Studies
Nung-tsun Chin-jung	Rural Finance
Nung-yeh Chi-shu	Agricultural Techniques
Nung-yeh Chi-chieh Chi-shu	Agricultural Machinery Techniques
Tsai-cheng	Finance
Shih-shih Shou-tse	Current Events
Tsai-ching Yen-chiu	Financial and Economic Research
Wen-yi Pao	Literary News

The reader will note that I have followed the somewhat unconventional practice of placing reference notes within parentheses in the text itself rather than at the bottom of the page. Once one becomes used to this system, however, I believe it will be found much less distracting than would a large number of short footnotes.

Acknowledgements

In the autumn of 1966, when Peking was in turmoil after Mao Tse-tung's mobilisation of the Red Guards, Dr. Han Suyin returned from China with a host of personal impressions of the new political upsurge. Derek Davies, editor of the *Far Eastern Economic Review,* allowed me to sit in on his interview with Dr. Han. In the middle of her description of the turbulent political scene in the Chinese capital, she narrated a fascinating discussion she had held with one of China's foremost economists. He had taken the trouble to interpret Mao's economic policies not only in the language of orthodox Chinese communism but also in the terminology of Western economists. Dr. Han's account of her conversation suggested it might be worthwhile trying to translate Mao Tse-tung's development programme into Western terms and to see how his thinking compared with the attitudes and experience of non-communist economists interested in the under-developed world.

In 1970, the *Review* had another visitor who is also a distinguished student of China, Mr Jack Gray. While listening to his analysis of Mao's economics, I was emboldened to make a serious effort to tackle the development stragegy of China's leader from a Western standpoint. I am indebted to Mr Gray for his encouragement on that and subsequent occasions to devote special attention to Mao as an economist. (My debt to him can be seen quite readily from the paper he published on Chinese development techniques in *Selected Seminar Papers on Contemporary China, 1.*)

I have enjoyed invaluable assistance in preparing this book from a great number of people from many countries. Fellow journalists, academics, businessmen, officials and diplomats from most parts of Asia, the two halves of Europe, North America and China itself have freely given me information, ideas and criticism. These favours were not offered to me personally but rather to the *Review.* It is a pleasure to record my thanks to Derek Davies not only for his friendship but also for establishing a reputation of integrity for his magazine which encourages its readers from a host of nationalities and a variety of political convictions to talk with such frankness to members of his staff.

I am also grateful to my editor for the working atmosphere within the *Review*. So many of my colleagues in all sections of the organisation have helped me that I could not list them all. However, I must express my gratitude to Bob Hawkins for his constant help, and I am indebted to Rosemary Righter for her efforts to straighten out my logic and my prose. The *Review's* 'China-watchers' over the years have taught me an immense amount. John Gittings, Colina MacDougall and, in particular, Harald Munthe-Kaas have allowed me to pick their brains quite ruthlessly — though they have no responsibility for the views I express in this book.

My wife and her mother have taken great care of me, going far beyond the demands of traditional Chinese family virtue! They have both tried hard to help me to understand Chinese society and culture and provided me with a large Chinese family and a vast circle of friends whose tolerance I have abused shamefully by breaking the Hongkong taboo on discussing politics. I owe a special debt for sound advice and a wealth of information to my 'Sincere Uncle'.

I apologise to one group of friends who are termed 'Chinese communists' in this book. They will rightly object that this term is a technical one, referring to members of the Chinese Communist Party, a formal status most of them do not have. However, I use the term in deference to their desire for anonymity and because the phrase to ordinary Westerners means no more than those who are supporters of the People's Republic. These friends have been invaluable in discussing my ideas and correcting errors of fact and interpretation of ideology.

Their assistance has ranged from points of minor detail to the authentication of two collections of Mao's writings I have drawn on heavily as more than unofficial Red Guard publications. (I would have used them in any case once Jerome Ch'en had vouched for them in *Mao Papers* but it was good to have their standing confirmed by people who belong to Peking-owned or -controlled organisations.) These friends also solved the problem of which version of Mao to use. I have taken their advice that since the Chairman's works are supposed to be programmes for action, the latest official editions are the ones which count, no matter how Mao's original pronouncements have been edited, amended, cut or expanded.

I must also thank Mrs. W.R. Norman for taking the trouble to go through the manuscript in a bid to spot as many of my infelicities of style as she could.

Prologue

A mere forty years ago, China was the helpless prey of foreign nations. American, British, Japanese and Italian gunboats could unite with impunity in the destruction of a Chinese city through a bombardment merciless in its disregard for civilian life. Wanton sadism was the response of China's government to a discontented peasantry during the same period, with thousands upon thousands condemned to die in whatever agonies perverted minds could devise. (Harold R. Issacs, *The Tragedy of the Chinese Revolution,* 227, 235, 296, 332.) Today, China can boast of successful satellite launchings after Western Europe's combined efforts to produce a space rocket ended in expensive flops in the Australian outback. Unlike most underdeveloped countries, China makes no appeals for foreign aid, pays its way in world trade and has begun to complain of a serious labour shortage.

The new China became so self-confident that its founder, Mao Tsc-tung, felt no compulsion to delete from his writings statements which he later contradicted with considerable vehemence. Such remarks, for instance, as the necessity 'to create terror for a while' and 'we have too little of capitalism' still stand in his official works, although both policies were repudiated utterly over the years. (SW I, 29; PW, 4; SW II, 353; III, 233; IV, 374.) With the exception of Liu Shao-chi, head of state from 1959 till his disgrace at the hands of the Red Guards, the host of leaders ousted during the Cultural Revolution which exploded in 1966 retained their claim to a place in history through Mao's continued acknowledgement in his essays of their role in his war to free China from foreign domination and the corrupt rule of Chiang Kai-shek's Kuomintang party. Even a commentator as caustic as Arthur A. Cohen admits Mao never employed Stalin's ruthless extermination of all political opposition. (*The Communism of Mao Tse-tung,* 193-98.)

Any nation which could change so dramatically in such a brief

1

period deserves assiduous study by a world concerned to eradicate international poverty and win true self-respect for the nations which have become independent since World War II. Unfortunately, Mao Tse-tung's strategy for the establishment of a modern industrial society has been barely mentioned by most analysts of China's economic record since Mao came to power. The handful who have resisted the fashionable approach of measuring statistically the function and performance of various sectors of the Chinese economy and have chosen instead to study Mao's formula for creating a prosperous industrialised society, have tended to be evangelists bent on extolling the virtues of the new China. This group's emotional sympathy for Maoism over-shadows the even tinier band with a more objective interest in the weapons Mao Tse-tung used to generate progress in the bankrupt and impoverished nation he inherited in 1949.

The task of laying bare Mao's ideas on the ingredients required to make China the equal of any other nation is frustrating. Mao Tse-tung is the colossus of modern China, and his influence on national policies grew to an enormous degree after the dismissal of all those suspected of deviations from his line during the Cultural Revolution. But the emergence of a modern community, for which manufacturing is the prime source of material well-being, from a primitive peasant community crippled by war, invasion, corrupt administration, superstition and disease is not to be wrought by a computer manipulated with mathematical economics. Political and social changes are needed to fertilise the seeds of an industrial revolution. Mao's economic thinking was set in a complex equation of prescriptions for China's total transformation. Mao elaborated this programme during four decades of political activity (though his supporters have quoted his works as a visionary blueprint without regard for the historical background of individual essays.)

Quite properly, economists are chary of over-extending themselves. To unravel the logic of a development philosophy conceived on Mao's sweeping scale demands an impossible familiarity with the whole field of social science. The economist has to exchange the safety of his professional expertise for a dilletantist review of ideological, social and cultural factors affecting economic progress. This dilemma is not new in economic science. Adam Smith and John Maynard Keynes, for example, took highly partisan stands on the proper ordering of life. But most economists prefer the cold calculus of economic abstractions to an assessment of the qualitative performance of their communities.

Alfred Marshall, a giant in English economics, took the largest question to be: 'Whether it is really impossible that all should start in the world with a fair chance of leading a cultured life, free from the pains of poverty and the stagnating influences of excessive mechanical toil.' This sentence sums up the aims of economic development. Marshall realised the answer depended 'partly on the moral and political capabilities of human nature' but he pushed these considerations aside as beyond his competence. (*Elements of Economics of Industry*, 4.) One of his foremost successors, A.C. Pigou, felt free to disclaim responsibility for prescribing policies although he was writing in 1928, the mid-point of one of the worst slumps his country had ever experienced. (*The Economics of Welfare*, 5.)

The luxury of neglecting those factors which cannot be assessed in hard cash is no longer possible for several reasons. I.M.D. Little has shown that discussion of economic welfare must involve an inquiry into value judgments. From his argument, it follows that analysis of controlled programmes of development must include more than a review of flows of goods and services measured in money. (*A Critique of Welfare Economics*, chapters I, V, XIV.) The goals set for society may be moral, political or strategic rather than financial. Again, economics by itself solves few problems. Thus West Germany and Britain have access to precisely the same economic theories and have similar economic systems. But their postwar performance has been markedly different for all the efforts of the British government to restore the country's fortunes. In poor countries, the situation is even more serious. Enough theories have been elaborated to show how plenty can replace misery if a nation operates as economists assume in their models. Yet international poverty persists. To be ruled by a communist party adds a new dimension. W. Keizer describes how under communism, economics is integrated with great firmness into a political system which seeks control over all aspects of life. (*The Soviet Quest for Economic Rationality*, 12.) Happily, Cyril S. Belshaw's *Conditions of Social Performance* demonstrates how the various branches of social science can be exploited within the framework of conventional economics and, more important, how this synthesis makes it possible for economists to analyse societies where the basic motivation is neither profits nor incomes, which are generally regarded as the mainsprings of Western economic activity.

Whatever the risks of seeming clumsy or shallow, an economist concerned with the validity of China's economic policies cannot disdain the social and political influences on the country's economic health. Mao Tse-tung did not map out the path to prosperity in narrow economic terms. Indeed, he would have been grievously wrong not to have taken account of every aspect of human behaviour related to growth. Study of China during Mao's rule cannot logically leave out Mao Tse-tung's own very broad terms of reference.

Nevertheless, recognition of the overall framework in which China has sought national development does not imply that Mao's ethics have to be examined. His blunt assertion that nuclear weapons had to wait upon general industrial advance showed a proper sense of priorities. (CS, 25.) Had he chosen to bleed the country dry and put atom bombs before hungry peasants, it would have been for the Chinese themselves to condemn him. All government decisions involve suffering for some individuals — hopefully for the greater good of the majority. Western government knows restrictions on funds devoted to medical services mean some people will die who could have been kept alive by artificial kidneys, for example. The budget for a police force is a calculation, in effect, of how much undeterred or undetected crime a public can tolerate. Such choices are even more distressing for an underdeveloped nation which counts itself lucky to feed and find work for all its citizens. The temptation for the outsider to moralise is strong, however, when a country embarks on the hazardous undertakings promoted during China's 1958 Great Leap Forward and the 1966 Cultural Revolution. The Great Leap, with its communes sprouting backyard furnaces which took peasants away from the fields for primitive industrial activities which produced practically no return, was a colossal waste. Hunger and a complete halt in economic momentum were the results. Similarly, the Cultural Revolution overturned the nation's administrative system; anarchy reigned in factories; violence flared in the cities; and utter chaos followed the Red Guards. As will be shown, the minister of defence in 1959 stated the country had cause enough to mount a revolution his troops could not have put down. Similarly in the Cultural Revolution, confusion was so complete that a national rebellion could have succeeded. China declined to overthrow Mao Tse-tung, and the country's tolerance of these events is a more accurate gauge of Mao's worth than a foreigner's judgement.

The key issue is what promise of a new and better life Mao could give his people after defeating the Kuomintang. From 1949 to 1955 he made the mistake of imitating the Soviet Union, although he well knew the Russian experience was not relevant to China. (Compare

Christopher Howe, *Employment and Economic Growth in Urban China 1949-1957,* 21; 108.) Mao then spent three years building development techniques out of the ideology born from his guerrilla days. But by the end of 1958, Mao was no longer head of state. Not until 1966 was he in a position to make a bid for complete control of the nation's economic destinies once more. The period in which pure Maoist economics prevailed did not start until 1969. Although ideologically without rivals in China after 1949, Mao's opportunity to apply his ideas on how to construct a modern nation through detailed policies was extremely limited.

Sufficient time has elapsed since the worst upheavals of the Cultural Revolution to be able to make an initial test of the logic of his approach, both from the standpoint of economic theory and from its practical results. These topics are discussed with only as much detailed reference to events in the first twenty years of China's communist government as is needed to set Mao's economics in context. To try to simplify the account of Mao's economic thinking and its application to the changing face of China, a story which covers an extensive timespan and continual shifts in national policies, each chapter has been made as self-contained as possible. This technique breaks the flow of narrative, irritatingly perhaps, but allows each phase of Mao's effort to remould his country's economy to be summarised as neatly as possible without waiting till the final chapter to draw all the threads together.

The story of Mao Tse-tung's attempt to create a new social and economic order in China became a moving drama in which disappointments and rebuffs created overtones of tragedy. He fashioned a concept of man's ability to master his environment and escape from the feudalism and superstition which had kept the nation in pawn to destitution for so long. His vision should have fired China's imagination. He realised, however, that China would accept his dreams for its future very slowly. He prophesied that his defeat of Chiang Kai-shek 'viewed in retrospect, will seem like only a brief prologue to a long drama'. (SW IV, 374.) In 1959, he forecast that the system he wished China to adopt would involve a struggle of 'at least twenty years and possibly half a century'. (RF, 13/1967.) Yet in practice, he seemed always over-optimistic about the chances of smashing the social and cultural forces opposing the radical reforms he viewed as essential to China's modernisation. His gradualist policies during the 1950s allowed traditional social institutions to recover from the shattering blows of the Japanese invasion, the campaign against the Kuomintang and the massive postwar collapse of the economy. The violent eruption of the Cultural Revolution seemed to strike a death blow at the attitudes and customs inherited from the past. But these old habits reappeared as anarchy spread across the country and were found flourishing again when Peking began to add up the results of the political convulsions which the Red Guards initiated in 1966.

Mao Tse-tung's views on economics have much to commend them. But what was his guarantee that the next generation of leaders would possess the iron will and patient sense of mission which Mao had displayed in fighting for his ideals? The odds are that the final heirs to Mao Tse-tung will espouse an easier life in which they do not have to battle against the basic instincts of their people. Maoism will then be diluted and must lose its force. Mao's philosophy allows no room for compromises, not because it was constructed as an inflexible logical edifice but because, in its creation, Mao Tse-tung had made all the concessions possible to the legacy of the past and the realities of the present if he was to work out a dream for the future.

Chapter One
'The Foolish Old Man'

The dreams of China and the minds of its 700 million citizens are shrouded in dense layers of prejudice and stereotype, some invented by the Chinese themselves, the rest outgrowths of the bias afflicting so many observers of a nation too proud to instruct mankind in its ways. China surrounds itself with conflicting images. A country once emasculated and mute, today emancipated but mad; a society formerly inhabited by fatalists, now captured by fanatics? Or China, once fettered by feudalism, now free to deride the superpowers and their miracles of military technology? A people formerly enslaved by poverty, today exploited no more but rising triumphantly from the ashes of towns and cities pillaged and put to the sword for a century by warlords and foreign armies until finally engulfed in the barbarism of the Japanese empire?

Those seduced by the splendours of China past forget the degrading misery whose pressure on a resourceless peasantry intensified from one generation to the next. Admirers of China present overlook the struggle waged unceasingly by one man over the last two decades to wipe out the ills he believed still burdened his people. This man, Mao Tse-tung, lacked the confidence of those who look forward to the future China as a society which will evade the trap of crass materialism which, in the eyes of so many, has undermined Western civilisation. 'Revisionism', the desire for ease and comfort without regard for either national or international social justice, was a temptation which tugged constantly, this man believed, at his people's hearts.

And what of China's future? Will Mao Tse-tung's belief in the power of the human will to conquer every obstacle and in man's capacity to find reward in moral as well as material accomplishments die with him? Will his 'Thoughts' become one more set of aphorisms the Chinese child memorises by rote as Sun Yat-sen's Testament was before the communists or, earlier still, the doctrines of Confucius? If

7

Maoism becomes just another addition to the roster of Chinese wisdom, the world may worry indeed about its fate when China has not merely 'stood up' as Mao put it, but flexes all the muscle which economic progress ultimately must bring to a massive and sophisticated people. Mao Tse-tung has described himself as a believer in man's essential goodness. If his optimism is well founded, the Chinese may accomplish the feat of absorbing modern technology without discarding the virtues and civilised standards they have honoured for so long.

To discuss China in the 1970s from most foreign standpoints is to abandon objectivity almost entirely. For the Japanese, China means guilt; for Indians, fear and rivalry; for the Russians, growing uneasiness; for the Americans, sad confusion. The Chinese are so large a part of recorded human history, possess so strong a culture and are so numerically overwhelming that the customary terms for summing up the characteristics and development of other countries seem too puny to encompass the Chinese panorama. Behind the anonymity which comes from being merely one cog in a machine of 750 million parts, the ordinary Chinese is repeating the experiences of many other parts of the world. His rulers are forced to find solutions for problems little different from those which have beset other governments. Only the scale is different.

Chinese resent any outsider's description of their life which makes them seem less than unique. Foreigners, both those opposed to the People's Republic and its sympathisers, have their own reasons for refusing to compare China with other lands. Analogies between China and the rest of the world make the average Chinese feel his cultural inheritance of such magnificence is impugned. Those hostile to Peking prefer not to see China classified as anything but a communist horde poised to enslave Asia, if not the world at large. Those who come to Peking's defence often feel drawn emotionally to a human experiment they want to believe is unprecedented. Nevertheless, since China is ruled by rational men, anxious to live free from a heritage of hunger and humiliation, its path inevitably criss-crosses that followed by nations who have already broken away from penury.

Over modern China, a lone figure cast a shadow, Mao Tse-tung, a rich peasant's son who personified the new nation. Although his troops marched into Peking in 1949, self-confident, disciplined soldiers and not the ragged rabble mustered into its previous national armies, Mao's real reign began some six years later. Only in 1955 was he able to begin the task of shaping the destiny of his countrymen according to his blend of

Chinese culture and imported marxism. In the following decade and a half, the obstacles to progress hardly changed, and his remedies altered only in their emphasis. Relentlessly, he pounded away at the 'mountain of feudalism', as he expressed it — at every trait which prevented the Chinese from breaking with the fatalism of the past and fighting for a different kind of future.

But a nation which suffered foreign domination centuries before the Europeans saw China as a prize worth despoiling, absorbs the shocks of strange philosophies and new political powers by bending rather than breaking. Mao had to undertake the task of preventing his nation from bowing before the force of the prevailing political tempest only to spring up undamaged when the storm had passed. He had to smash those very institutions which had enabled Chinese society to emerge from so many foreign whirlwinds intact and relatively un-scathed. He was battling against the people's most basic instincts for social survival. From the disastrous experiment of the 1958 Great Leap Forward when China vowed to catch up with Britain in a single bound but collapsed in three years of near-famine, Mao's struggle continued into the Cultural Revolution of 1966, when an awed world watched a pantheon of Chinese communist heroes topple because their ideas had not kept pace with the China represented by their old comrade in arms, Mao Tse-tung.

The lag between victory and the work of preparing China for its economic and ideological transformation may prove, in the long run, to have been Mao Tse-tung's greatest miscalculation. His reasons for moving so cautiously in the first years of his triumph were sound enough. The country had been devastated by almost two decades of war. An incredible inflation had halted all normal business. The outbreak of the Korean War, mounting American hostility towards the People's Republic and the intervention of Chinese soldiers in Korea called for a broad patriotic front within the country.

The need for national unity was not solely a question of healing the legacy of vicious conflict between the communists and the Kuomintang, and the latter fled to Taiwan. The regiments Mao Tse-tung assembled for his final blows in the civil war contained high proportions of captured Kuomintang troops who had been persuaded to switch their allegiance. These armies were the main military force at Mao's disposal when the Chinese swept across the Yalu river into Korea, driving the Americans and their allies back to the south. (Alexander L. George, *The Chinese Communist Army in Action,* 5-6.) In Mao's view

9

the crisis of war, and the fear in Peking of the United States' ability to retaliate directly against its cities, made draconian measures to instil communism into the people singularly inappropriate.

He was considerably alarmed too by the communist party's lack of experience in national administration as ultimate victory loomed larger. Although many observers believe Mao looked back to his guerrilla days as the ideal model for his new government, Mao Tse-tung's own statements reveal a less confident attitude. He recognised the paramount importance of postwar industrial and agricultural reconstruction, the shortage of skilled personnel and the need to absorb into the ranks of the government anyone with professional or technical qualifications. In 1944, Mao had urged: 'We must learn how to administer the industry, commerce and communications of big cities, or otherwise we shall not know what to do when the time comes.' (SW III, 172.)

The shortage of reliable and competent administrators grew more desperate as the communist advance developed in 1949. Mao put the problem squarely: 'As compared with urban work, rural work is easy to learn... We are preparing to send 53,000 cadres south with the army but this is a very small number. The occupation of eight or nine provinces and scores of big cities will require a huge number of working cadres, and to solve this problem the army must rely chiefly on itself. The army is a school ... We have to rely chiefly on the army to supply our working cadres.' (MW, 394.)

In the previous year, Mao had decreed the communist party was to employ all available talent, regardless of the individual's political background. (SW IV, 271, 274-75.) He summed up the tasks facing the communists at this time as restoring farm and factory production; controlling markets and communications; overcoming the serious shortage of supplies; and ending inflation. All these demanded considerable expertise. 'Production and construction' were to take priority over all other work, including consolidation of political power by the communist party. While state industry was to enjoy pride of place, capitalist enterprises were recognised as vital. The grave emergency facing the communists as they rolled across the country can be seen from Mao's command in mid-1949: 'We must overcome difficulties, we must learn what we do not know. We must learn to do economic work from all who know how, no matter who they are. We must esteem them as teachers, learning from them respectfully and conscientiously ... If we dig into a subject for several months, for a year ... or five years, we shall eventually master it.' (SW IV, 423.) Eventually, Mao's least optimistic estimate, five years, of the time required to learn how to direct China on lines both communist and Chinese proved to be the most accurate.

The costs of this policy of expediency proved considerable. The communist government found itself employing large numbers of individuals purely for their technical knowledge. The party had to work through officials, factory managers and businessmen with little natural taste for communism. They had not been purified through war and revolution which, before 1949, cleansed the minds of communist recruits from the bourgeoisie. Initially, the watering-down of the communist administration with an educated élite whose long-run personal prospects could only suffer from Mao's triumph was of small importance. The capture of Peking and the final rout of Chiang Kai-shek's forces in the south received a welcome verging on the euphoric. China was at last rid of decades of civil strife. The communist reputation was good, thanks to the rigid discipline demanded of the communist troops in handling civilians, contrary to the normal rape-and-pillage motto of Chinese soldiery. Mao Tse-tung offered a hope of the strong government and national independence most Chinese had longed for during a century and more of anarchy and foreign exploitation. In any case, rampant inflation and the havoc wreaked by the Japanese and civil wars had brought the middle classes, now mobilised to help administer the country, to the edge of ruin.

At this moment of enormous relief among the population and of immense prestige for the communist party, Mao Tse-tung was dealing with a shattered society. He could have introduced his own brand of communism quickly, counting on the tide of popularity running in his favour to make reforms acceptable to almost all classes, however radical his programme. He could have acted as the Russians did in their newly-acquired East European satellites after the war. If he had prevented the middle classes, whose prosperity had been undermined by war and inflation, from rising once more above the economic level of the common man, their discontent could have been averted by pointing to the ruined economy the communists had inherited. If Mao had been less anxious to build up an elaborate bureaucracy, the country could have kept going only through military rule. But the people would have understood the difficulty of finding idealistic, incorruptible civil servants overnight and accepted the necessity for a form of martial law. This approach would have been doubly palatable as the troops were under constant instruction to establish a good reputation and assist civilians, in obedience to Mao's belief that the army must belong to the people. (SW III, 214-15; IV, 273.) And it would have enabled the new administration to pick and train future officials with care, selecting cadres for their dedication to Mao's ideals.

The political dangers of concentrating on short-term problems, and these undoubtedly were of the most urgent nature, emerged almost immediately. Mao had to sort out party members who favoured giving the capitalist sector of the economy a completely free hand. (SW IV, 364.) The trouble was that Mao himself was facing in two directions. He called for 'a blanket policy of protection' for the economic interests of the middle classes, mainly because he wanted the allegiance of the 'enlightened gentry' and the intellectuals. (*ibid.*, 209-10.) In the countryside, his goal was equally moderate: 'The target of the land reform is only and must be the system of feudal exploitation by the landlord class and the old-type rich peasants, and there should be no encroachment either upon the national bourgeoisie or upon the industrial and commercial enterprises run by the landlords and rich peasants.' Absolute egalitarianism was denounced. (*ibid.*, 236.) However, Mao had also to direct: 'It is entirely wrong to think that at present we need not restrict capitalism and can discard the slogan of "regulation of capital".' (*ibid.*, 368.) Mao's conflicting demands were to cause him grave trouble for twenty years.

The capitalist sector revived with direct encouragement from the party. The Chinese communists lacked the Russian stomach for ruthless extermination of all who belonged to the 'exploiting' classes. Mao repudiated the executions of landlords and other members of the classes which had battened on rural poverty. (SW IV, 185-86.) In 1957, he ordered an enquiry into past excesses in dealing with the party's opponents. (PE, 98-99.) Consequently, once the economy had recovered substantially from war and inflation, a gradualist programme for abolishing capitalism was adopted which minimised disruption of management and output. In 1954, joint state-private ownership was begun on a national scale, leading to complete state control in 1958. This strategy (recounted in *The Socialist Transformation of the National Economy in China*, 183, 209-11, 217-26) was justified ideologically by a quotation from Lenin. He allowed for 'buying off the cultured capitalists who agree with state capitalism, who are capable of putting it into practice and who are useful to the proletariat as clever and experienced organisers of the largest types of enterprises'. The former owners were compensated with state bonds on which interest continued to be paid until the 1966 Cultural Revolution. Agriculture followed a similarly careful path. In his 'Report on the Question of Agrarian Reform' in June 1950, Liu Shao-chi, head of state from 1959 till overwhelmed by Red Guard criticism, called for the preservation of the rich peasants. Liu explained that the former policy of expropriating this class had been reversed because of the needs of the national economy. The process of bringing to an end individual peasant farming limped along until the 'mutual-aid teams' started on a large scale in 1953. (*Socialist Industrialization and Agricultural Collectivization*, 28-29.) Rural co-operatives came into fashion in 1955. The final step towards farming on a collective basis only began with the communes in 1958.

Significantly, Liu Shao-chi was attacked most savagely by the Red Guards for statements of support for capitalist producers. That China had adopted deliberately at the highest level a programme designed to make the transition to socialist ownership as painless and unopposed as possible was no defence. (SW IV, 168.) By 1966, the seeds of ideological heresy sown when private enterprise was still encouraged had borne bitter fruit in Mao Tse-tung's judgement. China had almost lost its faith in the austere socialist ethic which he deemed was the nation's only hope of avoiding the Soviet 'revisionist' betrayal of the true marxist gospel.

From Mao's point of view, the greatest evil of the initial compromise with rural and urban capitalism lay almost certainly in the demoralisation of the cadres and the consequent lack of enthusiasm for socialism among the masses. Communist officials had been prevented from enjoying the full fruits of their victory which collectivisation of agriculture and nationalisation of industry would have provided. Instead, they had been forced to pamper the rich, sacrificing marxist dreams to Maoist pragmatism. The situation frustrated Mao's attempts to transform the peasantry, the bulk of the population. Mao Tse-tung complained bitterly of the party's failure to back the rural co-operatives, denouncing not just the local branches but the 'higher authorities' as well. He lamented: 'Rural party branches in quite a number of places show this spineless attitude towards agricultural co-operation. Not only the party branches – it is possible that even some of the higher committees of the party do the same. This is the crux of the problem.' (SU, 138, 151, 206.) The typical cadre's low quality and poor motivation remained a permanent headache for Mao.

He was still reasonably hopeful about the overall situation, even to the point of almost reversing his long-held belief that a constant battle would have to be waged against the reactionaries' plots to stage a comeback. (Quotations, 16-17.) Thus in 1955 he said: 'By the end of this year the victory of socialism will be practically assured.' (SU, 160.) Liu Shao-chi made the mistake of expressing a similar optimism at the 1956 party congress: 'The question of who will win in the struggle between socialism and capitalism in our country has now been decided.' (CC, 174.) In November 1957 he retracted this statement, (CC, 396), following Mao Tse-tung's renewed claim that class struggle still existed and contradictions between the classes had to be eradicated through constant remoulding. But Liu's scramble to get back in step with his Chairman did not save him from denunciation by the Red Guards for his 1956 remarks.

The question of class struggle was not (nor is it today) some abstract ideological debate with little practical importance for those outside China's communist ranks. The very existence of the communist party was at stake. Teng Hsiao-ping, general secretary of the party, referred publicly in 1957 to a debate over whether the communist party's leadership was still necessary. He described the demands for the party's retirement from the political scene in terms which suggest they commanded solid support. (*Report on the Rectification Campaign*, 6, 16.) The attack on the party's role continued in 1958 and 1959 as 'Resolution on Some Questions Concerning the People's Communes' (NCNA, 18 December, 1958) and a *People's Daily* article (28 September, 1959) illustrate.

Toleration of private ownership and the recruitment of patent non-communists into the civil service inevitably led to doubts among some sections of the population as to what unique role the communist party could claim as its own when the country was making steady progress under a mixture of socialism and capitalism. Why should the ordinary citizen make strenuous efforts to imbibe communist doctrines or fall in with the government's mounting appeals for self-sacrifice (which reached a climax in the abortive 1958 Great Leap Forward) when all around private interests were allowed to co-exist with state undertakings? Furthermore, the encouragement enjoyed by capitalists and non-communists in the postwar period aggravated the problem of minimising their hostility when the time came to demote them forcibly to the level of the masses. Perhaps of overwhelming importance was the way the latent capitalist ambitions of the ordinary people, which Mao always recognised and feared, were fed by the modicum of prosperity given to the old privileged commercial, industrial and intellectual élites.

Mao Tse-tung's other major problem in the years immediately after assuming power was the correct road to attain prosperity. Once again, his modest assessment of the party's abilities to shoulder the enormous postwar burdens of China led him into a trap. He plumped for the Soviet economic model, declaring in a 1949 discussion of economic policy: 'The communist party of the Soviet Union is our best teacher and we must learn from it.' (SW IV, 423.) Aid from Moscow to build large-scale plants, its technical assistance and the facilities for Chinese students offered by Russian colleges were strong inducements to imitate the Soviet pattern. Thus in the initial stage of creating a modern socialist state in China, Mao Tse-tung took over an economic strategy evolved to meet the needs of a completely different type of society whose problems bore small relation to those of China. As Mao later confessed obliquely, Moscow's strategy had not been a striking domestic success in breaking the biggest bottleneck of all, agriculture.

Mao was far too sincere a Chinese nationalist and much too wise in the ways of his people to have copied the Russians indefinitely. But he felt short of time to learn the techniques of exercising national power despite his confident pronouncements when still a revolutionary philosophising in a Yenan cave. Mao's nervousness about how little he and his party knew of government when he marched into Peking in 1949 was striking. The Soviet Union, he believed, had the experience which could be put to work immediately — just as he had found jobs for Chiang Kai-shek's civil servants, soldiers and capitalist supporters. However, once the economy had set out on a Soviet-type course, the difficulty would lie in discovering which parts of the Russian model would need jettisoning and how to time the switch to a Chinese pattern of economic development. The process of abandoning the Soviet approach to industrial and agricultural progress was to prove extremely tortuous. Some elements admired Moscow, while other groups, frustrated by Russian methods, wanted to hasten the adoption of a Chinese development strategy.

The written record, which shows Mao Tse-tung trailing along behind the Soviet Union's economic policy, conceals the personal anguish this borrowing from Moscow must have involved. Mao had lashed out at members of his own party who aped the foreigner and swallowed their marxism undigested from overseas. (SW III, 19, 21.)

Particular contempt was showered in 1942 on his party's failure to develop 'economic theorists worthy of the name'. (*ibid.,* 37.) Yet in 1949, Mao Tse-tung found himself forced to look to another nation for solutions to China's problems. This fate must have been galling after the proud 1945 proclamation: 'The communist party of China has made the integration of the universal truth of marxism-leninism with the concrete practice of the Chinese revolution the guiding principle in all its work, and Comrade Mao Tse-tung's theory and practice of the Chinese revolution represent this integration.' (SW III, 177, 1965 ed.) Liu Shao-chi had spoken in similar terms about Mao in 1943. (Boyd Compton, *Mao's China,* 263.) Another senior cadre, Chen Po-ta, wrote of Mao's development of marxism in a Chinese context even more colourfully in 1951. (*Mao Tse-tung on the Chinese Revolution,* 1.) Mao had seen no alternative to learning from Stalin; but the betrayal of his long-term ambition to fashion out of marxism an ideology totally native to China must have tormented him considerably until he found a solution for this dilemma.

Fundamentally, Mao Tse-tung's decision to turn to the Soviet economic experience reflected his doubts about China's ability to hammer out its own policy. By contrast, in his own speciality, guerrilla warfare, he showed no desire to borrow from the Russians: 'Others hold ... that it is enough merely to follow the laws by which the civil war in the Soviet Union was directed and the military manuals published by Soviet military organisations. They do not see that these laws and manuals embody the specific characteristics of the civil war and the Red Army in the Soviet Union, and that if we copy and apply them without allowing any change, we shall also be "cutting off the feet to fit the shoes" and be defeated.' (MW, 79.) Similarly, in the ideological field where Mao had considerable expertise in developing propaganda attractive to Chinese nationalist sentiments, he could state: 'In applying marxism to China, Chinese communists must fully and properly integrate the universal truth of marxism with the concrete practice of the Chinese revolution, or in other words, the universal truth of marxism must be combined with specific national characteristics and acquire a definite national form if it is to be useful, and in no circumstances can it be applied subjectively as a mere formula.' (SW II, 380-81.)

At this stage, Mao believed that the laws of marxist revolution would lead inevitably to the creation of states on the Soviet model. Furthermore, China could not dispense with Russian aid. (*ibid.,* 350,

355.) In 1945, he had recognised the wide difference between Chinese and Soviet revolutionary backgrounds. (SW III, 234-35.) But he swung back four years later, insisting on the essential similarities between the two nations. (SW IV, 412.) Cynically, the contrast between 1945 and 1949 could be explained by his desire in 1945 to retain the support of non-communists for the party by convincing them of its moderation, while in 1949 victory was in his grasp. United front work was less vital, and flattery of the Soviet ego was essential to win Moscow's aid. Certainly in 1949, the slim chance of getting economic assistance from any other quarter but the Soviet Union was very much in Mao's thoughts. (ibid., 417.) However, judging from later developments, Mao was probably in two minds about the Soviet Union during these years. He genuinely believed in its economic prowess — it had survived the full brunt of Hitler's onslaught after all. Yet, simultaneously, he must have been aware of the special circumstances which faced his new administration in China.

Expressions of deep admiration for the Soviet Union's economic policies continued to be heard from Mao Tse-tung as late as 1955. In discussing the most effective method for introducing socialist farming to replace peasant agriculture, he tried to combat voices within the party calling for extreme caution in setting up co-operatives with appeals to Soviet experience, claiming: 'This road travelled by the Soviet Union is our model.' (AC, 18-19, 22.) He began to display a more critical approach to the Soviet bloc's economic achievements in 1956: 'On the question of agriculture, as the experiences of some socialist countries show, a poor job done in agricultural collectivisation also restricts production. The basic reasons for the failures in some countries in raising farm output are that state policy towards the peasants is questionable.' (CS, 23.)

Yet the break was gradual rather than abrupt. In 1957, learning from the Soviet Union was still in vogue, with the rider: 'There are two different attitudes towards learning from others. One is the dogmatic attitude of transplanting everything, whether or not it is suited to our conditions. This is no good. The other attitude is to use our heads and learn those things which suit our conditions, that is, to absorb whatever experience is useful to us. That is the attitude we should adopt.' (PE, 131.) At the end of that year, while in Moscow for the celebration of the fortieth anniversary of the Russian October Revolution, Mao felt confident enough to state: 'The Chinese revolution has its own national characteristics and it is entirely necessary to take these into consideration. But in our own revolution and socialist construction we have made full use of the rich experience of the communist party and the people of the Soviet Union.' (CC, 391.)

The later open breach between Moscow and Peking finally shattered any further possibility of following in the Soviet Union's footsteps. The entire economic relationship built up between the two countries was roundly denounced by China as either paid for in hard cash by Peking or as Soviet political blackmail and exploitation. (*Seven Letters Exchanged between the Central Committees of the Communist Party of China and the Communist Party of the Soviet Union*, 24-31.) But even without this split, Khruschev's revelations about Stalin's reign made further imitation of the Soviet development model embarrassing. In an article almost certainly written by Mao in December 1957, the point was made: 'All the experience of the Soviet Union, including its fundamental experience, is bound up with definite national characteristics, and no other country should copy it mechanically. Moreover . . . part of Soviet experience is that derived from mistakes and failure.' (*The Historical Experience of the Dictatorship of the Proletariat*, 45.) Stalin, temporarily at least in China, was no longer a name to conjure with. Interestingly enough, Mao never turned completely away from the lessons of the Soviet Union. He cited Russia (and the United States) as a model in a 1959 comment on pig-breeding. (LL, 33.) During the early days of the Cultural Revolution, he stated: 'At all times, our generation and posterity too will have to learn from the Soviet Union and to study its experience.' Those who spurned all things Russian because of its revisionism were mistaken, said Mao. Its people had positive lessons to teach China, while its leaders were a useful negative example. (*ibid.*, 65.)

Mao Tse-tung's slowly changing opinion of the Soviet Union was reflected somewhat more gradually in internal policy. The Chinese Prime Minister, Chou En-lai, referred in January 1956 to the technical progress made 'as a result of painstaking efforts in studying from the Soviet Union'. Nevertheless, he castigated those who argued that while production depended on Chinese workers, 'technique is dependent on the Soviet experts'. (CC, 132.) *The Proposals of the Eighth National Congress of the Communist Party of China for the Second Five-Year Plan* talked in 1956 of continuing to learn from the Russians. Premier Chou revealed at the same time the existence of a group which felt the prospects of co-operation with the Soviet Union and other socialist nations meant China had no need to build up its own comprehensive industrial system. (pp. 27, 59.)

By mid-1957, the prime minister faced a completely different climate of opinion: 'Some people are against learning from the experience of the Soviet Union, and even say that the mistakes and shortcomings in our construction work are also the result of learning from the Soviet Union. This is a very harmful point of view.' The question was whether China could borrow wisely from the first socialist state and thus 'avoid taking many unnecessary detours'. (CC, 309.) In 1958, the year of the first truly Chinese socio-economic experiment, the Great Leap Forward, the slogan remained: 'With the assistance of the various socialist countries, and especially of the Soviet Union, China can make use of the latest scientific and technical achievements of the world to avoid or reduce the many difficulties it may encounter in its march forward.' (*China Will Overtake Britain*, 45.)

As late as 1959, a major policy article stated: 'The question of how to combine the general principles of marxism-leninism with the actual conditions of China must be solved by ourselves.' But 'the construction experiences accumulated by the Soviet Union' were useful 'reference materials'. (RF, 17/1959.) The first five-year plan had been modelled closely on Soviet economic theories. But the second plan, also influenced by Moscow, was buried by the communes (which took Chinese agricultural co-operatives to a higher stage of socialism) and the Great Leap Forward, economic innovations untainted by Russian theories. China had ended its apprenticeship to a master whose techniques were of limited applicability to Chinese society and whose efficiency had always left much to be desired. The door swung open for Mao Tse-tung to show his nation how to reconcile marxism with China's historical, cultural and economic characteristics.

The legacy of the hesitant approach of the first six years under Mao can be summed up in a list of 'deviations' which still bedevil Peking today in mapping out development. Firstly, the principle that expediency and compromise with communist purity can be justified, provided they push forward national production particularly in an emergency (the collapse of the Great Leap, and the three subsequent years of crop failures, for example), carried considerable weight with policy-makers, as the five years immediately before the 1966 Cultural Revolution demonstrated. Secondly, the temptation to downgrade the importance of manning the bureaucracy with officials of unquestioned loyalty to communist ideals was allowed to flourish. Later attempts, and these were numerous and determined, to clean out the cadres' ranks never came near complete success.

The possibility of diluting full socialism with a limited degree of private enterprise was the third counter-communist tendency, still lingering on, which can be traced back to this early period. The value of capitalist methods was illustrated by the speed of China's postwar recovery and the undoubted growth under the first five-year plan. When in trouble, some of the party's leadership have tended naturally to look back to this postwar period for solutions to their immediate crisis despite the imperatives of marxism-leninism as propounded by Mao Tse-tung. Finally, the Chinese learnt the convenience of importing foreign technology to cut corners in their struggle for prosperity. This desire for 'things large and foreign' has persisted and is a direct result of the modern plant bought from the Soviet Union which helped to lay the foundations of Chinese heavy industry in the 1950s. The desire to make progress less painful by buying advanced equipment from overseas has been condemned since the Cultural Revolution as an expression of contempt for the talent possessed by the Chinese masses in the field of technical innovation.

As he turned his back on the Soviet Union, Mao found his standing in the party eroding rapidly. In part, this trend may have been a symptom of the discontent with existing leadership which affected the socialist world after Khruschev's denunciation of Stalin, exploding in the Hungarian revolt of 1956. During the 'Hundred Flowers Movement' of 1957, when Chinese intellectuals were urged to voice their criticisms of state and party, the claim was made that a massive protest had taken place among the audience listening to Mao's speech 'On the Correct Handling of Contradictions among the People'. (Roderick MacFarquhar, ed., China Under Mao, 258-59.) Such adverse reaction was to be expected since Mao argued that popular discontent with poor-calibre cadres should be allowed free expression, a proposal which threatened both the primacy and the privileged status of the party. Mao was forced to revise his essay before publication, drastically restricting the conditions under which public grievances against the party would be tolerated. (Cohen, The Communism of Mao Tse-tung, 156-58.)

In February 1958, Mao hit back at 'some people [who] say that the old cadres should be "bought over", paid some money and told to retire. This is because the old cadres do not know science and technology and are capable only of fighting and carrying out agrarian reform. We must certainly exert our efforts and we must learn to carry out the great technical revolution bequeathed to us by history.' This criticism he seemed to view as aimed in part at himself. (CS, 5.)

Under pressure, Mao used a standard political technique to enable him either to retreat gracefully from an unpopular position or to demonstrate that his backing within the party was still overwhelming. He asked the party at the beginning of 1958 to discuss whether or not he should retire as chairman of the People's Republic, retaining only the leadership of the communist party. (*ibid.*, 13.) This request suggests that although most people see Mao forced out of office in December 1958 because the Great Leap Forward was showing signs of proving a massive failure, the truth is that Mao could not round up enough party members to demand his retention as head of state. (In any case, it is highly doubtful if by the end of 1958 the evidence of the Great Leap's doom had surfaced in Peking.)

Thus, as Mao Tse-tung took the first steps toward implementing his personal economic philosophy, the power base from which he could operate was crumbling beneath him. Fortunately, he withdrew as head of state after completing the main blueprint for China's future and was thus able to concentrate on the struggle for a political comeback from his position as chairman of the party. His economic doctrines represent his thinking during a period in which he was in overall command of the administrative and power structure. Hence, he was not confronted with the dilemma of setting forth a popular programme which would win immediate national approval at the price of diluting a long-term campaign involving considerable personal sacrifices to overcome the obstacles to growth. In addition, he abandoned the post of head of state before the collapse of the Great Leap Forward became unmistakable. His retirement took place in circumstances which did not destroy permanently the credibility of his development strategy.

His prestige, according to foreign commentators, was shaken badly enough by the disaster of the Great Leap Forward. But much of the infrastructure which Mao would need at a later date to put his economic plans into effect remained fairly intact, especially in the countryside, despite the calamitous years from 1959 to 1962. At any rate, Mao Tse-tung had learned a great deal between 1949 and 1955 about the kind of policies China needed, and a great deal more between 1956 and 1958 about how these could be translated into solid political programmes.

Chapter Two

'Make the Past Serve the Present'

Already, a certain distortion has slipped into this portrait of China in the immediate postwar period. The evolution of Chinese economic policies has been isolated from the pattern of government as a whole. Thus, while Mao Tse-tung mistakenly picked Moscow as China's instructor in economics, the impact of the Soviet Union on Peking was reinforced by external events. China was dependent on the Russian nuclear umbrella once Peking engaged in open war against Washington in Korea and felt itself threatened by a ring of American bases stretching from Pakistan via the Philippines to Okinawa. Mao felt the Soviet army had little to teach his troops, yet the People's Liberation Army was remodelled on Soviet lines as a result of Moscow's involvement in Peking's defence. In addition, the personal admiration which Mao apparently felt for Stalin and the rude shock of Khruschev's sudden unveiling of Stalin's terror apparatus were other forces swaying China's leaders. Ambivalent attitudes developed among ordinary Chinese working side by side with Russian technicians and military advisers. A split appeared between those who resented the arrogant manners of China's latest set of foreign mentors and the group which felt Soviet support essential in building the new China.

Nevertheless, the description of the process of disenchantment with the Soviet Union over economic policies and the groping for a development strategy geared to China's situation has not been too incorrect. Mao Tse-tung by 1955 had returned to his true roots in the countryside. For all his approving references to the way Russia had handled collectivisation of its peasants, Mao was absorbed almost entirely by this time in rural problems where he felt utterly at home and in no need of a foreign guide. By returning to the villages which had been the source of his strength as a guerrilla leader, he laid hold of the heart of the nation's poverty. The peasants were the key to Chinese growth, and Mao now realised his dreams would be shattered unless he

22

could harness the energies of the enormous rural labour force to drag the economy by brute strength into the twentieth century.

The two hundred-odd plants erected by the Soviet Union looked impressive. Industrial centres such as Shanghai or Tientsin were nothing to be ashamed of in their new communist garb. Other cities were taking on a sleek look of well-being they had not known for years. But industrial prosperity was an illusion while the peasants continued to till the soil without deviating from the rules laid down by the inventors of intensive cultivation in the mists of antiquity. When rain and snow arrived on time, and the sun followed the farmer's almanac, the villages had a surplus to send to the cities after feeding themselves. When the weather was unkind, the margin for survival shrank alarmingly. The impoverished countryside offered little surplus capital to modernise the nation, since individual peasant farming already represented the highest level of efficiency to which traditional cultivation could aspire.

In addition, because the rural population represented the source of new factory labour for the future, the resilience of the outlook and habits of mind inherited from the past had to be broken at the point where they were reborn with every new generation, the self-contained villages. These communities were hostile to any outsider ignorant of the local dialect and customs, and their first loyalty was to family and clan. The villagers had learnt by bitter experience how to resist external pressures, to survive foreign invasion and local warlords.

This retreat by Mao Tse-tung to the peasants' custom-bound world took him full circle to the origins of his revolutionary career and his first inspiration as a mature communist. The rural and traditional background to Mao's thinking is of central importance in grasping his special brand of marxism. With the peasants, Mao brimmed with confidence. His ability to lead, to understand the ancient cultural forces which moulded social forms and to speak a language touching the imagination of his audience surfaced powerfully when he caught the peasants' smell of sweat and earth. This element in Mao's make-up helps to explain why the bulk of his published writings dates back to the period before he left the hills to take over Peking. Their validity remains as long as China's countryside moves only slowly towards socialism. Roughly half his post-1949 officially published work deals exclusively with agriculture. The two central documents on overall economic policy which he drafted in the 1950s were released very apologetically and lack the force so apparent in the bulk of his essays. (CS, 1, 21.)

Mao Tse-tung at the end of 1958 was in deep political trouble; he had decided to dispense with his Russian teachers but was replaced as head of state by Liu Shao-chi. The obvious question is what formed Mao's power base. Throughout his career, he spent most of his time at war with the party, a fact clearly demonstrated but not sufficiently emphasised by his biographers Schram and Ch'en. In the wilderness early on because he refused to obey the party's foolhardy policy on rural problems; at loggerheads in the 1930s with Moscow-trained and backed party leaders; forced to mount a rectification campaign in the middle of the war with Japan; disappointed by the party's attitude towards co-operative farming in the 1950s; left without a party mandate to stay on as head of state in 1958; wildly angered by the party's economic policies from 1962; and finally in open combat with the party which he smashed in the Cultural Revolution from 1966 to 1969, Mao never loved his party wholeheartedly.

Mao was not a communist ruler whose authority depended on total control of a pliant party apparatus, as Stalin was. Mao Tse-tung's indestructibility stemmed from his unrivalled comprehension of the Chinese mentality. As Edgar Snow put it: 'It was Mao's ability to analyse the experience common to his own generation, rather than the uniqueness of his own experience, plus his messianic belief in the correctness of his own generalisations of that experience which distinguished him from compatriots who became his followers.' And as Snow added, 'Mao understood his own country better than any national leader in modern times.' (*Red China Today*, 165, 166.) As a guerrilla theoretician of the highest order, Mao was well aware of the power derived from an intimate knowledge of the society for whose control battles were being fought. (MW 93-94, 109-10.)

The extension to politics and economics of the military 'appreciation-of-the-situation' logic followed easily: 'Only those who are subjective, one-sided and superficial in their approach to problems will smugly issue orders or directives the moment they arrive on the scene, without considering the circumstances, without viewing things in their totality (their history and their present state as a whole) and without getting to the essence of things (their nature and the internal relations between one thing and another). Such people are bound to trip and fall.' (SW I, 302.) Earlier in the same passage, he argued that a cadre who felt unable to cope with an assignment would gather confidence as he studied the problem set him.

In most other countries, knowledge of a society's basic aspirations and its reactions to policies are to a large degree accessible to any reasonably perceptive and impartial observer. The vastness and diversity of China make immensely difficult the task of uncovering those national social features of major significance for official programmes. Experience of one district's conditions often distracts attention from what is common to China as a whole, as Mao observed. (SW III, 20.) Anyone, for instance, who used Fukien province's traditional treatment of women (the swift murder of baby girls in families where they threatened to outnumber boys, the restriction of women's diet to leftovers from their menfolk's meals) as a guide to the general status of women would find their conclusions invalidated by the relative equality of the sexes throughout much of the nearby province of Kwangtung.

Mao Tse-tung evolved his ideas not in an artificial realm of marxist-leninist notions imported from the West by way of Russia and Japan nor from the restricted experience provided by his upbringing in Hunan province. His philosophy grew out of a sustained effort to listen to the voice of the entire Chinese community. This aspect of his personality persisted after he came to power, as Edgar Snow related in an account of Mao's taste for long and unheralded visits to all parts of China, his hunger for knowledge, and his voracious appetite for books both Chinese and foreign. (*Red China Today*, 176-77.)

This description of Mao by no means implies that what the people most desired, he gave them. No revolutionary bent on transforming a tradition-ridden society could afford this luxury. Mao's strength was a capacity to gauge fairly accurately the nation's mood and to predict how Peking directives were likely to be received and applied. Such a claim could not be made for the bulk of those who came to power with him. His erstwhile secretary and marxist theoretician of some repute, Chen Po-ta, wrote in a dull, abstract manner which must have left most readers sighing for the apt classical quotations and salty personal touches which leaven Mao's essays. The only figure who approached Mao in his impact on China was Liu Shao-chi. But his works were aimed at party members and were formerly the basic training manuals for cadres. Mao Tse-tung alone dared to stake his survival on a gift for penetrating the hidden collective ideals of 750 million people.

From a superficial survey of traditional China, based on unpretentious essays by scholars mainly out of sympathy with the People's Republic, Mao Tse-tung's response to yearnings which stem from the earliest periods of Chinese history can be demonstrated dramatically. (Deliberately, this analysis make no pretence at depth; scissors and paste interpretation, perhaps, but the historical parallels seem too obvious to require elaborate review here.) To the Westerner, Mao's place in the roll of Chinese reformers may seem of mere intellectual interest. In fact, the Chinese nation has a propensity to relate the present to events of antiquity which is an added complication in political life. The ruler in Peking must measure up as worthy to govern not only in contrast to his contemporary rivals but by comparison with legendary heroes.

This characteristic is partly the product of the preservation in ordinary speech of the ethical codes laid down by such sages as Confucius. In addition, the profession of story-telling to entertain an illiterate peasantry found its most popular material in the epic quality of China's history. Even a Chinese of minimal education has the kind of outlook on life which a Greek might possess if quotations from Plato and Aristotle slipped naturally into his everyday conversation and if he could recite not only the order of battle before the walls of Troy and the wanderings of Odysseus but the religious rites of Minoan Crete as well. Mao himself is proof of this trait as he strewed his essays and speeches with historical allusions and classical quotations. Etienne Balazs argues: 'In the last of the great and victorious peasant wars, the one that led to the founding of the empire of Mao Tse-tung, historical parallels have, either consciously or unconsciously, played as important a part as the new foreign doctrines.' (*Chinese Civilization and Bureaucracy*, 160.)

These historical roots of Mao's ideology can be tackled under three headings: the peasant world, the civil service and the ultimate source of authority in China. Since Balazs has made such a bold assertion about the marriage of tradition and marxism in Mao, he is an appropriate source of information on the peasants' greatest longing — enough land to maintain their families. Balazs shows with great clarity that an integral aim of almost every Chinese reformer's programme had been some brand of rural socialism for two thousand years. He mentions an official calling for agrarian reform at the end of the second century B.C. through 'limiting private estates'. In 485-86 A.D., Li An-shih urged: 'The aims of agrarian reform should be to have no land out of cultivation, and no hands left idle; to ensure that the best agricultural land should not be monopolised by the rich; and to ensure that the poor should reach a minimum subsistence level.' Li Kou in the eleventh century traced low agricultural productivity to the unequal distribution of land. The national economy he believed should be enriched by 'strengthening the foundation (the peasantry) and cutting down expenditure, so that below there is no one who does not have enough, and there will be a surplus for those above'. (*ibid.*, 103, 108, 280.)

Speaking of the peasants' role in Chinese society, Balazs points out: 'The agrarian problem, of primary importance in any agricultural society, has always been China's major problem. Its solution determined the well-being of the peasant masses and of the ruling minority, the fate of governments and, in the last analysis, the rise and fall of dynasties.' (*ibid.*, 113.) Mao's comment was very similar: 'So the peasant problem becomes the basic problem of the Chinese revolution and the strength of the peasants is the main strength of the Chinese revolution.' (SW II, 367.)

The rural population's characteristics have shaped China's economic thinking to the present day. As a result of invasions by barbarian tribes in the north and of Chinese colonisation as the population spread southwards, the villages had to become self-supporting units and meet virtually all their own needs for both food and consumer goods. Yet China also had an urban population. Between town and country, a conflict emerged which still persists. The towns needed food, yet the urban areas had few products to trade with the villages which could contribute to farm output.

This factor accounts for the traditional respect the peasants were supposed to enjoy and the contempt to which, in theory, the mercantile classes were condemned. The rural population was recognised as of such vital importance that, traditionally, its exploitation was forbidden. In practice, the merchant class and the bureaucrats formed alliances at the expense of the peasants. Nevertheless, the villages were the one sector of the community over which the government assumed least direct control. Commerce, regulated through guilds, was subject to state interference. Copper and salt were but two examples of major industries run as national monopolies. State control of trade and industry is thus hallowed by tradition in China. The government occasionally attempted land reform and compelled villages to contribute labour for the construction of irrigation works. But the farmer, by and large, was expected to run his own affairs through the family and the clan, as Mao hoped the 'masses' would manage the rural communes. The introduction of marxism into China in this century represents no catastrophic conflict with essential cultural values in China.

Significantly, Chinese still identify themselves today by their 'native place', the village from which their forefathers came. Respect for the individual's rural origins represents more than a recognition of the peasant basis of economic and family life. It reflects a peculiarity of Chinese civilisation. The countryside, until relatively modern times, was not culturally deprived or primitive. As Frederick W. Mote has noted, only recently have the villages ceased to be the homes of private academies, great libraries and the storehouse for a fair share of the nation's works of arts. (*Traditional China*, 47.)

The dominant role of the peasant world left its mark on social attitudes. The family, social relations between individuals in a group setting and an emphasis on membership of a social unit became of paramount importance in the Chinese world of ideas. A mistrust developed of situations in which the individual could not build well-defined personal attachments to those with whom he dealt. The urban areas split into groups which reflected the intimate nature of village life where every family knew the history, virtues and worth of its neighbours. Associations based on such features as employment in the same trade, graduation from the same school, fluency in the same provincial dialect (or one of its variants) sprang up in the towns. To prosper outside the village, the individual had to form personal ties which allowed him access either directly or through relatives and friends (often given courtesy kinship titles) to these closed groups which wielded considerable power.

The nation was fragmented into a myriad of villages which never lost their original character as bulwarks against hostile outsiders. The towns were splintered into a host of overlapping but at the same time select groups designed to protect their members' interests. To hold this divided community together required a special system of administration. The country, threatened by constant pressures from the tribes on its northern borders and highly atomised internally, was in perpetual danger of falling into anarchy. The capital's control depended on an army of civil servants whose outlook was national and whose loyalty, in theory at any rate, was directed towards the central government rather than local demands. The nature of Chinese society accounts for the rise of a bureaucracy whose membership (for all its corruption, pedantry and privileges for the ruling élite's offspring) was open to all. The criterion for entry into its ranks was a competitive examination whose basic aim was to test the candidate's knowledge of the classical documents which formed the civil servant's ideology.

Generally corrupt because of the miserable stipends allocated to them, frequently lacking in zeal and justice towards their constituents, nevertheless these civil servants under a strong central administration assumed a role similar to that of the tiny band of men who held the Indian Empire for Britain. They were expected to adapt to any part of China, to undertake the building of roads and waterworks, to use their astronomical lore to assist the farmers in planting their crops, to mete out justice, to maintain law and order, and to defeat invaders. The reality was usually far from this ideal. But whatever the dynasty, Chinese, Mongol or Manchu, the bureaucracy survived because it formed the only structure, apart from the majority of the population's feeling of a common Han racial origin, capable of binding together the diverse immensity of China and of imposing a national ethos and identity on its multitude of groups seeking social and economic autonomy.

Above the law and privileged beyond all other classes, the civil servant nevertheless was always a tool of the throne. He could be purged, humiliated or savagely punished at the emperor's whim. By becoming an official, an individual was lifted above the ruck of the anonymous masses and made subject to increasingly intensive scrutiny and hostile intrigue as he climbed up the hierarchy. A civil service, trained throughout by study of the same subjects, heavily indoctrinated with the same ideology and united by a common profession, should have been able to hold the government to ransom. When the monarch was weak or a dynasty disintegrating, the bureaucracy was the sole force keeping the nation intact as a legacy for the next imperial potentate of any worth. Yet the Chinese civil service as a class never seems to have been able to escape from its bonds of loyalty to the ruling house and to set up an alternative administration of its own.

The educated élite, expected to undertake any task, civil or military, selected initially for its ideological expertise, and liable to be thrown out of office at a nod from the capital remained the norm under Mao. He expected the cadres who replaced the old officials to dedicate themselves entirely to the masses' welfare. He demanded a complete break with the mandarin tradition by which a civil servant gave his first concern to the emperor, provided China was under strong rule, and his second to the aggrandisement of himself and his family. But these changes were matters of style and emphasis rather than function. The cadre remained an extension of the central government either in his capacity as a party member (the status of most key officials) or as a functionary in a ministry or other state organisation. His duty was defined as guardian of the masses' welfare because, as

29

marxists, the central authorities of the People's Republic were committed to seeking first the protection of the masses' interests. However, a well-known confucian aphorism shows that even this distinction between past and present is less striking than many imagine: 'When a ruler loves what pleases his people, and spurns what they spurn, then he indeed deserves the name of father of his people.'

Close examination of Mao Tse-tung's views on the role of the cadre and the party member brings out the parallels between the old and the new Chinas. His duty to knit the country together Mao stated specifically: 'It is only through the unity of the communist party that the unity of the whole class and the whole nation can be achieved.' (SW I, 292.) The need for training in a common ideology was also felt: 'All communist party members who can do so should study the theory of Marx, Engels, Lenin and Stalin, study our national history and study current movements and trends . . . No political party can possibly lead a great revolutionary movement to victory unless it possesses revolutionary theory and a knowledge of history and has a profound grasp of the practical movement.' (SW II, 208.) The names of the sages changed; the call for intellectual grasp of their wisdom remained.

Mao appreciated the importance of the academic élite. 'Without the participation of the intellectuals victory in the revolution is impossible', though he insisted they shed their feelings of superiority towards the rest of society. (*ibid.*, 301; III, 87.) The peasants and workers were to be excluded no longer from the bureaucracy but again education was called for: 'The central committee of our party now emphatically requires that our cadres of working-class and peasant origin should obtain an elementary education because they can then take up any branch of study — politics, military science or economics.' (SW III, 41.) The list of skills needed by a cadre was no less comprehensive than those attributed to the old mandarins: 'To help the peasants draw up their household production plans, to set up labour-exchange teams, salt transport teams and multi-purpose co-operatives, to organise production in the army, the schools and the government and other organisations, to organise production in the factories, develop emulation in production, encourage and reward labour heroes, and arrange production exhibitions', and to carry on the war to conquer China as well. (*ibid.*, 157.)

Even the shadow of demotion and disgrace were in the great tradition: 'The composition of the leading group in most cases should not and cannot remain entirely unchanged . . . the activists who come forward in the course of the struggle must constantly be promoted to replace those original members of the leading group who are inferior by comparison or who have degenerated.' (*ibid.*, 118.) On the question of purges, Mao stated in 1962: 'I think such demotions and transfers, irrespective of whether they are justified or not, are useful. Your revolutionary determination can be tempered. You can investigate and study many new situations and can increase your stock of useful knowledge.' (LL, 37.)

The Chinese political system required power to flow from a single supreme authority to symbolise the unity of a society which had little natural cohesion. A common cultural tradition in an illiterate society split into isolated geographical units was hardly enough to bind the country together. A common ethnic origin could have disappeared as a significant unifying factor under the strain of a variety of mutually incomprehensible dialects. The social pecularities of the Chinese people demanded the community be gripped by a strong hand at its centre, capable of making its influence felt at the outermost limits of the empire and in every village however remote. The Chinese have never been able to afford the luxury of political forms in which personal liberty was a principle of the greatest weight. The individual in his isolated village, or sheltered by the self-contained urban groups o., if necessary, protected through outright nepotism and corruption had enough means of refuge from the worst excesses of an essentially despotic and totalitarian system of government.

From the emperor, the officials derived their status; through the emperor, national programmes could be imposed on a people whose first instinct was to give pride of place to family or personal interests. In the relatively small Western countries, most of which have achieved democracy since the invention of modern means of transport, communications and mass media, the state can explain its difficulties and achieve the compromises between personal freedom and national needs which the more serious emergencies of history make inescapable. In China, whose governments on an imperial scale have lasted since Rome first fashioned a military machine to conquer and hold down a great empire, liberty of the individual would have been an invitation to anarchy. Moral teaching had to concentrate on enshrining the social rather than the personal obligations of virtue.

While the emperor was technically a tyrant and invested with a semi-divine aura through elaborate court rituals, ostentatious expenditure and a gulf dividing him from every other class, the classical philosophers set limits to the Chinese concept of the 'Divine Right of Kings'. Dynasties rose and fell, while China survived. History was a constant reminder of the mortal nature of even the Sons of Heaven. To the confucian and, indeed, the people at large, a monarch's downfall could be accounted for in moral terms. He had lost the 'mandate of heaven' by his failings as an emperor. John C.H. Wu has summed up in almost romantic terms a dynasty's need to earn its mandate by visible proofs of its superior virtue, especially when a new imperial line began. Wu also emphasises the obligation which tradition imposed on the masses to rise in rebellion against an unjust emperor. (*The Chinese Mind*, 213-14.)

The ruler earned obedience in the ideal Chinese world by his total dedication to the interests of his people, exercising power as a burden of service to the nation rather than as an opportunity to impose his will upon millions. In practice, a more cynical view of life was fostered by the 'Legalists', philosophers who saw men not as naturally good and thus responsive to their sovereign's virtues but in need of constant coercion through a severe code of laws.

Mao Tse-tung's view of life tended to the confucian, according to Snow, seeing mankind as essentially good. (*Red China Today*, 350.) The correct political line veered from left to right as Peking dictated. The communist party was the ultimate judge of what was permissible. Attempts to establish personal rights and impartial justice, as Stanley Lubman has illustrated, made little progress under Mao because of the party's need for total control over the individual to protect its power. (*Columbia Law Review*, April 1969.) Yet Mao insisted: 'In treating an ideological or a political malady, one must never be rough and rash but must adopt the approach of "curing the sickness to save the patient".' (SW III, 50.) Thus, Mao Tse-tung's rule represented a compromise between the two political traditions of China, the idealistic and the pragmatic, where control over the individual was concerned. But his personal inclination seemed to be a view of man's innate capacity to reform his nature.

Ritual, obeisance to imperial edicts (whether implemented or not), and total respect, externally at least, for the emperor marked the past. Hypocrisy and time-serving undoubtedly diminished the imperial charisma in practice, as comparison between the current ruler and his predecessors was so easy for the Chinese. Nevertheless, a measure of excellence was set for the omnipotent ruler, and Balazs has summarised what this standard implied. His list is of considerable interest as it offers a model of what Mao had to compete with in Chinese history to justify his right to govern. Balazs quotes from a description of one of Mao's military heroes, Tsao Tsao (SW I, 213; II, 164), though this figure has not been treated kindly by most of China's historians.

Tsao was depicted as preferring simplicity to elaborate ceremonial; loyalty to manipulation; firmness to leniency in maintaining order; brusque trust in others to smooth-tongued confidence in no-one but relatives; self-assurance rather than hesitancy in planning; sincerity rather than fine manners in winning followers; genuine compassion towards the unfortunate rather than empty condolences; controlling supporters through virtue rather than intriguing to divide and repress them; real military skill to sham parades of strength; justice and correct judgement. (*Chinese Civilization and Bureaucracy*, 228-29.) Whether or not a Chinese communist would accept a comparison with Tsao as complimentary, Mao's character as drawn by Edgar Snow accords strikingly with this list.

Whatever Mao Tse-tung's conscious desire to project an image modelled on the heroic characters of his country's past, a charismatic personality is of paramount importance in the survival of a Chinese leader. He must symbolise to a far-flung nation the essence of China. Snow is very frank in his examination of the use made by Mao Tse-tung of the 'personality cult' fostered around his name and admits Mao's concern for its role in maintaining political influence. (*Red China Today*, 170-71, 330-32.) Mao himself expressed his understanding of the need to establish a national reputation before a communist party leader could hope to win the people's loyalty. (LL, 71.)

Handsome and charming to a remarkable degree in the classical Chinese pattern as a youth; well educated, articulate and a master of the highly-developed Chinese rules of polemic; a writer whose essays even in the bleakest days of his revolution had the ring of a man who foresaw eventual triumph; avuncular but with a glint of hardness in his eyes in old age, Mao Tse-tung had more than enough qualities to build up his image. Besides these external assets, Mao was able to inspire a reputation for openness by his free confessions of past failings: his distaste for peasant dirt and manual labour as a young intellectual; his ignorance of local conditions in his guerrilla base; his initial unfamiliarity with marxism and his personal need for remoulding; his blunt admission of past unpopularity with the party central committee; his candour in acknowledging non-communist friends. Such frankness generated an image of striving for righteousness despite the weaknesses to which all men are heirs. (SW III, 73, 45; PE, 106; LL, 72, 45.)

Can it be true that after two decades of Mao's rule, the old social patterns still survived, compelling the nation's leader to adopt a role similar to that of China's former rulers? In fact, the lingering influence of tradition has resisted even the Red Guards, as radio and press admit. The *People's Daily* (14 February, 1970) referred to the scandalous situation in one part of Kiangsu province where a political rectification drive was sabotaged by an appeal to village loyalties: 'People with the same surname are of the same family.' The clan was expected to pull as much weight as official directives. In Honan province, a similar attempt was reportedly made to shield political heresies from investigation: 'Family disgraces should not be made public.' (RS, 26 February, 1970.) Blood ties in rural areas were still a sturdy shield against prying official eyes. In a third province, Anhwei, attempts have been made to establish close bonds with local cadres by inviting them as guests of honour to feasts on which public funds were lavished. (RS, 30 January, 1970.) The perquisites and temptations of office still flourished, except Peking no longer tolerated such abuses as an inevitable feature of government.

Country customs change slowly all over the world. But even in as modern and sophisticated a city as Shanghai, and a long-standing problem for the new China, the old guilds and associations proved powerful, as the local newspaper, *Wen-hui Pao,* revealed: 'So-called organisations exist of drivers and bus conductors, cooks' associations, societies made up of college and university contemporaries . . . formed to push the narrow, selfish economic advantages of some individuals.' (14 March, 1967.) The *People's Daily* (15 March, 1967) described these groups as capable of resisting the onslaught of the Cultural Revolution: 'People who are motivated by the guild outlook fail to define their targets for political struggle by looking at the overall and extensive interests of the workers and the labouring class . . . They organise themselves on the basis of occupation and industry and set their targets for political struggle in accordance with the narrow and immediate advantages of workers in the same job or trade.' The need to project a sense of a dynamic personality at the nation's helm to unite these isolated and self-seeking, small social groups who put loyalty to their fellow-members first was as urgent for Mao Tse-tung as for any previous ruler.

Even without the survival of these ancient social forms and even if Mao had not been conscious of a past to which he must live up, he would have been forced to encourage a personality cult. Apart from the widespread mistrust of any leadership with which personal relations or some kind of identification cannot be established, the Chinese have always shown a great longing for order and strong rule during the collapse of one dynasty and the rise of a new ruler. (Pye, *The Spirit of Chinese Politics*, 87, 97-98.) The veneration heaped on Mao by the communist party symbolised for the nation an end to the era after the Manchus' overthrow in 1911, when factions, parties and armies had struggled for power. The Chinese could find reassurance in the leadership of a powerful figure backed by a stern moralistic ideology and a monolithic party in running the country. C.P. Fitzgerald has summed up this phenomenon succcintly: 'The return to orthodox and authoritarian government fulfils the unexpressed desire of many, and does so, by using a modern form, in a way which is more acceptable to the educated than any outright return to some kind of monarchy could ever be.' (*The Birth of Communist China*, 188.) (Mao's own formula for creating unity, it must be pointed out, was not charisma but political struggle.)

But the charismatic leader is found elsewhere than just China in the modern world. Most countries approaching modernisation long to be reassured that the violent transformations sweeping away their inherited society are being directed by a personality they can respect. The pain of abandoning the past for a future governed by unaccustomed rules creates tensions which such tradition-bound communities have no formulas for overcoming. The strain can be eased if the people are induced to believe the leader whose personality represents their national or ethnic identity is the deliberate contriver of the radical changes they are experiencing. In addition, the industrialised nations have increased the pressure on their politicians to become public personalities. Whether this trend is the result of television's importance in today's political life or whether it is a remedy for the facelessness of administrations whose influence grows from year to year in modern societies, who can say?

However, a distinction must be drawn between the cult surrounding Mao Tse-tung and the adulation showered on Stalin, de Gaulle, Gandhi and Nasser, or the image-building of Richard Nixon and Harold Wilson. Although Mao busts have been everywhere, his public appearances marked by hysteria and Mao himself referred to with fervent awe ('the red sun in our hearts', for example), the essence of the Mao cult was not the man but his 'Thoughts'. His wisdom as a teacher, the inspiration of his writings, the correctness of his personal decisions

35

were taken by press and radio as their constant theme. The reason for this may have been a distaste in Mao for emotional exhibitions which are deemed repugnant by Chinese. He told Edgar Snow in December 1970 that while personality cults were necessary and indeed inevitable in all societies, China had taken its veneration of himself (Mao) to extremes, sometimes expressing a purely hypocritical respect while the floods of tears and applause from the thousands upon thousands who marched past in perfect order to the beat of the martial music on major festivals in Peking smacked of a feudal past he had condemned. (*Asahi Evening News,* 6 May, 1971.) The crowds roared 'A long, long life to Chairman Mao'. Unhappily, the phrase they had to employ to demonstrate their wishes for longevity was formerly a salutation to the emperor and one which, said Mao, became a synonym for imperial majesty. (SW I, 57.) Perhaps a more valid explanation lies in a possible recognition by Mao Tse-tung as he grew older that the worshipping crowds of the present were of less moment than an ability to so instil his ideals in the cultural soul of his people that they could not wither upon his death. The summit of ambition, surely, is not merely to sway the destinies of today but to stretch out a hand of authority from the grave − a goal well within the imagination of Mao Tse-tung, reared on Confucius whose works still had their uses for China's communist government.

The shift in Chinese custom from official adulation of the national ruler to veneration of his philosophy suggests that the roots of the Mao Tse-tung cult demand analysis at a deeper level than Chinese social traditions. For two decades the country has been dedicated to the masses both in name (the People's Republic) and in fact. Mao defined the popular nature of his new state vividly: 'It is only the working class that is most far-sighted, most selfless and most thoroughly revolutionary. The entire history of the revolution proves that without the leadership of the working class revolution fails and that with the leadership of the working class revolution triumphs.' (SW IV, 421.) Mao was the creator of the ideological framework which gave a moral force to this characteristic predicted of the new China.

From this angle, 'Mao Tse-tung Thought' and its constant invocation could be interpreted as the veneration of itself by a China now in the possession of the masses. The concept of worship has been attributed by some sociologists to 'the quality of sacredness ... attached first of all to the collective and impersonal force which is a representation of society itself ... societies are inclined to create gods or religions when they are in a state of exaltation, an exaltation which occurs when social life itself is intensified'. (Raymond Aron, *Main Currents in Sociological Thought* 2, 63.) Aron observes that the originator of this theory, Durkheim, claimed: 'Exaltation at the time of the French Revolution was not sufficient to create a new religion. But ... other upheavals will occur, the moment will come when modern societies will once again be seized by the sacred frenzy, and out of it new religions will be born.' (*ibid.*, 62.)

Exaltation and intensification of social life have been very much in vogue since the first shouts of acclaim when Peking fell to Mao. Through the years, national pride has grown to fresh heights, fed by such triumphs as the 1970 space satellite (ahead of Britain and a host of other developed nations), and such defiant comments on international affairs as: 'Those who refuse to be enslaved will never be cowed by atom bombs and hydrogen bombs in the hands of US imperialists.' (Mao Tse-tung, *People's Daily*, 3 September, 1967.) The communes of 1958 and the 1966 Cultural Revolution were dramatic examples of intensified social life and nation-wide ecstasy. However, they were but crests in the wave-like advance of revolution, which was Mao Tse-tung's own view of political campaigns. (SW IV, 202.) Durkheim's approach seems, on this reckoning, useful for putting the cult of Mao into perspective. This approach is especially interesting in the Chinese context for the Chinese characters for society, *she-hui*, contain both a religious and community meaning. As Noah Edward Fehl notes, *she* is derived from the name of a primitive earth god. (*Rites and Propriety in Literature and Life*, 21-22, 206-7.) The original character meant both the deity and a small grouping of families. More important than the derivation of the character are the facts that in historical times, *she* was the name of a major religious festival and that even today part of the word is used as a 'prefix' in characters having religious overtones. The link between worship and the organisation of individuals into social groups is conveyed very directly by the actual word 'society' in Chinese.

Marx's works may contain a concept of man's attitudes to the state similar to Durkheim's. Jean Hyppolite certainly implies so. In a telling comment, he interprets communism as: 'The Idea in actuality, the divinisation of man, authentic man, fully aware that he is the one who makes his own history', a situation which will only cease when society moves beyond the communist stage of evolution. (*Studies on Marx and Hegel*, 103-4, 111-12.) However, this statement basically reinforces the idea that Mao's philosophy is the summation of the new

China and thus a natural cause of rapture verging on the religious. Omitted from the analysis is the other aspect of Maoism, its public expression of ideas proferred to China for its education. 'Mao Tse-tung Thought' is a form of communication between ruler and citizen, and between China in the abstract and the reality of its millions.

By following Hugh Dalziel Duncan's invaluable synthesis (*Communication and Social Order*), analysis of the dialogue which Mao has carried on with his people can be taken a stage further. Psychoanalysis is a useful starting point (though not in the pugnacious style of Robert Jay Lifton in *Revolutionary Immortality*). Communication depends on symbols, on dreams, mythology, language, the total cultural heritage which Mao Tse-tung exploited so deftly in his writings. For Freud, authority is concerned with solving conflicts, and power is represented by a father figure. Mao Tse-tung does not fit into this paternalistic category. China is too ancient a community and remembers its past too well to see Mao as its creator, unlike most modern nations with their short histories of independent statehood.

Another tack could be taken here. Social interaction may be seen as a sort of game, no bad description of Chinese social life, with its elaborate forms of correct behaviour and verbal response for every kind of social situation whether favourable or adverse. Sociologists who take this view of human relations maintain equality is essential to bring out the fullest potential of social interaction. Equality, of course, was the goal of Mao's China. But the communist party, on his own admission, formed an élite mobilised to lead the people to solve all problems. (SW II, 197.) This reduces the validity of this theory when applied to a China for which equality remains a distant aim.

The ritual patterns of much Chinese conversation point to a third hypothesis developed by sociologists: that language is an attempt to bind together individual members of society. This theory is particularly striking as Mao stressed the need to find an effective form of communication through absorbing communist doctrine: 'In the past some of our high-ranking cadres did not have a common language even on basic theoretical problems of marxism-leninism, because they had not studied enough.' (SW IV, 378.) In 1957, Mao stressed again the importance of 'speaking the same language'. (PW, 8-9.) The quotation on every conceivable occasion of some passage from Mao's writings made possible a standard speech pattern for China, helping to reduce ambiguities in discussion and action through the correct application of Mao's aphorisms to specific problems.

Close scrutiny of official news media and regular discussions with Chinese communists reveal a tendency to produce the appropriate Mao phrase as a conditioned response to situations rather than as the rational application of his theories to complex problems. The danger for those schooled in Mao's works is the temptation to exploit ideology 'to avoid a direct confrontation with the realities of their politics', as Pye describes the function of political theories in Chinese life. (*The Spirit of Chinese Politics*, 31.) Mao Tse-tung was not blind to this trap: 'There are not a few people who still regard odd quotations from marxist-leninist works as a ready-made panacea which, once acquired, can easily cure all maladies . . . It is precisely such ignorant people who take marxism-leninism as a religious dogma.' (SW III, 43.)

Adulation of 'Mao Tse-tung Thought' perhaps stems partly from Mao's vision of the proper use of political power. To communicate is to persuade, the first step towards political success. His philosophy used Western (marxist) tools for understanding society, but applied them creatively to a society in which they were never meant to be employed, acting as a modernising agent. 'Mao Tse-tung Thought' was to bridge the gap between the old peasant China and modern developed communities. This aim Mao emphasised more than once. (SW II, 381; III, 21.) He saw too that ideology was a weapon to defeat opponents through conversion: 'Our comrades must understand that ideological remoulding involves long-term, patient and painstaking work . . . We must learn to conquer erroneous ideas through debate and reasoning.' (PW, 16.) His ideology never lacked targets stubbornly resistant to his ideals. He remarked rather wistfully that the creation of a genuinely socialist society was not easy. (AC, 6.)

To bend the wills of a people which had forced every previous alien influence which crossed its frontiers to retreat or to adopt Chinese ways, Mao fought a constant battle for his Chinese version of communism. His cult enshrined what for him represented an assault against an isolationist and tenacious culture to smash tradition's brake on progress. Every slogan set in banner headlines, quoted with reverence on the radio or shouted adoringly by the faithful was a commitment to China's transformation. The fortifications erected around the Chinese mind over the centuries were so stout that the blows, the Mao slogans, had to be relentless. If Mao quotations could be woven into the fabric of political ritual, they would acquire validity and compulsion, no matter how strong the countervailing forces of tradition. How many ever lived by the letter of confucianism? Yet

Confucius for over twenty centuries influenced behaviour and thought and erected a standard for character and action to be judged impartially. Mao Tse-tung would be probably content with just this fate.

The role officially assigned to 'Mao Tse-tung Thought' has been complex. Lin Piao, Mao's official heir until disgraced in September 1971, described Mao's philosophy as 'a unifying thought, revolutionary thought, correct thought'. Lin went on to explain how it would transform the nation's mentality and assist economic production. 'Through the living study and application of his works,' Lin claimed, '[and] only [thus] can the mental outlook of the working people be changed and spiritual forces be transformed into tremendous material strength.' (ID, 240-41.)

In the lives of ordinary people, the study of Mao's philosophy provided a set of rules for analysing and solving problems. The official press and radio have poured out examples of obstacles overcome in factory and farm through applying Mao's ideas. In a Shanghai chemical works, Mao's philosophy showed the party secretary why his factory had failed to cut production costs. (RS, 28 October, 1970.) Mao Thought helped a group of peasants to boost their harvests. (NCNA, 16 November, 1970.) Classes in Mao Thought apparently have taught ordinary peasants and workers how to produce their own solutions to local difficulties and conquered their lack of experience in the use of abstract theory to master novel situations. With the whole country embracing identical logical techniques through Mao study sessions, life has become easier for Peking; the pattern of popular response to economic bottlenecks and social change has been made more predictable.

The unity in national life to which Lin Piao referred has an importance which extends beyond politics to embrace economic development. If growth is seen as a total process, involving the release of new forces to provide the momentum, hitherto weak or absent, towards economic transformation, social change in some degree must take place. A key feature of modern industrial communities is specialisation through division of labour and administration counterbalanced by a high level of co-ordination and co-operation between the various stages of production and, indeed, the different sectors of the economy. Barrington Moore, in tracing the emergence of free as opposed to totalitarian régimes, has commented: 'Economic co-operation among any set of individuals in the Chinese village lacked permanence or the institutional basis' observable in India or Japan. He also underlines that in China, unlike Japan or pre-industrial Europe, the major decisions in the farming cycle were left to the individual household instead of being a collective responsibility. (*Social Origins of Dictatorship and Democracy*, 210-11.)

These facets of rural life have blocked social innovation, and thus economic progress, for as Morris Ginsberg maintains, 'An important factor in social change is the emergence of a common purpose'. He sees the formulation of a 'general will' as increasing in difficulty with a community's size, though this obstacle can be overcome in a democracy where a community has a long history. (*Essays in Sociology and Social Philosophy*, 148.) China is old but suffers both from large numbers and a lack of democracy. Hence, to achieve general acceptance of radical changes in living patterns, a forced development of a national consensus is necessary, another reason for adopting Maoism as the sole Chinese ideology. The cult of Mao Tse-tung, in short, had implications beyond the aggrandisement of personal power, the satisfaction of exercising a charismatic influence over a country or even of knitting together the community's semi-autonomous social units. Maoism was part of the total thrust towards social and economic revolution.

A major issue in weighing up how long Mao Tse-tung's ideological dominance can survive is the acceptability of his philosophy to China. James R. Townsend observes: 'Political change in modern China has, therefore, been gradual and partial, rather than abrupt and total as the [Chinese communist party] and foreigners sometimes suggest.' Yet he emphasises the political participation and commitment demanded from every citizen, in striking contrast to the imperial era. (*Popular Participation in Communist China*, 213.) The strain of adapting to the communist style of rule has however been reduced since so many of Mao's principles can be traced back to the nation's most respected political ideals. More important than the hotly-debated question of how far Mao created a brand of communism owing less to Marx than to his own culture, is the extent to which a Chinese can feel Mao has been faithful to the inheritance of the best in Chinese philosophy. Some examples of the similarities between Maoism and China's historical values have been offered already. Nevertheless, Mao Tse-tung's attempt to turn ancient ideals into modern realities deserves closer examination.

The old duty to rebel against unjust governments was mentioned earlier. In 1939, Mao stated: 'All the truths of marxism can be summed

41

up in one sentence: to rebel is justified.' (LL, 10.) A right to demonstrate openly in protest against oppressive cadres had been implicit ever since 1957 when he called for understanding and not repression, 'if disturbances do occur as a result of bad work on our part'. (PE, 123-24.) At the start of the Cultural Revolution, he made this principle more than just another fine-sounding slogan. He urged: 'It is necessary boldly to arouse the masses and to let the masses rise up in revolution, educate themselves, run their own affairs and liberate themselves.' (PD, 20 August, 1966.) The people were encouraged to take him at his word. He restated his message the following year: 'Erroneous leadership, which brings harm to the revolution, should not be accepted unconditionally but should be resisted resolutely.' (PD, 1 January, 1967.)

By the end of 1967, Mao was concerned with discipline: 'Comrades of the whole party must unite around the central committee and any act of sabotage against unity is a crime.' (Wen-hui Pao, 27 November, 1967.) But by this stage of the Cultural Revolution, anarchy and factional violence had reached an alarming pitch. However, cadres were to respect views which clashed with theirs. (PD, 6 February, 1968.) Mao still insisted: 'The basic thought of marxism-leninism is to make revolution.' (KMD, 5 May, 1968.) An ancient right, rarely exercised before, had been integrated into basic Maoist philosophy and implemented in practice.

One of Mao's constant injunctions was: 'We should at no time divorce ourselves from the masses. In this way we shall be able to know the masses, to understand them.' (PD, 17 August, 1966.) The concept is by no means alien to Chinese society, even though the educated have despised manual workers. One philosophical school (the Mo-ists), however, venerated the sage who could undertake the most brutal labour, battling with his hands against natural disaster, living plainly and practising total self-sacrifice. (Sources of Chinese Tradition, I, 80-81.) Balazs claims officials manning the outposts of the empire in the first century A.D. had close links with the peasantry. (Chinese Civilization and Bureaucracy, 206.) Charles O. Hiller recounts how officials were sent to pacify the disaffected by persuasion and personal contact. (The Traditional Chinese State in Ming Times, 1368-1644, 75-76.) Mao's theories about personal contacts changing behaviour seem similar: 'We must have faith in the ability of the labouring people to surmount or correct their shortcomings and mistakes when political work has been properly carried out.' (PD, 24 December, 1967.)

Barrington Moore also suggests the upper classes (defined by official position and not just by wealth in China) kept in contact with the ordinary people through the clan institution. The clan was run by the gentry, but the peasants who composed the majority of its members could not be ignored. (*Social Origins of Dictatorship and Democracy*, 207.) Mao praised the ties which cadres could establish with the masses even on visits of only a few hours to rural or workers' communities. (CS, 8.) He insisted: 'No matter how high an official anyone is, he should be like an ordinary worker among the people. It is absolutely impossible for him to put on airs.' (PD, 19 November, 1967.) This directive cut across centuries of mandarin behaviour, but the Chinese have never expected their bureaucrats to be completely cut off from the masses. Indeed, one of a new dynasty's strengths was the ability to win support through its awareness of the popular grievances which had swept away the previous imperial house. (*The Chinese Mind*, 214.)

Maoist China frequently has compelled officials to face scrutiny and censure from the party and the people. The masses, Mao stated once, even enjoy the right to dismiss cadres from office without fear of reprisal. (SW IV, 186.) Similarly, provision was made in imperial China for commoners to lodge complaints against officials, and special institutions were established to make this system work. (*Traditional China*, 69-70.) (The redress obtained in practice was undoubtedly minimal.) In addition, reformers frequently reminded their imperial masters of the ancient custom of choosing officials through popular selection. One seventh-century document complained: 'Appointments to office are not based upon the recommendation of the village communities.' Another figure in the same period, Wang An-shih, asked: 'What is the way to select officials? The ancient kings selected men only from the local villages and through the local schools. The people were asked to recommend those they considered virtuous and able, sending up their nominations to the court, which investigated each one.' (*Sources of Chinese Tradition*, I, 401, 415.) Mao Tse-tung's search for popular control over the bureaucrats was of ancient lineage. China has accepted for some two thousand years the value of protecting the commoner from the arbitrary excesses of a totalitarian administration. Mao Tse-tung, in a sense, simply took the principle to its logical conclusion in 1966 and, through the Cultural Revolution, broke down fear of the civil servant and state power. The people could attack the highest in the land, and head of state Liu Shao-chi lost office.

While Mao Tse-tung would prefer the nation to struggle with its duties out of self-dedication, he never overlooked the importance of material benefits in safeguarding the party's influence. (For example, SW II, 445.) In the agricultural development programme drawn up under his supervision, the rural areas were ordered to accumulate as much as eighteen months' grain reserves, while the state would build grain stocks to cover up to two years' consumption. (*National Programme for Agricultural Development, 1956-1967*, 22.) Barrington Moore has noted the importance attached in imperial times to maintaining well-stocked local and national granaries as a defence against famine. (*Social Origins of Dictatorship and Democracy*, 205.) Mencius, like Mao, put the people and their prosperity at the top of the virtuous ruler's obligations. (*The Chinese Mind*, 155.) This teaching of over two thousand years' currency was honoured almost entirely by lip service. Yet the maxims of Mencius were drummed into student heads well into this century. Mao Tse-tung's attitude to the masses' comfort was not judged by a primitive community intrigued by the novelty of social welfare but by a nation which had recognised and remembered through centuries of education the responsibility of governments for their citizens' well-being.

A striking parallel between Mao Tse-tung and the Chinese philosophers who preceded him is his use of the marxist theory of 'contradictions', the conflict or opposition of various social and economic forces. Chinese find little difficulty in appreciating this notion, although Cohen comments how communist discussion of 'contradictions' often seems 'a stupid and tiresome verbal game'. (*The Communism of Mao Tse-tung*, 140.) The criticism is well founded in a Western context. For Chinese, however, the argument that life consists of antagonistic influences in need of reconciliation is almost pre-historical. Male and female forces (Yin and Yang) are the outstanding examples of this idea of contradictory influences governing the world. Huston Smith sums up the notion of 'contradictions' in Chinese philosophy very cogently: 'The mutual reciprocity that pervades all things is in most instances between unequals, the relations that link man and nature are not symmetrical.' (*Traditional China*, 114.) Wing-tsit Chan quotes some vivid historical phrases on this subject, for instance, 'the process of fusion and intermingling, of overcoming and being overcome, and of expansion and contradiction'. (*ibid.*, 129.)

Since the theory of 'contradictions' expounded by Mao has been hailed officially as a beacon which 'illuminates the course of China's socialist revolution and socialist construction and ... has laid the theoretical foundations for the current Great Proletarian Cultural Revolution', its long acceptance in the nation's philosophy is of great significance. (ID, 4.) Mao took care to quote examples of 'contradictions' from his country's traditional culture to prove that this basic marxist concept was reasonable. (PE, 65, 68.)

A telling illustration of past and present combined in Mao Tse-tung is the commune. Although he did not invent the institution, he encouraged it. The word represents for Westerners the most radical form of Chinese communism. Wolfgang Franke examines the characters for commune, *kung-she*, and observes: 'For the Chinese, both characters immediately start a whole chain of associations. The first *kung* depicts an ideal stage of primitive communism.' (*Modern World, 1963/64*, 79.) He cites a moving passage from a famous work written three or four hundred years before the Christian era portraying the commune in terms of virtue, affection, economic security and social justice. This is not unlike Mao's own conception of commune life − he referred in 1939 to this ideal primitive commune. (SW II, 306.) Some outsiders may be alarmed by China's communes, by their echoes of the 1871 Paris revolution and the brutal collectivisation of Soviet peasants. But the word originally had almost idyllic overtones for Chinese of any education. The modern commune may fall far short of its ancient predecessor but what counts is that Mao's people have known for so long what a commune should offer its inhabitants.

The assertion that Chinese use the events of twenty centuries ago to judge their present government sounds fanciful if not pure whimsy. In 1966, Mao's adherents showed the devastating impact of comparing modern China to its past. They picked on a feature series in the Peking press written by a group they accused of ridiculing Chairman Mao and his policies. These 'counter-revolutionaries' were denounced in a revealing indictment: 'In the guise of recounting historical anecdotes, imparting knowledge, telling stories and cracking jokes, they launched an all-out and venomous attack on our great party, using ancient things to satirise the present.' (GSCR (2), 2-3.) To prove these allegations, large chunks of the offending articles were reprinted with the crucial passages set in bold type. This technique brought into sharp relief what seems to have been a deliberate attack on the communist party and on Mao Tse-tung personally. The anecdotes chosen to ridicule Maoist polices were drawn from the earliest periods of China as well as later dynasties.

The list of historical events used 'to satirise the present' was extensive. Wise monarchs who listened to all shades of opinion, officials brave enough in defence of virtue to face dismissal, extracts from traditional philosophers on the proper management of state affairs were quoted in one article after another. (*ibid.,* 12-49.) Maoist theories were bruisingly attacked by means of parody camouflaged as innocent historical discussion. The drama lay in the contrast between the behaviour of the current leadership and the graces or follies of ancient emperors. One item devoted to the correct method of employing labour on public works ended with the bold remark: 'If a man of the seventh century B.C. understood this truth, we who live in the sixties of the twentieth century should naturally understand it even better. We should draw new enlightenment from the experience of the ancients.' (*ibid.,* 25.) The detailed rebuttal of the series implies the average Peking reader understood only too well the message his newspapers had wrapped up in diverting fables and references to the sages.

Given Mao Tse-tung's respect for long-standing Chinese ideals and the careful garbing of marxism in a dress which China would not find alien, what can be predicted about his philosophy's survival as a vital and modernising influence? The easiest answer is the cynical observation that Maoism is so Chinese it will be swallowed up eventually into the body of national political philosophy. If Lenin and Stalin could be watered down to the relatively benign Soviet policy of more bread and some circuses for the citizenry at home and peaceful co-existence with capitalism abroad, the Chinese, with long experience of drowning foreign elements in their culture, should have no difficulty in reducing 'Mao Tse-tung Thought' to a latter-day version of Confucius. But times have changed. A modern China, industrialised and much further removed from its rural heartland, must inevitably evolve new social and cultural forms to suit a community dependent on machines rather than battling with nature in scattered villages. Mao Tse-tung's philosophy offers his country an answer to this challenge. It could refuse his solution, but human beings usually take the easy way out. The Chinese are pragmatic enough to grasp a ready-made guide to life which preserves something of their proud past. Furthermore, despite the failure of the Great Leap Forward and the chaos of the Cultural Revolution, Mao Tse-tung had given his people independence, alleviation of the periodic famines, nuclear weapons, space satellites and, above all, unity and order. In future crises, he will be remembered as a source of solutions to grave emergencies. Equally important was Mao

Tse-tung's unique position as the only Chinese political philosopher of major importance to become his country's ruler. This fact gave him a leverage never possessed by Confucius, Mencius and the rest of those who sought to teach men what produces a healthy society and good government.

In the period of undiluted Maoism following the Cultural Revolution, Confucius and his ilk were roundly denounced. Is this evidence that Mao Tse-tung had tried to build a political framework untainted by the 'ghost of the confucian shop'? One major analysis of why respect for Confucius should be stamped out seems to have been inspired by anxiety that Confucius might be promoted as a rival to Mao Tse-tung. (PD, 10 January, 1967.) Another essay in the same vein denied the benevolent ideals usually attributed to Confucius and his spiritual descendants. Confucius was also intolerable because of the use made of his teachings by imperial tyrants. But more important seems to have been the fear that if confucianism were tolerated, the country would never cease to hanker after its comfortable but obsolete customs: 'The reason why the reactionary class is still able to restore the old by exploiting respect for Confucius is that the reactionary influence of the "confucian and mencian doctrines" still harms people . . . If we look back to 1962 when the remnants of the feudal landlord class still used feudal clan relations to continue the feudal family records, we can recognise the long-term nature and large scale of this ideological struggle.' (RF, 6-7/1969.)

Before 1966, considerable debate took place on how the cultural heritage could be employed by the modern era. One writer used the classics to illustrate Mao's theory of contradictions and the importance of heeding the masses in framing policy. (PD, 12 June, 1962.) Another commentator argued that although the classics contained some merit if studied from a marxist standpoint, essentially they reflected the feudal outlook of their age. (Wen-yi Pao, 11 December, 1963.) But some writers were agitated because Confucius and other notables in Chinese philosophy had inculcated a feudal morality used to suppress the people. For instance, the emphasis on chastity had turned women into inferior creatures; filial piety encouraged obedience to the emperor. (Hsin Chien-she, 20 November, 1963.) Philosophical terms, it was claimed, have a meaning derived from the class situation in which they are applied, causing considerable problems in absorbing the past. Traditional ethics could be useful in a communist state only if stripped of their feudal elements. (ibid.) These views may make the sages appear an embarrassment to the new China. However Mao's own familiarity with the classics and his apt quotation from them were emphasised by one author to refute the call for the past to be consigned to 'the dustbin of history' – as long as the country's cultural legacy was employed to propagate marxism-leninism. (*Che-hsueh Yen-chiu*, 25 July, 1965.)

Mao Tse-tung's approach was entirely practical. 'To venerate all the trappings of confucianism as religious dogma' was backward. Yet he called on the party to 'learn whatever is alive in the classical Chinese language' to improve its publications. (SW III, 54, 60.) Quite properly, Mao was proud of his people's achievements: 'Our national history goes back several thousand years and has its own characteristics and innumerable treasures. But in these matters we are mere schoolboys. Contemporary China has grown out of the China of the past; we are marxist in our historical approach and must not lop off our history. We should sum up our history from Confucius to Sun Yat-sen and take over this valuable legacy.' (SW II, 209.) Not surprisingly, he rejected those who worshipped Confucius or his canons. (*ibid.*, 369.) Mao was concerned to fashion a new society, an impossible goal if people refused to turn round and face the future. His line was: 'A splendid old culture was created during the long period of Chinese feudal society ... To reject its feudal dross and assimilate its democratic essence is a necessary condition for developing our new national culture and increasing our national self-confidence.' (*ibid.*, 381.)

Obviously appreciative of the old culture's sway over the minds of modern Chinese, and a skilful writer himself, Mao displayed his good taste in declaring: 'We must on no account reject the legacies of the ancients.' He proudly claimed they represented 'the difference between crudeness and refinement, between roughness and polish, between a low and high level, and between slower and faster work'. (SW III, 81.) From his own gift for using history, the classics and ancient Chinese ideals to rub away the most foreign elements of marxism, nobody seems to have been more aware than Mao Tse-tung that any Chinese who rejected contemptuously the cultural treasures handed down through generations of reverent guardians would find his people a hostile audience.

Chapter Three

'A Future of Incomparable Brightness'

Mao Tse-tung did not take to revolution because he was a rebel by nature or psychologically at odds with his own society. His writings long before he came to power had the ring of a man drafting policies for a party already in control of the country. He lacked the typical insurgent's nonchalant acceptance of violence as the answer to political problems. His first serious split with the communist party arose, significantly, over his refusal to accept central committee rebukes for his tendency towards 'too little burning and killing'. (SW I, 98.) 'A bloodless transition is what we would like and we should strive for it', he declared. (*ibid.*, 290.) He also expressed his hostility to army elements which clung excessively to the old guerrilla mentality. (MW, 278.)

Like the rest of his nation, peace and order meant a great deal to him. 'War, this monster of mutual slaughter among men, will be finally eliminated by the progress of human society . . . But there is only one way to eliminate it and that is to oppose war with war.' (SW I, 182.) Again, as with so many Chinese radicals of his period, Mao's anger boiled over at abuses repugnant to all observant citizens: denial of freedom to such groups as women (Mao's first political campaign); brutal exploitation of peasants and workers; official corruption; foreign domination. No genius was required in the 1920s to diagnose China's national sickness. Mao's contribution lay in mobilising the forces to overthrow the prevailing system and substitute a vastly superior régime on any estimate except the blindest anti-communist reckoning. All China groaned under the same woes; Mao schemed for their permanent cure.

Unlike most revolutionaries, personal administration of his country was not Mao's ambition. Communist sources and Western visitors with access to information about the power structure in Peking after 1969 agreed Mao Tse-tung was concerned not with the details of government but with overall policy. His true ambition appears to have been heady enough but somewhat unusual in a man whose potential authority was unlimited, that is to act as the country's conscience. Mao's postwar pronouncements concentrated on the whole on pulling party and people back to the proper path whenever he believed them to be straying.

Nevertheless, as Bernard Crick points out: 'In Marx himself, right from the beginning, the theory of ideology furnished a plan of action aimed at a total change of society, not simply an academic means of understanding society as it was.' (*In Defence of Politics,* 39.) Mao Tse-tung was no different. Ideology must be directed towards a specific end: 'Any ideology – even the very best, even marxism-leninism itself – is ineffective unless it is linked with objective realities, meets objectively existing needs.' (SW IV, 457.)

Mao sketched a vague picture of life in the new China. Probably however, he was not concerned with the danger that the more specific the promises made before victory, the greater the risk of disappointing popular expectations later on since Mao displayed an odd attitude towards material conditions. He did not emphasise the people's misery (around a dozen passages in the official selections from his works) in arousing support for the communist party. His descriptions of the socialist nation to come were confined to some ten pages in his writings. Perhaps this peculiar feature of Mao's propaganda work could be explained by the simple truth that China's sufferings spoke for themselves. No future could be bleaker than the present under which the country groaned until 1949.

Mao Tse-tung in 1945 offered the nation hope of 'a China which is independent, free, democratic, united, prosperous and strong'. (SW III, 201.) Most of his specific aims were concerned with economic development, the only sensible priority in a community so destitute. 'The abolition of the feudal system and the development of agricultural production will lay the foundation for the development of industrial production and the transformation of an agricultural country into an industrial one . . . We believe that revolution can change everything, and that before long there will arise a new China with a big population and a great wealth of products, where life will be abundant and culture will flourish.' (SW IV, 238, 454.) Communism was not an end in itself for Mao: 'In the last analysis, the impact, good or bad, great or small, of the policy and the practice of any Chinese political party upon the people depends on whether and how much it helps to develop their productive forces.' (SW III, 251.) To evaluate a new economic structure, rural co-operatives, Mao Tse-tung laid down the simplest criterion: 'The main indicator by which all co-operatives should measure their health is — is production increasing, and, how fast?' (SU, 28.)

Mao rejected the role of hidebound political theorist and felt no compulsion to swallow unquestioningly the dogmas of marxism's patriarchs: 'Marx, in the era of *laissez-faire* capitalism, could not concretely know certain laws peculiar to the era of imperialism beforehand, because imperialism, the last stage of capitalism, had not yet emerged and the relevant practice was lacking.' (SW I, 299.) This passage is but one of several declarations of Mao's independence. The object of studying marxism-leninism, he observed, was 'to seek from this theory the stand, viewpoint and method with which to solve the theoretical and tactical problems of Chinese revolution'. (SW III, 22.) Mao regarded himself as free to innovate. Furthermore, while scorning the failure of Western learning to solve China's problems (SW IV, 413), Mao Tse-tung saw the merit of borrowing from every possible source of knowledge. He warned: 'China has suffered a great deal from the mechanical absorption of foreign material.' Yet he advised: 'We should assimilate whatever is useful to us today not only from the present-day socialist and new-democratic cultures but also from the earlier cultures of other nations ... We should not gulp any of this foreign material down uncritically, but must treat it as we do our food — first chewing it, then submitting it to the working of the stomach and intestines with their juices and secretions, and separating it into nutriment to be absorbed and waste matter to be discarded.' (SW II, 380.)

Mao Tse-tung thus laid down standards by which he must be judged. How far did his theories show his people how to smash the fetters of their poverty? Were they consistent with increased production and the growth of a modern economy? Did they adapt international experience of economic development to China's needs?

To put Mao Tse-tung's prescriptions for national prosperity on trial is a complicated exercise. Few studies of the Chinese economy contain much critical analysis of the philosophy of the new China. Most scholars seem to deny, by implication at least, the existence of a Maoist school of coherent economics. Some have gone further and denied that Mao has any deep concern with economic growth, among them Dwight H. Perkins. (*Current Scene,* 7 January, 1971.) Scholars who take this attitude are not to be blamed for their view of Mao's aims. Mao was essentially a politician and concerned with economic questions as

51

problems to be tackled by political means. Thus the task of extracting his development strategy from his essays is a tedious process in which they must be stripped of Chinese ideological jargon and translated into the colourless prose of conventional economics.

The maturest expression of Mao Tse-tung's economic theory was set out in his 1957 essay, 'On the Correct Handling of Contradictions among the People'. This might seem an odd assertion; at first glance, the work appears chiefly concerned with political problems: domestic discontent, the Hungarian revolution of 1956, potential clashes between a communist government and its subjects. Nevertheless, a host of Chinese authorities have employed this essay in economic debates, indicating its exceptional importance for those concerned with economic policy. The best Chinese summary of Mao's economic teachings was a long *People's Daily* article on 25 February, 1960. The writer explained Mao's slow evolution of a national development programme from 1949 and 1955 and went on to show the enormous influence of 'On the Correct Handling of Contradictions' in shaping China's growth strategy from 1957.

Teng To, overthrown as propaganda chief by the Red Guards for criticising Mao's economic programme (ER, 6/1966) among other sins, hailed the essay in 1960. He asserted in a commentary on its significance: 'Comrade Mao Tse-tung has once again creatively combined the truth of marxist political economy with the realities of China's socialist construction, and thus socialist economic theory has been further enriched in content.' (*Hsin Chien-she*, 2/1960.) Vice-Premier Li Hsien-nien, minister of finance, who survived the Cultural Revolution, quoted extensively from this 1957 essay in a feature on finance and banking. (RF, 1/1960.) References to 'On the Correct Handling of Contradictions' appeared in dozens of other major articles on economic policy during the early 1960s.

For Mao Tse-tung the barriers to economic progress had their origins in a lack of harmony between economic realities and the social institutions involved in generating growth. He had first analysed this conflict between the social system and the economy twenty years earlier (1937) in an another work entitled 'On Contradictions'. It seems that development, to him, resembled a set of scales with three weights in each pan, but never quite in balance. Each weight was paired with its opposite on the other side of the scale. The first of these conflicting pairs was the capacity for production ('productive forces'), and the social units, farms and factories, through which production is organised

52

('productive relations'). The second was the practical problems to be solved, and the ideological theory available for their analysis. The third pair was the 'superstructure' (the political and cultural apparatus), and the stage of development through which the economy was passing ('the economic base'). (PE, 58.)

Mao Tse-tung in 1957 highlighted specific conflicts ('contradictions') within these three pairs. The maximum capacity to produce ('productive forces') was reduced to some extent by the two social forms of production which then co-existed in China. The economy contained a state-owned sector whose regulation and adjustment were easy enough. But this sector could develop along different lines from the collectively-owned production facilities (chiefly the rural co-operatives which became the 1958 communes). Where the means of production – land, equipment, buildings and capital – were owned by a group such as an agricultural co-operative, government control of its activities had to allow for the members' freedom to make their own decisions, for example, about investment of communal savings. Mao Tse-tung claimed the 'superstructure' (the administration and its regulations) was basically suitable for the current socialist stage of the Chinese economy. But he warned that bureaucratic defects had not been eliminated, and the state system was still not completely in harmony with the country's economic needs. The overall ideological position was good in his opinion, so that the theoretical tools for resolving basic problems were available. But bourgeois ideas antipathetic to socialism still lingered on. (*ibid.*, 94.)

He quoted examples of the principal contradictions to be overcome. The money to be allocated to the public for personal consumption and the amount to be saved for investment represented a conflict affected by the different conditions under which the state-owned and the semi-autonomous collective sectors of the economy operated. (*ibid.*) Again, the government sometimes threw progress out of gear by faulty planning when 'subjective arrangements do not correspond to objective reality', that is the targets set by the plan could not be achieved with existing resources. (*ibid.*, 95.) On the ideological plane, time was needed 'for the masses to become accustomed to the new system, and for the government workers to learn and acquire experience'. (*ibid.*, 95-96.) The 1957 essay continued with a detailed programme for solving fundamental contradictions in such areas as agricultural policy, the intelligentsia and 'overall planning'.

Mao Tse-tung neglected to restate some principles he had

promulgated in his earlier work, 'On Contradictions'. In deference to marxist orthodoxy, Mao had acknowledged in 1937 that the decisive factors normally must be the existing capacity for production, the economic problems facing the community and the nation's stage of development. However, he argued, on occasion the various forms of social organisation blocked growth and thus played the key role. Again, if faced with a problem previously unforeseen by marxist theory, advances would depend on developing the ideology to a new level. If the political system obstructed economic progress, then the first priority must be changes in the realm of politics. (*ibid.*, 58.) He bowed politely to orthodoxy and stated his belief that generally mental and social attitudes grew out of economic and social realities. Yet he was also convinced erroneous ideas stood in the way of the nation's economic and social breakthrough: 'We also — and indeed must — recognise the reaction of mental on material things, of social consciousness on social being and of the superstructure on the economic base.' (*ibid.*, 59.) This conviction of the power of the human mind to influence events was to prove of prime importance in Mao's later thinking.

Mao Tse-tung was concerned with attacking poverty on three fronts. To build up economic momentum Mao believed the technical, economic and social relations within the nation had to be sorted out. New methods had to be evolved to overcome technical problems, such as the ceiling on output if agriculture continued to be organised according to primitive peasant formulas when national demand for food and raw materials was expanding. Economic factors had to be tackled if, for example, low prices for farm produce reduced the villages' purchases of industrial goods to modernise agriculture. For farming would remain backward and factories be left without markets unless price policy altered. Society might also require drastic transformation if inherited conservative attitudes meant that the masses were unwilling to use modern machines and advanced technology. Mao Tse-tung, in other words, was seeking solutions for the technical limit on output caused by a lack of skills, shortage of economic resources and other restrictions on growth; for the obstacles created by faulty state economic policy or administration; and for the hurdles raised by the survival of unprogressive ideas and customs in society. His own summary was: 'Any given culture (as an ideological form) is a reflection of the politics and economics of a given society, and the former in turn has a tremendous influence and effect upon the latter; economics is the base and politics the concentrated expression of economics.' (SW II, 340.)

A number of Western social scientists have argued along very similar lines. Mao regarded 'contradictions' as the prime cause of social change. (PE, 27.) Morris Ginsberg has analysed the failure of a community's formal institutions to cope with changes in the basic characteristics of society (a sudden population increase, for example) as a major force compelling a community to transform its structure. (*Essays in Sociology and Social Philosophy*, 140-42.) Ginsberg's subsequent attack on the marxist theory of contradictions does not mean his discussion of changes produced by social institutions' inability to meet community demands differs materially from Mao's position.

Albert O. Hirschman proposes an assault on economic bottlenecks through a technique implict throughout Mao's 'On the Correct Handling of Contradictions'. (PE, 125-26 in particular.) Balance and harmony can return to development by seeking out elements favourable to growth which can be exploited to remove the bottleneck — the 'contradiction' — indirectly through progress in other sectors. Hirschman urges, for example, that if poor government is a handicap, calls for administrative reform are not enough. Ways should be explored to force improvement in the government's performance by pushing forward in the sectors least affected by official incompetence. Thus, 'additional pressure (economic and political) could be brought on the obstacle to give way'. (*Development of the Emerging Countries*, 41.)

An example of how this might work in practice would be a nation whose badly-paid civil servants cannot afford to refuse bribes. This could affect economic performance if import restrictions under their control were not enforced on luxury goods (for which the rich will make corrupt payments) but operated to keep out equipment required by state industries. Better salaries would ease the problem, but higher government revenue to finance improved pay scales has to wait upon economic expansion. The remedy would be to encourage first the economy's private sector which is willing to buy off civil servants. Then once the growth of national income allowed decent wages for bureaucrats, corruption could be eliminated.

Mao Tse-tung's conviction that contradictions exist everywhere (PE, 91) finds an echo in Milton J. Esman's commentary on 'transitional societies'. The process of modernisation sets up economic, political and social pressures which constantly demand adjustments in the distribution and exercise of power. Esman can be read as stating that economic progress alters the foundations from which political

55

authority grows. The shifting power base cannot be ignored in organising the state. (*Approaches to Development,* 61.) Is this assertion at odds with Mao's prediction that in China, protracted ideological struggle would persist between the former ruling class (the bourgeoisie) and the new proletarian administration of the communist party? (PE, 116.) Wilber Scramm notes the strains resulting from the gap between the demands made on organisations and their ability to meet their obligations. He observes the value of such tensions in forcing vital adaptations on a community, with regular rhythms of uncomfortable strain followed by relaxation as five-year plans and similar campaigns are implemented. (*Communications and Political Development,* 36-37.) Mao Tse-tung's remarks on planning were very similar. Balance is a temporary phenomenon continually disrupted by 'struggles' between opposing elements in the economy. (PE, 95.)

Mao Tse-tung and Western development economists share a remarkable identity of views on the conflicts which arise as societies strive to transform poverty into plenty. Even more striking is the way Mao Tse-tung's practical plans for progress were rooted in principles accepted by a significant group of conventional Western economists. The gulf dividing China from the rest of the world is reflected painfully in the ignorance of this unity of thinking shown by Chinese communists (who are incredulous when the parallels are demonstrated) and by ordinary economists whose familiarity with Mao Tse-tung rarely derives from a first-hand study of his works. However, the way Maoist and Western economists, completely out of sympathy ideologically, arrive at similar programmes for prosperity is strong testimony to the basic validity of their conclusions.

Mao Tse-tung tackled the balance between the growth of production and the social organisation of economic activities, his 'technical engineering', with imagination. He laid down the priorities for national development in the simplest terms in 1957. Heavy industry, he described as 'the core of China's economic construction'. But this was to be a long-range aim. In practice, he shifted the balance subtly away from the former obsession with the growth of heavy industry derived from imitation of the Soviet economic model. Mao put his finger on the implications, so often overlooked, of moving forward from an overwhelmingly agricultural base. He claimed China understood the connection between farming and heavy industry. The peasants formed the market for heavy industry, though their potential demand for its products, machinery, power, fertilisers, transport facilities and the like, was hidden by the still primitive nature of Chinese farming. Mao predicted that with agricultural modernisation, farming's link with heavy industry's performance would come into focus. He remarked that, as China well knew, light industry was totally dependent on agriculture because light industry's direct source of raw materials and its immediate customers were the farms. He thus envisaged a three-tier development process. Faster expansion of agricultural output would allow light industry to grow at an increasing rate. Improved performance in these two sectors would create the savings for heavy industry's investment in new plant and equipment. The first two sectors' prosperity would ensure adequate purchasing power to buy the supplies turned out by heavy industry. In the last resort the overall rate of growth, according to Mao, depended on the peasants. (PE, 129-30.)

Mao saw the replacement of individual farming by agricultural co-operatives as essential to a breakthrough in the countryside. (*ibid.*, 101.) He had explained as early as 1955 his reasoning on this subject. The shift from traditional cultivation to large-scale farming with machinery and other inputs was, he judged, the only hope for a substantial increase in supplies of food and industrial raw materials. At the same time, a rural boom would raise peasant incomes and demand, while leaving a surplus for industrial investment by the state. Co-operative farming would start a social and technical revolution. (AC, 19-20.) Scientific farming through better seeds, more fertilisers and irrigation works, and improved techniques, equipment and management became a favourite theme. He returned to it constantly long before the 'Green Revolution' and its introduction of high-yield rice forced the rest of Asia to press for similar technical advances on its farms. (AC, 12; CS, 2, 12-13; LL, 34-35.)

Asia as a whole began to think along the same lines some ten years after Mao drafted his programme. And once awakened to agriculture's significance for development, the region started to speak in startlingly similar terms. The United Nations Economic Commission for Asia and the Far East (ECAFE) drew attention in 1964 to the historical association between the transformation of farming and successful industrialisation. The commission outlined how better farming raised export earnings and national savings for investment in factories, allowed the establishment of industries based on agriculture (Mao's 'light industry') and it noted the rural sector's potential as the major market for industrial output. (*Economic Survey of Asia and the Far East,*

1964, 112-16.) This United Nations body was dominated by such anti-Peking nations as Malaysia, Thailand, the Philippines, Taiwan and Australia. Its membership is proof that the similarity of its conclusions to Mao Tse-tung's recommendations a decade earlier was the result of economic necessity rather than any ideological sympathy with China.

Independent economists have expounded theses on developing countries which contain several notions found in Mao Tse-tung's writings. The general Asian preoccupation with heavy industry was dismissed as 'a somewhat romantic view' by Bert F. Hoselitz (*Sociological Aspects of Economic Growth*, 124.) Rainer Schickele has analysed the effect of low village incomes on production and pointed to the rigid ceiling imposed by limited rural spending on purchases of inputs to modernise farming. The market for factory output remains tiny, thus restricting investment opportunities in the industrial sector. (*Agrarian Revolution and Economic Progress,* 44.) Johnston and Mellor, though critical of sweeping claims for the superiority of co-operative farming over individual cultivation, admit the existence of highly efficient large-scale farms. (Plantation agriculture is their example.) They also believe reforms in land tenure are an urgent consideration. To some extent, their outlook runs parallel to the social revolution Mao began with the rural co-operatives. (*Economic Development: Challenge and Promise,* 191, 195-96.) When it came to agriculture, Mao Tse-tung was well ahead of other Asian leaders, and his ideas tally with the sort of thinking found among non-marxist economists.

Many development specialists would disagree with Mao Tse-tung's views on population. These were bound up very closely with his general economic ideas and with his agricultural approach in particular. While the Chinese government's policy on birth control has been far from consistent, Mao himself has been rude to prophets of over-population, dismissing their predictions as the 'the absurd argument of Western bourgeois economists'. 'It is a very good thing,' he declared, 'that China has a big population. Even if China's population multiples many times, she is fully capable of finding a solution; the solution is production.' (SW IV, 453.) Here Mao echoed Confucius' advice when asked what to do with a numerous population: 'Give them prosperity . . . educate them.' The possibility of escaping the danger of unemployment both open and disguised (seasonal farm workers, for example) by using more manpower and resisting mechanisation failed to attract Mao. He believed: 'The social and economic physiognomy of China will not undergo a complete change until . . . machinery is used, wherever possible, in every branch of production and in every place. (AC, 28.) He did not deny China's vast population created problems but he rejected any pessimism on this score. (PE, 112.)

Mao encountered opponents at home who claimed: 'The spread of co-operation would produce a vast pool of surplus labour for which there would be no outlet.' He admitted jobs disappeared when agricultural co-operatives were first formed, but insisted that a labour shortage then developed rapidly. The explanation for the initial drop in rural employment was 'because the co-ops there had not yet launched into large-scale production, had not yet begun additional money-making activities, had not yet started intensive cultivation'. When the co-operatives began functioning properly, demand for workers shot up. The labour shortage would worsen, he forecast, after mechanisation of farming. His confidence was founded on the prospects for expanding the scope of agricultural production far above current levels, together with mounting pressure on labour supplies through general economic development. SU, 151, 285-86.)

Clark and Haswell take issue with Mao's labour policy. They insist China lacked enough manpower to handle all the work available at such peak farming seasons as harvest time. They hold that Mao Tse-tung was misled by seasonal unemployment into setting up rural industries in 1958 and expanding cultivation beyond the capacity of the local work force in some areas. (*The Economics of Subsistence Agriculture*, 130-32.) Their criticisms in fact support Mao's analysis: any labour surplus could be absorbed by increasing both agricultural and industrial production. The difficulty lay in finding a formula to create seasonal work for the months when the rural population traditionally had little or nothing to do. This dilemma Mao Tse-tung attacked directly by encouraging double and triple cropping, sharply raising the amount of manhours required on the farms. He called, too, for new irrigation works and land reclamation, which could be carried out in the slack winter months. (AC, 12.) At a later stage he was to support rural industrial complexes which increased the calls on manpower in the countryside.

In a sense, Mao Tse-tung's emphasis on mechanisation was deceptive. His initial approach to the question of agricultural co-operatives was one of caution. As he observed in counter-attacking those who opposed co-operatives because of Soviet blunders in collectivisation, the process of winding up individual farming was to be gradual and voluntary. (AC, 21-25.) 'Technical transformation', he felt, 'will take longer than the social'. (*ibid.*, 28.) Mao warned: 'We will need several decades of intensive efforts to raise the standard of living of our entire people step by step.' (PE, 103.) He did not envisage any substantial shortcuts to prosperity. On this reasoning, though urging mechanisation which might have cut employment levels in the countryside, Mao was not expecting machines to supersede men in the short run. (LL, 35.)

Since mechanisation was a long-term plan, why introduce collectives if their main advantage, large-scale mechanised farming, was remote? The answer was far from simple, and many in China found his policy confusing, as one writer observed: 'Some people held that, without tractors, co-operation could not be achieved, or at least it would be slowed down. Or they maintained that, without tractors, production could not be increased and land could not be used to the full ... Some misguided people thought that our programme, namely, first co-operation and then mechanisation, was meant to slow down the mechanisation of agriculture so as to avoid a labour surplus.' (Tung Ta-lin, *Agricultural Co-operation in China*, 41, 49.) In 1956, Mao himself commented: 'Some people take the view that since the peasants were given land in the course of land reform and have been very enthusiastic in production, there is no reason why co-operation should be introduced.' (CS, 47.) These passages indicate the serious split over agricultural collectivisation.

Mao Tse-tung's support of the co-operatives was based partly on the political situation but it was mainly a matter of economics. He was deeply concerned that 'the spontaneous forces of capitalism have been steadily growing in the countryside in recent years'. The rich peasants had made a comeback. Poor peasants were not enjoying higher living standards. On the contrary, they were getting deeper into debt and giving up their land. (AC, 26.) This dangerous trend could, in Mao's opinion, only be halted through co-operatives. But economics took pride of place. Mao was convinced expansion of light industry and farming, which formed the main source of government revenue to pay for new industrial investments, could not be achieved through small-scale, peasant production. (*ibid.*, 20.) Unless output rose, 'what point, then, would there be in having co-operatives at all?' he asked. (*ibid.*, 12.)

The special growth element co-operative farming possessed compared with individual cultivation, Mao never explained clearly except for references to the advantages of large-scale production. He contented himself with the bald assertion: 'The change-over from individual to socialist, collective ownership in agriculture . . . is bound to bring about a tremendous liberation of the productive forces.' (Quotations, 26.) He even admitted the cadres lacked the experience necessary to make the transition to co-operative farming painless. (AC, 6, 17.)

One commentator has made the valid point that the pre-1953 communist land reforms had upset the balance between the size of a household's plot and the quantity of draught animals and implements at its disposal. Previously, the unequal distribution of land allowed the rich to hire out essential equipment in exchange for the poorer peasant's labour. This was no longer possible. Again, land reform made no demands on the peasants for the purchase in any manner of their extra fields. The complete abolition of rents raised the average peasant's income by reducing farming expenses. His family could thus afford to eat more and sell less grain. These factors made some form of pooling of land, labour and equipment essential. (Kang Chou, *Agricultural Production in Communist China, 1949-1965*, 43-44.) The same writer also shows the co-operative's advantages. Plots could be combined into more efficient units, with each field devoted to the crop most suited to its soil. Since all co-operative members had a right to be maintained from its earnings, cadres had an incentive to employ surplus labour on such activities as irrigation schemes. But he notes the well-known problem of trying to apply industrial-type management to farming, where success is determined as much by nature as human ability. (*ibid.*, 47-49.) On this last point, Mao felt cadres would learn to solve the admitted management weaknesses of co-operatives in the course of taking part in farm work. (AC, 1-2.)

While these comments are convincing enough and prove co-operatives had their own logic, some drawbacks and a number of virtues, the analysis has to be put into a larger context. Kang Chou shows how co-operatives ease the risks of adopting modern techniques with which peasants are unfamiliar and are likely to bungle on their first trials. These innovations become less daunting when shared by a group rather than borne by a single household. (*Agricultural Production in Communist China, 1949-1965*, 50.) This factor is important, but underneath it lies an even weightier consideration.

Many sociologists accept as commonplace that a group tends to choose more adventurous policies than an individual. (For example, Peter B. Smith, ed., *Group Processes*, Reading 18.) Although Mao

Tse-tung never displayed any overt awareness of this behaviour pattern, he apparently grasped by instinct the importance of getting groups to take decisions when implementing radical policies. Mao insisted on the group technique because he believed in leading the people through persuasion and example and in unleashing the innate abilities of the masses by making them partners in decision-making. At the same time, meetings dominated by one person, he asserted, would never produce real unity for action. (SW III, 191; IV, 242, 267-68.) Mao's views came quite close in practice to a deliberate bid to awaken the courage ('daring' was the word Mao used frequently in this context) which several researchers believe a group develops when it functions collectively instead of as disunited individuals.

In reorganising agriculture on a collective basis, first through the co-operatives, and from 1958 through the communes, Mao Tse-tung was following a world-wide trend to diminish the importance of individual land ownership and household farming. Land reform and agricultural co-operatives are popular programmes in many countries. Furthermore, while Mao was acting as a marxist, the tendency in the United States for land ownership to be divorced from farm management had already begun. The American situation developed because the land itself combined with a given amount of labour no longer determined the level of output. Of growing importance in regulating yields were the quality of grain, the quantity of fertiliser applied, and the technical expertise required by modern agriculture. (*Readings in the Economics of Agriculture,* 26.)

But the other side of modernisation, the use of machinery, has a very different effect. In industry, machines smash the old pattern of the artisan who has the satisfaction of creating a product from start to finish, deciding how best to use his raw materials and dependent on his personal skill. The assembly line creates repetitive work in which the employee cannot identify the finished article with his own labour. Farming is just the opposite. A machine makes ploughing easier, but the farm worker still has to know the right depth of furrow to get the best yield. He may plough, plant and reap with machines, yet management of the cultivation process and production of the final crop are no less the fruits of his effort than with hand-farming methods. Machines, though reducing the physical strain of farming, increase the level of skill required. Improved farm technology thus produces far less direct change in the farmer's life and outlook (except through higher incomes) than the total revolution involved in the replacement of handicraft industries by modern factories. (*ibid.*, 6-13.)

This is of great significance in assessing the forces working to produce new social patterns in China's villages. An interesting point here is Mao's dislike of specialisation. He preferred the all-rounder, the factory worker who could till the fields, the peasant able to run small rural industry. (LL, 56.) This view reflected Marx's vision of the communist Utopia: 'To hunt in the morning, fish in the afternoon, rear cattle in the evening, criticise after dinner, just as I have a mind.' At the same time, Mao surely was recognising the impossibility of intense specialisation and division of labour in agriculture. Farming depends on intimacy with the local environment and the ability to adjust to weather, pests, blights and a host of biological factors. Rice cannot grow on an assembly line. (Rainer Schickele, *Agrarian Revolution and Economic Progress*, 101.) Mao's opposition to specialisation also took into account the obsolescence which overtakes the craftsman's skills in an industrial revolution. His call for the masses to acquire competence in various fields helped to persuade them that the painful process of making redundant the old-fashioned artisan was compensated by a new range of abilities and not just an unskilled mechanical routine. (Compare E.P. Thompson, *The Making of the English Working Class*, 289.)

A final point concerns the kind of modern scientific agriculture Mao Tse-tung pressed upon the peasants. Indian experience indicates that mechanisation by itself reduces demand for farm labour. One solution is the adoption of hybrid grains, 'miracle' IR-8 rice, for instance. But small Indian farmers find high-yielding strains too risky because of their vulnerability to pest and disease. Modern seeds also require more financial credit because the new hybrids devour fertiliser. (Gogula Parthasarathy, *Agricultural Development and Small Farmers*, 34-38, 62-67.) This evidence casts doubts on such unqualified assertions as: 'The new seeds are bringing far-reaching changes in every segment of society. They may be to the agricultural revolution in the poor countries what the steam engine was to the industrial revolution in Europe.' True, as Mao foresaw, 'farmers who wish to realise the genetic potential of the high-yielding seeds must prepare seedbeds more thoroughly, apply fertiliser more frequently, weed more carefully, and use more pesticides. All these operations require additional labour.' (Lester R. Brown, *Seeds of Change*, 10, 103.) The rural labour surplus can be made to disappear, but farming's rhythm and its dependence on individual skills remain.

The problem is to find a bridge between safe, traditional cultivation and the novel techniques which are always a gamble when first introduced. Mao understood something of this difficulty and observed: 'With regard to administrative staff and, further, with regard to material resources, such as the ability to raise loans, the co-ops have a hard time if the party and the government do not give them a hand.' He gave a high priority to state subsidies for the poorer peasants joining co-operatives. (SU, 137-38, 220.) However he had enormous, perhaps excessive, confidence in the peasants' ability to create the resources needed for improved farming out of their own sweat. (*ibid.*, 13-14.) In *National Programme for Agricultural Development, 1956-1967*, the main burden of improving agricultural standards was pushed firmly on to 'the hard work of the peasants themselves', though the government promised 'from now on gradually [to] give more and more of whatever assistance is necessary for carrying out the numerous measures to increase agricultural production'. Definite pledges of help were not made, and vague injunctions to promote rural credit organisations and strengthen co-operation between agriculture and industry replaced promises of solid material assistance. (4, 26-29.) The mere re-organisation of the social units for farming, the creation of co-operatives and then communes, seems to have struck those responsible for implementing Mao's policies as virtually all that was required to free the villages from penury, provided they worked hard enough.

Chapter Four
'Poor and Blank'

'Chinese socialism is something new in the world. The Czech reformers claimed to establish socialism with a human face. The Chinese have set out on the more ambitious course of establishing economic development with a human sense of values.' (Joan Robinson, *Freedom and Necessity*, 104.) This comment by a distinguished though not entirely impartial English economist sums up China's own view of its development pattern. The statement is slightly inaccurate, not because it stressed China's human values but in its implication that under Mao growth was not fuelled by the universal pains of bending low over the crops and the agonies of learning to surrender the familiar patterns of the past for the strange industrial techniques of the present. All that a government can do, whatever its political colour, to lessen the strain of living through an industrial revolution is to ensure its own efficiency and offer its people some equality of sacrifice. Investment in new factories tomorrow still has to come out of what can be snatched from peasants' rice bowls today. The search for efficiency in the administration's regulation of industry was a major preoccupation of Mao Tse-tung when he explored the mechanics of industry's contribution to China's future.

Mao Tse-tung tackled the engineering of 'technical' change in the industrial sector only after mapping out the future development of agriculture. He struck out on a path of his own in 1957 by ending the overriding priority for heavy industry and calling for development of the light industrial sector. (PE, 129.) His first feeling of distaste for 'unrealistic and unacceptable' demands for the development of heavy industry (including armaments) was expressed during the war. (SW III, 113.) He rejected in 1956 total concentration of resources on heavy industry's expansion through his study of the Soviet bloc, which revealed waste resulting from the neglect of light industry and agriculture, creating shortages of the basic necessities of life. He spoke of

65

sinking 'a bit more investment in light industry', but denied this policy meant China was not interested in heavy industry. As he saw it, without the food and goods to satisfy the needs of the workers and the capital raised from taxing light industry and agriculture, heavy industry could not progesss. (CS, 22-23.)

Mao's logic was hard to fault. The factory work force had to be kept alive, and new capital equipment had to be paid for. With an economy as close to subsistence level as postwar China, a furious race for large, modern factories would have courted disaster. Even if foreign credits (from the Soviet Union) financed the construction of these plants, the peasants could not afford, as Mao knew, industrial products until a substantial rise had taken place in rural incomes. Mao Tse-tung's preference for light industry was thus a child of necessity. But the policy had important implications he did not trouble to enumerate but which others spelt out for him. Only slowly did Mao become acutely aware of the long period which the country would need to achieve a reasonable standard of economic development, although time is a key consideration in a realistic programme of development priorities. Before coming to power, Mao Tse-tung refused to regard 'economic construction as the centre of all our work'. The war and its needs came first in setting economic priorities. (SW I, 133.) Mao had little background in large-scale economic planning before 1949. Hence, in the final stage of the battle for control of the nation, Mao felt able to assert: 'The day is not far off when China will attain prosperity. There is absolutely no ground for pessimism about China's economic resurgence.' (SW IV, 370.) This rosy picture soon faded when he confronted the country's economic confusion as its new leader. By 1955, he forecast twenty to twenty-five years would be necessary to transform farming. (AC, 28.) A prosperous China would not be achieved for 'several decades' was his estimate two years later. However in 1956, the time factor became of crucial political importance. In that year, 'small numbers of workers or students in certain places went on strike. The immediate cause of these disturbances was the failure to satisfy certain of their demands for material benefits'. (PE, 122.) The signs of restiveness at continuing poverty were menacing, with the example of Hungary's revolt vividly before all developing communist countries. The remedy had to be found in increasing output so fast that rising government revenue would allow new factories to mushroom and therefore permit still more production.

For Mao, the answer was simple. The materials to expand light industry were to hand. He argued that factories in this sector could frequently be built extremely quickly. Once in production, their annual rate of return would range from twenty to a hundred per cent. If the initial investment could be liquidated at this pace, capital turnover would be so high, Mao reckoned, that returns from one new plant would allow between one and four additional enterprises to be established in every five-year period as a result of the first factory's profits. (CS, 24.) The arithmetic of light industry's profits and the prospect they offered of cutting short the period required to get the economy progressing rapidly enough to underwrite the costs of modern large-scale manufacturing were so impressive that light industry became a cornerstone of Mao's economic philosophy.

To the public, he explained this new priority essentially in terms of his desire to speed up national growth. But Mao's reference to the contribution from light industry (chiefly small workshops in the villages, Mao was to urge) to better living standards hinted at another motive to which he dared not allude openly. Marx had described the brutal effects on the family of modern factory industry: 'However terrible and disgusting, under the capitalist system, the dissolution of the old family ties may appear, nevertheless, large-scale industry by assigning an important part in the production process to women, young people and children of both sexes outside the domestic sphere creates a new economic basis for a higher form of the family and of relations between the sexes.' In the same passage, Marx refers to the destruction of parental authority which followed the introduction of factory enterprises. Mao Tse-tung might have been willing to believe modern methods of production would eventually improve family relations and eradicate the petty tyranny which prevailed in so many Chinese households obedient to corrupted versions of the confucian ethic. But to Mao as a Chinese, the results of modern factory life depicted by Marx must have been appalling, a denial of every comfort and virtue the nation had sought from time immemorial in its private life. In his analysis of the obstacles facing the development of heavy industry, Mao Tse-tung alluded to the mistaken policies which had harmed the people's livelihood in Eastern Europe. (CS, 22.) Two essays on Stalin never ascribed officially to Mao but almost certainly from his pen, summed up the Russian despot's faults as the failure to allow the masses to control the state apparatus, including economic enterprises. (*The Historical Experience of the Dictatorship of the Proletariat*, 49.) Soviet experience offered little reassurance that a socialist state would

67

avoid the evils of industrialisation as depicted by Marx. Mao Tse-tung may well have calculated that to introduce heavy industry first – even if China could afford such a step – would rip apart the social fabric. A modest start with light industries (linked to agriculture as Mao pointed out) would permit gradual adjustment to a modern, industrial society. With just such caution Mao approached the first stage of creating agricultural co-operatives to avoid too much social disruption. A more gentle transition from a peasant to a manufacturing economy would give the communist party time to learn how to keep ahead of the inevitable social tensions and to avoid the mistakes committed in the Soviet Union and its European satellites. In a 1958 speech attributed to Mao Tse-tung, he expressed his belief in the value of the current form of family life although, with a bow to orthodox marxism, he suggested the existing family structure might become an obstacle to development in the future. (*Translations on Communist China,* No. 90, 47.)

The logic of Mao Tse-tung's development programme was expounded with considerable verve by one commentator. He revealed that about half the national income was derived from farming, highlighting the peasants as a source of investment funds. The countryside produced some eighty per cent of the nation's consumer goods. A rise in living standards must start therefore with a boost in rural output to permit increased consumption by the public. Because natural factors, largely beyond human control, determined the harvest and because of the shortage of farm equipment, agricultural progress and that of light industry (dependent upon the state of farming) were still unsatisfactory. Without a prosperous peasantry, he went on, heavy industry would not be able to find markets for the bulk of its wares. Finally, to allocate more funds to agriculture or light industry implied no down-grading of the overall importance of the heavy sector. The rate of growth of heavy industry was naturally so much faster than the rest of the economy (except for 'temporary periods) that Mao's policy should be viewed as accelerating agricultural and light industrial progress rather than retarding the development of heavy industry. (TKP, 11 December, 1961.)

Another Chinese observer took up the question of heavy industry's place in the development programme, indicating how anxious China was to avoid charges of discarding the proper socialist emphasis on heavy industry. He argued that agricultural equipment and inputs such as chemical fertilisers and pesticides were included in the heavy sector, yet their production strengthened farming. (RF, 21/1962.)

Another essay explained the circular connection between farming and heavy industry. Output for consumption and production of capital goods and equipment have to be balanced. Without food and the other basic consumer goods, the factory work force could not exist. But without the modern implements and chemical aids to farming, agricultural modernisation would be impossible, holding back progress of both light and heavy industry. (RF, 11/1962.)

The slow returns from large plants were also underlined: 'The bigger the scale of capital projects, the longer the lag before they go into production. They also call for higher initial inputs of material, equipment and labour. The wages paid out to workers engaged in capital construction will soon affect the market in the form of increased demand for consumer goods.' (ibid.) A danger arose, therefore, of throwing the whole system out of balance if the rural and light industrial sectors failed to supply the resources for capital works and proved unable to maintain workers engaged on construction projects. The turnover of capital was examined carefully to demonstrate that although heavy industry's profit margins were higher than in other sectors, this advantage was offset by delays in recovering the funds invested in large undertakings. But the writer also grasped the difference between long-term gains — superior in heavy industry — and short-term costs which would be lower for the smaller plant. (RF, 23/1961.) Location came into the picture. This factor bothered Mao Tse-tung. He understood the economies of building new factories in existing industrial areas already equipped with the infrastructure required for manufacturing. Yet location of the bulk of new plants in such areas would be inimical, he said, to the balanced development of the nation's resources as a whole. (CS, 24.) Less investment was needed to erect factories close to existing plants, just as extensions to old enterprises cost less than building new ones, one writer noted. But these benefits had to be set against the disadvantages of over-concentration of industrial development in a handful of districts. (RF, 23/1961.)

China's economic journalists picked up and expanded another Maoist idea: 'Marxists hold that in human society activity in production develops step by step from a lower to a higher level.' (PE, 3.) This principle implied technical revolution should take place from the bottom upwards and that modernisation should be achieved by transforming small primitive establishments into large modern undertakings. In addition, Mao Tse-tung declined to concentrate investment on large-scale modern plants in either the light or the heavy sectors.

Though admitting big factories were indispensable for turning China into an industrial power he still insisted: 'We should set up more small and medium enterprises.' (*ibid.*, 128.) His economic policy thus meant a change in overall priorities away from heavy industry, accompanied by a move to smaller-scale factories.

A shift away from large enterprises was inevitable if heavy industry — manufacturing the equipment the rest of the economy needed for its production processes — was no longer pre-eminent. A relative decline in the capital for heavy industry meant the supply of machines would be reduced, calling for smaller undertakings with less advanced assembly lines. This approach made it necessary to ensure smaller plants did not give China an industrial base too crude to justify the money spent on its creation. Again, the point was made by a Chinese economist that: 'The claim that the medium and small enterprises, especially the latter, are uneconomical is actually an excuse to justify the fetish of large modern undertakings. The small enterprise requires less investment, takes less time to build, comes into production faster and can benefit from employing total utilisation of its raw materials.' (RF, 12/1960.) Mao Tse-tung saw several ways of preventing small plants from lagging behind in efficiency and thus failing to contribute the maximum to national development. Increased labour productivity was essential. Mao believed many of the regulations governing industry reduced the workers' initiative. He also denounced gross waste of labour. (CS, 7-8.) Since marxists believe a product's value is determined by the labour input (direct and indirect) used in its manufacture, constant reference by Chinese economists to the need to raise workers' productivity was natural. One of the best summaries of the importance of increasing output per worker emphasised: 'Where society is concerned, low labour productivity results in poverty and backwardness. If a society wants to free itself from poverty and backwardness, if a new social system is to be consolidated and developed, the community's labour productivity must be raised.' (RF, 17/1962.) The writer warned that whereas in capitalist societies (according to marxist theory), increased output per worker led to fewer jobs and more unemployed, a socialist economy suffered only when productivity fell. Productivity and living standards went hand in hand; they could rise only in tandem. The truth of this assertion for China is obvious without its marxist background. Any economy short of machinery can only grow through constant increases in the efficiency of its main natural resource, human energy.

The author continued by recognising with Mao Tse-tung (CS, 5) the contribution to be won from improved technical knowledge among the work force. The *Red Flag* article stated: 'A skilled worker can produce more and better goods, with a smaller quantity of raw materials and at a lower cost.' It went on to show that publicity for pace-setting enterprises would demonstrate to less advanced undertakings how to improve their performance. 'Emulation' was also one of Mao's favourite slogans; he believed that: 'Under identical conditions, the advanced and the backward are compared, and the backward are urged to overtake the advanced.' (*ibid.*, 7.) At the same time, Mao Tse-tung realised innovation was an important element in modernising his nation even if this process meant turning to foreign countries for models which could be adapted to China's conditions. (*ibid.*, 33.) A major editorial, in calling on the population 'to be brave in experimenting', commented: 'National science and technology bear no class characteristics.' (RF, 11/1962.) In plain English: grasp any technical knowledge useful to China whatever its origins.

Tao Chu, one of the country's senior administrators until disgraced in the Cultural Revolution, was thoroughly in tune with Mao when he illustrated his master's theories at work in an article on a photochemical plant in Kwangtung province. The factory began as a laboratory soon after the communist triumph. The plant, he claimed, never employed trained technicians but its products managed to match world standards. With a minimum of state finance and equipment but a constant series of experiments by the work force, an incredible increase in output was achieved: from between Yuan 100,000 and Yuan 200,000 a year to Yuan 70 million annually. Tao claimed: 'The progress of this factory's growth shows the greatness and the correctness of our party's line for building socialism and represents an impressive demonstration of the law of development from small to large and from indigenous methods to modern techniques.' (*ibid.*, 12/1960.)

Mao Tse-tung's biggest enemy was waste. He put the issue very simply: 'We want to carry on large-scale construction, but our country is still very poor – herein lies a contradiction. One way of resolving it is to make a sustained effort to practise strict economy in every field.' (PE, 127.) A host of statements on this issue show precious resources were thrown down the drain out of pure negligence. The chairman of the state planning commission, Li Fu-chun, attacked those who believed waste either 'inevitable' or 'a trifle'. (CC, 83.) Chou En-lai raised the same problem, castigating those responsible for money sunk in unproductive projects, over-expensive undertakings, poor production standards, loss and damage to materials and inefficient use of labour.(*Proposals of the Eighth National Congress of the Communist Party of China for the Second Five-year Plan,* 100.)

A study of accounting procedures revealed a tendency to spend investment funds on grandiose plant and unnecessary replacement of old machinery. Another temptation was for factories to make excessive requisitions for raw materials, stockpiling the surplus in warehouses. One difficulty the survey's authors tried to tackle was the extent to which an enterprise should be permitted to raise efficiency by substituting capital for labour. The article referred to the need for a minimum volume of finance to underwrite and expand the economic activities required to provide the labour force with full employment and rising living standards. (ER, 4/1962.) But their conclusions failed to establish a definitive standard for spending money on using machines instead of men. Idleness among the workers was another source of loss to the state. (PD, 11 April, 1962.) Two economists dramatised the costs to China of avoidable waste with the revelation that ninety per cent of the budget was derived from the state enterprises, and seventy per cent of national expenditure went on economic development. Labour productivity, for the usual marxist reasons, was their first priority, followed by more efficient use of technicians to spread available talent over a greater number of factories. Warehouses full of unused fuel, machines and raw materials and the failure to exploit industrial wastes for secondary use were also attacked. A happy disregard of the rules laid down for the spending of funds also provoked their wrath. (ER, 10/1962.)

One form of waste to which Mao Tse-tung had drawn constant attention was the proliferation of bureaucrats. He popularised the motto: 'Better troops and simpler administration.' This slogan came from a non-communist Chinese, as Mao stated. (SW III, 177.) His dislike of an administrative octopus was derived from the necessities of war and not from Marx's famous passage which denounced the basic selfishness of bureaucrats: 'Taken individually, they make the purpose of the state their own private end, the race for promotion and getting ahead.' Mao had been forced to dismantle the administrative apparatus the party had built up in its guerrilla retreat because of growing enemy pressure, a necessity many party members opposed bitterly. (*ibid.,* 99-101.) He later elaborated his objections to an over-sized bureaucracy in terms of stark efficiency. Cadres were a drain on productive resources, a burden on the people. Administration had to be simplified to reduce this cost and to allow for greater co-ordination and cohesion. Better organisation of government functions would raise efficiency, and attention could be given to thrift and the eradication of graft, corruption and meaningless 'red tape'. (*ibid.*, 115-16.)

The bureaucratic birthrate mounted in the early years of the People's Republic despite Mao's strictures. Premier Chou En-lai in 1956 described how 'Generally speaking, the state administrative organisations at different levels are at present still inflated and overstaffed'. The prime minister had as little effect as Mao. In the following year, the order was issued: 'All units should rapidly formulate plans for retrenchment and mobilise large numbers of personnel to production posts, to basic level units which need reinforcement, or make other provisions for the reduced personnel.' (CC, 240, 362.) Mao Tse-tung also demanded cadres be transferred to productive work. (PE, 129.)

By this stage, the pressure to simplify government work was inspired by three motives. The first was to reduce the cost of the administrative service. The reasoning here was not solely that a poor nation needed to save every possible resource for the direct development effort. Marxism denies that administrators contribute to national income. One article saw a link between the growing complexity of the economy as it advanced and recruitment of extra managerial staff. But the relative number of these 'non-productive' workers should be held constant it urged. More serious were the 'health, cultural, educational, scientific and service organisations'. These tended to grow much faster than the administration as a whole and 'even faster than the number of workers in the productive sector'. The argument was that if the administrative and social services were not kept to a minimum, they would reduce the number of workers who contributed directly to the nation's wealth. (KMD, 25 September, 1961.) This point translates easily into non-marxist language: China could not afford to permit a diversion of human energies from the main task of meeting basic material wants to the expansion of laudable but non-essential social and cultural activities.

The second factor, the strengthening of the basic administration, followed from the establishment of agricultural co-operatives. Mao Tse-tung rejected the pessimists' contention: 'The peasants were uneducated and so lacked people who could act as book-keepers ... co-operatives were growing too rapidly for the political consciousness of the people and the level of experience of the officials.' Yet he acknowledged: 'If a co-op cannot get leadership from the party, of course its affairs will be in confusion.' He expected cadres, through personal participation in the co-operatives, to provide them with educated leadership. (SU, 150, 266.) John Wilson Lewis states the cadres ordered to production posts were usually assigned to backward units. (*Leadership in Communist China*, 223.) Thus retrenchment tackled an obstacle to progress long foreseen by Mao – the low cultural level of the peasantry. (SW IV, 419.) The policy of transferring officials away from their offices at the higher echelons of government to take part in physical labour did not end their official careers. They remained cadres, organising the basic production units and earning their official salaries through their own productive labour. This strategy aimed at establishing a civil service operating at the basic level on which overall national growth depended and where the shortage of expertise of every kind was most acute. And this bureaucracy earned its own keep.

The third factor was an old worry of Mao Tse-tung. He noted in 1957: 'A dangerous tendency has shown itself of late among many of our personnel – an unwillingness to share the joys and hardships of the masses, a concern for personal fame and gain.' (PE, 128.) The war had taught Mao the importance of equal treatment for leaders and led when living conditions were at their toughest. (MW, 31.) By sending the civil servant to a job where he had to share the sufferings of the people, morale would be raised by this physical symbol of a whole nation mobilised to battle for prosperity. Just as important was Mao Tse-tung's realisation that without mixing with the people and learning their difficulties at first hand, cadres risked issuing directives in complete ignorance of actual conditions. (SW III, 11.) He also had an enormous faith in the wisdom of the ordinary individual, 'while we ourselves are often childish and ignorant'. (*ibid.*, 12.)

Maurice Zinkin has written a critique of Asian bureaucracy which echoes, with less colour, Mao's comments: 'Most Asian countries cannot afford a civil service of adequate size . . . The administration in underdeveloped countries, and particularly the economic development part of the administration, cannot be conducted on paper or at a desk. It must be carried on in the field, by talking to people; and talking over a very wide range of subjects, from contributions for a new school for the village, to the use of a fertiliser of which the villagers have not previously heard, or the need to build a road to the local market.' (*Development for Free Asia*, 89.) Zinkin's remarks illustrate once more the common sense Mao used in tackling a development problem of universal concern.

The drive behind Mao Tse-tung's economic strategy, with co-operatives replacing the individual peasant, emulation campaigns to share out knowledge, cadres labouring with the masses, was the search for a means of making a communal spirit effective in practice. He was aware of the long tradition of individualism which affected the peasants' outlook. But he understood an even greater temptation which obstructed mutual help: 'The tendency towards selfish departmentalism by which the interests of one's own unit are looked after to the exclusion of those of others. Whoever is indifferent to the difficulties of others, refuses to transfer cadres to other units on request, or releases only the inferior ones, "using the neighbour's field as an outlet for his overflow", and does not give the slightest consideration to other departments, localities or people – such a person is a selfish departmentalist who has entirely lost the spirit of communism.' (SW III, 156, 46.)

The first five-year plan called for 'co-ordination and mutual support in the construction of these various types of enterprises, so as to guarantee not only construction of the priority projects but also quick returns from investments in many enterprises'. (CC, 60.) With Mao Tse-tung's plea for more consideration for the smaller-scale enterprise, co-ordination between factories became vital. The correct relationship between different-sized undertakings was laid down in 1956 by Premier Chou: 'There should be some large enterprises to serve as the backbone, and there should also be many small and medium enterprises to support the large ones.' (*Proposals of the Eighth National Congress of the Communist Party of China for the Second Five-Year Plan,* 70.) This call amounted to a policy of setting up large factories supported by a network of smaller branch units. The prime minister pushed this concept a stage further. Plants, he indicated, need not be built on a large scale when first erected. Rather, they should evolve into bigger factories 'stage by stage', and he added that small and medium enterprises should be planned to allow for expansion into large undertakings once available resources and other factors permitted. Chou insisted that co-ordination of large plants with smaller-scale factories should be organised through exploiting the productive potential of small and medium-sized units already in existence. (*ibid.*) Co-operation between large and small factories and the steady transformation of small undertakings into large factories became integral elements in official economic philosophy. This policy imaginatively attacked the problem of ensuring small-scale operations were married not only to general expansion of overall output and advances in the agricultural, light and heavy industry sectors but to growth at factory level as well. Economic development was viewed in total terms. Small undertakings had to be so closely linked in their operations that although a set of industrial units was located in different streets or even towns, they worked together in perfect concert with an efficiency equal to the standards found in a large unified works built on a single site.

Maximum co-operation was necessary to implement another of Mao Tse-tung's ambitions: a measure of local self-sufficiency. He had expressed his support in 1956 for each district forming an economic base suited to local conditions. (CS, 28.) This proposal developed a wartime theme: 'It is imperative for the revolutionary ranks to turn the backward villages into advanced, consolidated base areas, into great military, political, economic and cultural bastions.' (SW II, 316-17.) This idea first bore fruit in 1958 in establishing the communes and reached full bloom in the 1969 programme for national development. But Mao had learnt as early as 1928 the strength of local loyalties which hindered mutual co-operation. He had observed: 'Localism exists to a serious extent between counties and even between districts and townships in the same county.' (SW I, 93.) Any significant decentralisation of economic authority or self-sufficiency at the grass-roots, and Mao advocated both, required an effort to preach the virtue of combining local initiative with a sense of responsibility for the national interest. As power was transferred in 1958 from Peking to the regions, the slogan 'the whole country a co-ordinated chess game' became a theme in domestic propaganda. (PD, 24 February, 1958.) The alternative was for the economy to break up into competing elements, each concerned with its own narrow, local well-being.

To permit each district to frame policies to meet its own needs and to dismantle the central control apparatus seemed on the surface to discourage co-ordination. However, Soviet experience indicates decentralisation of the economy has disastrous results unless wedded to some measure of regional self-sufficiency. P.J.D. Wiles has illustrated how Russian factories with a simple target to produce a given quantity of nails instead of detailed instructions on the year's production activities react by making the nails as small as possible. The factory meets its target with output to spare, but its products represent a waste of national resources. (*Communist International Economics*, 293-94.) If a region is forced to consume the defective products it permits its industries to turn out, the local authorities are soon compelled to end such costly abuses. This was the strategy proposed for China.

Mao Tse-tung's industrial policy was summarised neatly in 1962. 'The communist party and Comrade Mao Tse-tung long ago pointed out that in economic development we should follow a policy of "walking on two legs" — simultaneous development of large, medium and small plants and a combination of indigenous and foreign techniques . . . Why must large, medium and small plants be developed at the same time? Firstly, individual areas are endowed with different natural resources. In some localities, natural resources are abundant and therefore conditions favour the establishment of large-scale enterprises. Resources in other districts are scattered, and conditions favour small and medium units . . . Again the law of development of things is from small to large. A small or medium-scale undertaking of today may grow into a large plant tomorrow.' The article then veered away from Mao Tse-tung's views on local self-sufficiency, though the writer could excuse this deviation since Mao had not detailed his thinking on this subject. After stating the advantages of each district accelerating the establishment of its own economic system, the author maintained that full implementation of this policy would be possible only after considerable economic development on a national scale. Manpower, investment funds and raw materials were scarce and thus had to be devoted to meeting national rather than local needs. But, the article added, national development also expanded industry, farming and transport facilities at district level. 'This will pave the way for individual localities to set up their own economic systems at a later stage.' (TKP, 27 June, 1962.) This commentary brings out how closely Mao Tse-tung's economic strategy was tailored to the practical requirements of his underdeveloped country.

Standard economic textbooks, by and large, urge economic policies violently at odds with Mao's prescriptions. The more popular economists stress the advantages of large-scale plants over small enterprises. This attitude can be found in a general work such as John F. Due's well-known text *Intermediate Economic Analysis.* (140-45.) A more sophisticated analysis — by Tibor Scitovsky, for instance — acknowledges that some factories may be either too large or too small for efficiency but concentrates on the defects of the smaller concern. (*Welfare and Competition: The Economics of a Fully-Employed Economy,* 31-32.) Economic development specialists exhibit a similar bias. One example is Charles P. Kindleberger whose outlook is summed up in a single sentence: 'Costs and prices decline as the scale of output increases with development.' (*Economic Development*, 94.) Harvey Leibenstein follows a similar line. In a discussion of the 'critical minimum effort' needed for economic breakthrough, he states: 'The essential aspect of the argument is that firms have to be above a certain minimum size in order to be reasonably efficient . . . For size of plants is a kind of absolute matter and is not relative to the size of a country or its national income.' (*Economic Backwardness and Economic Growth: Studies in the Theory of Economic Development*, 106.)

Mao Tse-tung emphasised the need to boost light industry – which serves consumption needs – rather than heavy industry which makes the equipment needed for production activities throughout the economy. Mao did not call for an abandonment of the growth of heavy industry. He wanted an alteration in priorities without upsetting the balance between the light and heavy sectors. To keep the two in equilibrium was not easy. The call for smaller plants came as a corollary to this policy. However, size of factory was the key factor, whichever sector of the economy was under consideration. Shirts can be manufactured in small workshops quite efficiently. The construction of machine tools requires a minimum quantity of equipment for transforming raw steel into finished goods. If stress is placed on the smaller enterprise, a shift to light industrial products is tempting because of the small quantity of machinery available. Mao's economic programme as explained by Premier Chou En-lai could overcome this tendency, provided co-operation between small plants was organised so superbly that any co-ordinated group of smaller concerns added up in productive capacity and efficiency to a large-scale undertaking.

Size was also a crucial issue because of the notion of small firms gradually increasing their scale of operations and growing in size as they pushed up output. Mao Tse-tung thought in dynamic terms. The small factory was but a stepping stone to large enterprises, with light industry the first stage along the road to advanced heavy industry. (CS, 23.) Mao Tse-tung anticipated in early 1958 that the country would pass through a technical revolution. (*ibid.*, 5.) Small size with minimum investment in plant and equipment had a special merit on this view of China's future. Less capital would be wasted when industrial capacity became completely obsolete and had to be scrapped as China outgrew its primitive economy.

The need to make sure investment pays for itself before technical advances render equipment obsolete has been analysed by Kaldor and Mirlees. They indicate that technological progress can create pressure to reduce investment per worker (and thus, presumably, average factory size) below the level apparently best suited to existing conditions because equipment bought today will become outdated in the future. (*Growth Economics*, 349, 364.) A. Lamfalussy has drawn attention to the way rising wages lead to more capital per worker, since increased labour costs make machines cheaper than men. (*Investment and Growth in Mature Economies*, 75.) Mao believed wages and productivity should rise together, thus making increased labour costs a factor for the future. (CS, 25.) But improved living standards would have to take second place to frugality for years to come: 'China is a big country, but it is still very poor. We shall need a few score years before we can make China prosperous. Even then we still will have to be diligent and frugal.' (SU, 67.) Thus a direct choice between a higher wage bill and investment in machines could be postponed. The immediate need was flexibility — the creation of an industrial base which could be modified constantly to meet the changing economic demands of the rapid development Mao envisaged.

Hla Myint echoes points made by Chinese economists in his conservative approach to the underdeveloped world. He takes issue with those who insist on heavy capital investment and who argue this will eventually ensure faster rates of growth. They forget, in his opinion, the equally strong humanitarian reasons for immediate increases in output in a poor society through less costly projects yielding more immediate profits. (*Economic Theory and the Underdeveloped Countries*, 18.) Joan Robinson also tackles the problem on the basis of a 'a choice between jam today and more jam the day after tomorrow'. Highly mechanised production, she states (as have Chinese economists), offers higher profits. The drawback is that an industrial system with advanced technology offers less employment opportunities and a smaller initial increase in output. (*Economic Philosophy*, 115.) Mao Tse-tung was thus keeping respectable company in outlining his economic theories even though a large number of Western economists prefer the large and expensive when it comes to factories.

Even examined from the way a socialist economy (that is, a communist nation) operates, Mao Tse-tung's approach had an essential validity, as R.M. Goodwin brings out. He demonstrates that a smaller amount of machinery for each worker can lead to a higher potential growth rate in an underdeveloped country. Wages, he continues, affect the decision to use more equipment. Under capitalism, industrial wages are usually higher than in traditional crafts even if a labour surplus exists. So the pull towards replacing men with machines is relatively strong. But in a planned, socialist state, Goodwin maintains, society must meet the consumption needs of the work force whether employed or not. A socialist country can thus afford to disregard the labour costs of expanding output to a much greater extent than capitalist economies when it plans investment. The socialist government can adopt production techniques which use the minimum capital compared with their capitalist rivals, since the difference between living standards for both employed and unemployed in the socialist world should be zero. (*Elementary Economics from the Higher Standpoint,* 111-12.) Thus, under communism, big plants with large inputs of equipment are relatively less attractive. This reasoning does not solve the contradiction between small-scale plants with only a basic technology and the need to produce enough machinery to equip the economy for growth, in theory, ideally produced in big plants. But Mao Tse-tung with small branch factories serving large enterprises − an arrangement popular in the British car industry − could forget this problem.

More convincing than glancing through a sample of economic texts is the practical experience of other Asian countries. The classic example is Japan where, Eleanor M. Hadley estimates, small and medium firms account for two-thirds of employment in manufacturing. She states that a considerable proportion of small and medium-sized enterprises act as subsidiaries for large concerns by producing or 'finishing' component parts. (*Anti-trust in Japan,* 16.) The Japanese enjoy one of the most efficient economies in the world. Indian evidence on the efficiency of small plants is somewhat confusing. But a recent study concluded: 'With two or three exceptions, small units generate larger income (value added) per unit than either medium or large units.' (B.V. Mehta, *Bulletin of the Oxford University Institute of Economics and Statistics,* August, 1969, 189-204.) In Ceylon, the data point conclusively to the merits of small factories. (*Small Industry Bulletin,* No. 5, 97.) Experience from other areas in the region such as South Korea and Taiwan reflects the same pattern. As with agriculture, Mao Tse-tung seems to have chosen a course for industrial growth consistent with at least some prominent economists' conclusions and which makes sense when tested against Asian experience of development problems.

'Economic engineering' presented Mao with much more complex issues. In laying down the guidelines presented above for crashing the barriers to increased national income, Mao was dealing with technical relationships, actual situations which could be investigated and tackled through practical suggestions to stretch to the utmost China's meagre development resources. But economic relationships involve imponderables; tackling them means laying down policies on planning, profits, prices and incomes whose success can be measured only by their results. Mao faced the dilemmas confronting him over basic economic relations with appropriate modesty. Even though he saw quite clearly by the period from 1955 to 1958 how to organise production, he openly admitted that his search for the techniques to control the economy at this time was far from finished.

Planning was central to Mao Tse-tung's formula for directing the economic fortunes of his nation. What else was to be expected of a marxist leader? However, in Mao's case, planning's merits became a personal conviction not from academic research into marxist economics but from experience in the hard school of war. Through the ebb and flow of combat and the uncertainties of guerrilla warfare, Mao perceived the value of coherent plans but was forced to grasp their defects: rigidity and the danger of a strategy based on less than perfect intelligence about the enemy. His remarks on a commander's plan deserve quotation: 'In carrying out the plan from the moment it is put into effect to the end of the operation, there is another process of knowing the situation, namely, the process of practice. In the course of this process, it is necessary to examine anew whether the plan worked out in the preceding process corresponds with reality. If it does not correspond with reality, or if it does not fully do so, then in the light of our new knowledge, it becomes necessary to form new judgments, make new decisions and change the original plan so as to meet the new situation.' (MW, 87.)

Mao Tse-tung was fortunate in having this experience of the way plans require constant adjustment and total flexibility. The gross waste experienced by the Soviet Union because of over-centralised planning, inadequate information and the continual search for balance as demand outstripped supply for both consumption and production purposes is notorious and needs no documentation. Sir Arthur Lewis implies that a centrally planned economy of its very nature leads to mistakes in setting targets and allocating supplies; to unwillingness by the authorities to recalculate their complicated sums and adjust their programmes to changing circumstances; to unnecessary delays as the importance of adequate reserves and stocks is overlooked; to excessive product standardisation to reduce the variety of goods the administration must handle; and to a stifling of initiative. He notes the impetus planning gives to the proliferation of bureaucrats. (*The Principles of Economic Planning*, 16-19.)

Apart from Mao's general recognition of the perils of inflexibility, this last defect could not be ignored by China, desperately short of skilled personnel and anxious to pare administration costs to the bone. J. Wilczynski quotes the forecast that if the Soviet Union's planning staff continued to grow at the same rate as between 1928 to 1963, the whole adult population would be employed in planning agencies by 1980. (*The Economics of Socialism*, 43.) Mao Tse-tung's first grasp of what made a good plan came from the sternest of tests: a plan's cost could be reckoned by the bodies left behind on the battlefield. His view of economic plans was thus quite different from the self-imposed strait-jackets found in other socialist countries.

Economic plans were for Mao the principal weapon for over-coming 'the contradiction between production and the needs of society'. The balance between investment and consumption, between demand and supply 'is partially upset every month or every quarter, and partial readjustments are called for'. Mao believed the superiority of a planned economy lay in its ability to strive continually to overcome the forces throwing the system out of gear. (PE, 95.) He maintained: 'True revolutionary leaders must . . . be good at correcting their ideas, theories, plans or programmes when errors are discovered . . . In a revolutionary period the situation changes very rapidly; if the knowledge of the revolutionaries does not change rapidly in accordance with the changed situation, they will be unable to lead the revolution to victory.' (SW I, 306.) Mao's remarks applied to adjustments in plans during such movements as the 1958 Great Leap Forward and the 1966 Cultural Revolution as well as the revolution which brought him to power. Although foreseeing that political upsurges would lead to radical policy changes, he demanded that cadres 'plan everything on a long-term basis'. (SW IV, 248.) To predict the future was hardly possible in a country where changes of ideological campaign could occur so abruptly; but for Mao, long-term programmes could be adapted to new circumstances because plans were not sacrosanct.

Furthermore, Mao was unimpressed by the mediocre official's servile obedience to his superiors' commands and his reluctance to undertake planning on his own initiative. Mao also condemned overlapping and contradictory orders from the centre. He was aware perhaps of the old complaint made by Chao Tso in the second century B.C. against the waste caused by arbitrary and conflicting official edicts: 'Orders promulgated in the morning are altered by evening. Faced with such levies, the people must sell their property at a loss.' Mao urged a measure of freedom for the individual cadre to relate the priority for implementing various instructions from above to local conditions, and he condemned the practice of issuing targets without clarifying how they ranked in order of importance. (SW III, 121.)

'Overall planning' was another Maoist maxim. The slogan meant taking into account the interests of the total population. This principle, he stated, must guide all economic activities. However, he insisted that 'overall planning' was not an excuse for the concentration of all authority in the hands of the central government. Much could be left 'to the care of the public organisations or of the masses directly — both are quite capable of devising many good ways of handling things'. (PE, 112-13.) This instruction reflected his general concern to decentralise authority. For agriculture, unified economic planning was to be modified by 'retaining a certain leeway and independence' for the co-operatives (and later, the communes) as long as the national interest was not injured. (*ibid.*, 102-3.)

Mao Tse-tung was under no illusion about the difficulties of drawing up plans in an underdeveloped country, especially in the rural sector. He advised in 1956: 'Every county, district and township in the land should draw up comprehensive plans ... Even if they are a bit crude and not entirely practical, at least they will be better than no plans at all.' Mao seemed to regard the plan as a tool for spotlighting obstacles to progress. He observed: 'Conservatism seems to be making trouble everywhere now. To overcome it and allow production to take a big step forward, every locality and every co-op should make its long-range plan.' Mao was correct, provided the plans were subject to scrutiny at a higher level by officials capable of deducing from these documents the output potential and actual performance. To raise planning standards, Mao fell back on 'emulation'. 'If a province can produce relatively presentable plans from one or two counties, one or two districts, and one or two townships,' he believed, 'they can immediately be publicised and serve as models for the plans of other counties, districts and townships.' To boost morale, he added: 'People talk a lot about the difficulty of planning, but actually it's not particularly hard.' (SU, 361, 389.) This bold assertion was hardly consistent with the tone of Mao's other remarks on the subject, but he always preferred optimism to wariness.

Mao Tse-tung liked cadres to tackle their own difficulties and adjust official directives to the local situation. He never defined the precise demarcation line between the central government's domain and what could be left to the good sense of the lower administrative levels. The temptation to concentrate all authority in the capital had attracted attention in imperial times. A seventeenth-century writer, Ku Yen-wu, had commented: 'The demands on the government are so enormous that no one man has the capacity to deal with them all . . . What is most required now are local officials who will personally see to the people's welfare, yet these local officials today enjoy the least power.' Mao first faced the dilemma of retaining overall direction of events while encouraging local initiative as a military commander. Guerrilla war required both central command and maximum flexibility for the combat unit.

The correct balance, Mao discovered, lay in control of general strategy and co-ordination between units from the top while leaving soldiers in the field fairly free in implementing instructions passed down the chain of command. He insisted subordinate units inform their superiors of developments to ensure concerted action. But Mao disliked 'hard and fast commands' from the upper echelons. The longer the chain of command, either geographically or in terms of formal hierarchy, 'the more advisable it becomes to allow greater independence to the lower levels in their actual operations'. (MW, 183-85.) Unfortunately, while autonomy for party and military junior leaders encouraged enthusiasm, discipline deteriorated leading to 'anarchy, localism and guerrilla-ism'. Mao was obliged to return power to the party central committee. (SW IV, 273.)

Mao struggled to resolve this contradiction which would prove important in civil as well as military affairs once he came to power. He still advocated: 'Except where conditions call for centralised management, we must oppose the wrong view which favours centralising everything, regardless of circumstances, and which dares not give full rein to decentralised management.' (ibid., 124.) He sought a remedy through the party structure. Within the communist ranks, the individual was subordinate to the organisation; the minority to the majority; the lower level to the higher echelon; and all party members to the central committee. 'Whoever violates these articles of discipline disrupts party unity.' At the same time, Mao insisted on 'initiative' among the cadres which he defined as: 'Their readiness to assume responsibility, in the exuberant vigour they show in their work, in their courage and ability to raise questions, voice opinions and criticise defects and in the comradely supervision that is maintained over the leading bodies and the leading cadres.' To achieve these goals, democracy was required, said Mao, but the party itself reflected the undemocratic nature of China caused by its 'small-scale production and the patriarchal system'. (SW II, 204-5.)

Mao tried to prevent conflicts of authority by instructing that a state agency should not give orders to its junior cadres without advising the official in charge of the district or institution concerned. 'Both the person in overall charge and the person with specific responsibility should be informed and given responsibility. This centralised method, combining division of labour with unified leadership, makes it possible, through the person with overall responsibility, to mobilise a large number of cadres ... to carry out a particular task, and thus to overcome shortages of cadres in individual departments.' (SW III, 120-21.) In the land-reform campaign, for all his approval of personal initiative, Mao had to demand total obedience to the central committee's instructions. Cadres were allowed to suggest amendments only where party policy was inappropriate to their district. (SW IV, 255.) In setting up agricultural co-operatives, however, Mao took a different line. Work teams sent out by a 'higher organisation' – their functions, Mao indicated, puzzled him – 'go to help local party organisations, not to replace them, not to immobilise their hands and brains, not to let them rely on the work teams for everything'. (SU, 206-7.)

While ideological and moral issues could not be settled by administrative orders, Mao argued: 'The people want their government and those in charge of production ... to issue appropriate orders of an obligatory nature.' (PE, 86-87.) In fact, respect for authority was excessive, as Mao Tse-tung had noted years before coming to power. He attacked bitterly the peasants' respect for the written word, matched by party members who always asked 'show me where it's written in the book'. Directives from the party leadership were only correct, stated Mao, if they conformed to reality. 'It is quite wrong to take a formalistic attitude and blindly carry out directives without discussing and examining them in the light of actual conditions simply because they come from a higher organ.' (SR, 34-35.) In his 1956 blueprint for national development, Mao had to confess the right balance still had not been struck between the central and local administrations.

He explained the subordinate role of the lower administrative organs, but argued that to remove all freedom from such basic units as factories would stifle enthusiasm. Furthermore, in expanding both supplies of raw materials and markets for industry, local administrations had an important part to play. Yet confusion prevailed at the bottom of the bureaucratic ladder as each central government department passed down its own instructions without bothering to inform the party central committee or China's state council. Mao believed in some circumstances (left undefined) the centre could control enterprises directly. In other cases, the central authority need only outline broad policies and targets, leaving the details for subordinate units to work out on their own responsibility. Above all, consultation between Peking and the basic administrative bodies was as essential as flexibility in supervising the lower echelons.

Mao Tse-tung could find no clearer solution than these general principles and admitted the party's failure, because of its inexperience, to produce a masterplan for harmonising the national government's authority with the need to decentralise the hierarchy. (CS, 26-28.) The economic world presented Mao with the same dilemma as rural warfare. In civil affairs, his solution amounted to striking a rough balance of interests which could be adjusted as conditions altered. In Mao's defence, it must be said the same dilemma has baffled politicians all over the modern world. The failure to find a solution to relations between central and regional governments has caused crises in such Western nations as France and Italy and civil wars in Nigeria and Pakistan. Economists in the non-communist world have discussed the impact on progress of tensions between the central and regional authorities. Their researches have not led to any clear indication of the ideal solution to clashes between national and local interests. (*Federalism and Economic Growth in Underdeveloped Countries* examines this problem in detail.) As with planning, so with decentralisation, war had taught Mao where the dangers lay. But his guerrilla days could not provide him with the concrete solutions he needed to run a vast but dispersed national economy.

In human terms, the real strain in the drive to turn a primitive economy into an advanced, industrialised community comes with the battle to increase investment funds without reducing living standards to an unbearable degree. As Gunnar Myrdal bleakly puts it: 'There is no other road to economic development than a compulsory rise in the share of the national income which is withheld from consumption and devoted to investment. This implies a policy of the utmost austerity.'

(*Economic Theory and Under-developed Regions,* 82.) What is spent on consumption cannot be set aside from national income to build factories or to buy modern agricultural equipment. The Soviet Union under Stalin, thanks to an incomparable terror apparatus, found a solution in squeezing consumption to bare subsistence level. Erich Strauss sums up the Soviet pattern neatly: 'If the village was bled white of resources, this was not done in order to provide the workers with cheap food; they had to pay the "market price" for the necessities of life, while the government, as the guardian of the long-term interests of Soviet society, collected a swingeing turnover tax.' (*Soviet Agriculture in Perspective,* 292.) Mao Tse-tung dared not adopt a policy of perpetuating rural destitution to commandeer resources for urban industrial growth. He had watched the Chiang Kai-shek régime crumble through exploitation of the peasantry, the bulk of China's population. Mao stated frankly: 'Another mistake is "draining the pond to catch the fish", that is, making endless demands on the people, disregarding their hardships and considering only the needs of the government and the army. That is a Kuomintang mode of thinking which we must never adopt.' (SW III, 114.)

Incomes, investment (accumulation is Peking's term), profits and taxes form an equation which regulates the pace of overall economic growth. With his face set firmly against a sweated labour force, Mao was left in a quandary. Crushing taxation was out of the question as this policy would have slashed incomes. The alternative was to acquire the cash for investment from the profits the state could earn from economic activities. The profit level depended on official prices. If the public were charged too much for essential goods, living standards would be static or actually fall. Yet without a healthy margin between production costs and prices, the government would lack the profits to pay for modernisation. A compromise had to be found. Reasonably stable prices and improved living standards had to be achieved as worker and peasant earnings rose with increased productivity. Simultaneously, sufficient profits must be obtained to provide the national revenue for development.

Mao's effort to clarify his policy in this complex field was protracted and never produced a set of rules which could be translated directly into a rigid programme. While deeply convinced of man's power to overcome all difficulties if adequately inspired, Mao Tse-tung was under no delusions abut the consequences of empty bellies. At the outset of his guerrilla campaign, he warned that economic strain would eventually prove 'too much even for the workers, poor peasants and Red Army men'. (MW, 37.) He realised how economic conditions affected party loyalties: 'If the workers and peasants become dissatisfied with their living conditions, will it not affect the expansion of our Red Army and the mobilisation of the masses for the revolutionary war?' He stressed this point strongly: 'Do we want to win the support of the masses? . . . If so, we must be with them, arouse their enthusiasm and initiative, be concerned with their well-being, work earnestly and sincerely in their interests and solve all their problems of production and everyday life.' (SW I, 130, 149.)

Mao's attitude to rewards for work sounds paradoxical in view of the condemnation after 1966 of those officials who saw higher incomes as the best way of raising output. His approach to wages was in fact hard-headed. Output would grow, he stated, if the people were rewarded with adequate rises in income. 'To stimulate production we should also institute a system of individual bonuses, graded according to the quality of the work, for all who participate in it directly.' (SW III, 193.) But Mao was alive to the dangers of putting too much money in the public's pocket: 'We must strictly guard against being ultra-leftist; there must not be excessive increases in wages or excessive reductions in working hours.' Another comment from Mao in the same vein was: 'The workers' livelihood must be appropriately improved, but unduly high wages and benefits must be avoided.' The costs of liberal income policies were noted in another passage: 'Do not foster among them the psychology of depending on the government for relief.' (SW II, 445; IV, 184, 248.)

The balance in his statements between a call for improved incomes but a slow introduction of higher wages was adroit. Mao's published remarks on this sensitive topic are in line with W. Howard Wriggin's advice to politicians on buying power through promises of prosperity: 'If economic development could be promoted without detailed and defined statements of vaulting purpose or if specific steps could be implemented without definite targets or publicity, efforts to promote economic development would be less ambiguous political assets.' (*The Ruler's Imperative,* 202.)

Mao Tse-tung's sensible approach came to the fore again when he began the task of pushing agricultural co-operatives in 1955. 'No one should be allowed to suffer a loss' through co-operation. He commented realistically: 'When people see that large and advanced co-operatives are better than small and elementary co-operatives, when people see that long-range planning brings them a life of a much higher material and cultural level, they will agree to combine their co-ops and build advanced ones.' (SU, 238, 478.) In 1956, Mao decreed factories should enjoy access to higher living standards and in the countryside, 'unless irresistible natural calamities are encountered, the peasants should be enabled to receive every year an income higher than the one in the previous year on the basis of agricultural production'. (CS, 26.) But in the same passage, he confessed the government had little experience of how best to stimulate industrial workers' morale. He endorsed provincial leaders' arguments that 'with the worker's productivity raised and the output value per workday increased, wages should be readjusted accordingly. It is improper to ignore this.' (ibid., 25.)

Productivity was, it seems, the major determinant of wages for Mao Tse-tung. His discussion of the gap between rural and urban incomes claimed: 'The productivity of the workers is much higher than that of the peasants, while the latter's cost of living is much lower than that of workers in the cities, so the workers cannot be said to have received special favours from the state. However, the wages of a small number of workers and some government personnel are a bit too high, and the peasants have reason to be dissatisfied with this, so it is necessary to make certain appropriate readjustments.' (PE, 104-5.) If agricultural productivity rose, the villagers were to benefit: 'We should do everything possible to enable the peasants to raise their personal incomes year by year in normal years on the basis of increased production.' (ibid., 103.)

In outlining his thinking on earnings, Mao Tse-tung also discussed the proper division of national income between the state and the individual. In 1956, Mao was prepared to skate over difficulties in a fair allocation of output between consumption (the individual) and investment (the state or the co-operative until 1958 and then the commune). He respected the need for accumulating funds for investment but recognised that sums saved for this purpose could be excessive. Direct government levies on various types of enterprise earnings rather than juggling officially-controlled prices was the correct way to build up a surplus to finance development. Industry and agriculture should exchange goods on the basis of the value of labour used directly or indirectly in their production. Mao apparently saw this principle would put the peasant at a disadvantage since his productivity was so much lower than the average output of an industrial worker. A farm would have less to trade with a factory employing the same

89

number of workers. Mao wanted to end the differential between rural and urban incomes, so he advocated stable industrial prices with factories operating on slim profit margins. He demanded proper regard for the interests of both the individual and the state in slicing up the economic cake. (CS, 27.)

Mao Tse-tung had not found the answer he sought by 1957: 'To decide the proper ratio between accumulation and consumption . . . is a complicated problem for which it is not easy to work out a perfectly rational solution all at once.' (PE, 94.) His main concern was the countryside: 'On the question of the distribution of income, we must take account of the interests of the state, the collective and the individual. We must properly handle the three-way relationship between the state agricultural tax, the co-operative's accumulation fund and the peasants' personal income . . . Accumulation is essential both for the state and for the co-operative, but in neither case should it be excessive.' (ibid., 103.) Mao was far from satisfied when he returned to the subject in 1958: 'The correct ratio between accumulation and consumption in China's national economy is an important question which affects the pace of our country's development. It is hoped that everyone will study this issue.' He disliked the current situation in which sixty to seventy per cent of rural households' incomes came from their spare-time activities and the cultivation of their private plots. This situation, Mao stated, must diminish the peasants' enthusiasm for agricultural co-operatives which produced the smaller portion of their earnings. (CS, 4.)

If Mao Tse-tung could not propose a comprehensive formula, applicable to all sectors of the economy in determining prices, profits, incomes, investment and savings, his failure was understandable. The economy lacked direct state control of the vital farming sector and was also affected by large regional differences in natural resources, soil fertility and levels of industrialisation. A policy covering fundamental economic issues defined in very precise terms could have meant a dangerous lack of flexibility in coping with local conditions. His tentative views on resolving the various conflicts of interest left open the door for discussion and for the application of the party's growing experience of regulating the national economy. Mao can be criticised for leaving questions of such crucial importance unsolved, since the party was obliged by Mao's role as the national ideologist to make policies conform to his guidelines. Mao's principles were too vague to form the immediate inspiration for economic policy-makers, as debates in the first half of the 1960s were to demonstrate.

Yet he had laid emphasis on the right issues. Angus Maddison argues in favour of the same degree of protection for peasant incentives as Mao. Maddison underlines the significance of ensuring rural incomes encourage peasants to adopt modern methods of cultivation, and he suggests governments 'even subsidise new inputs of fertiliser and seeds whilst the new farm technology is in its infant stage'. He adds that farming should be taxed with care to avoid discouraging increased production. (*Economic Progress and Policy in Developing Countries*, 159.) Mao Tse-tung did not express his ideas in such concrete terms. But his call for respecting the individual's interests and for smaller profit margins in industrial output – and thus, in practice, lower prices in sales to the countryside – reflected a similar attitude.

Again, Mao's desire to equalise agricultural and industrial earnings by applying the same basic principle – labour costs and productivity – to both sectors of the economy was entirely correct in terms of conventional economic analysis. W.E.G. Salter in his classic, *Productivity and Technical Change,* explains with great clarity the pitfall of basing wages on what an industry can 'afford' – a tempting policy in a socialist economy. He shows how the labour market should comprise all employees regardless of whether they work in progressive or inefficient industries. If this principle is abandoned, he maintains, those sectors of the economy with the greatest growth potential will find themselves starved of labour. (153.) If through control of migration and its ability to rig prices and taxes, the state's pressure on the villages to raise productivity to industry's standards were relaxed, the Chinese government would have insulated farming from competition with the rest of the economy. Overall progress would have been impaired. Although Peking has used direct controls to maintain the number of peasants and forced large numbers to leave the towns for the countryside, agriculture, on the whole, has formed an integral part of the economic system. The peasantry were neither ruthlessly exploited nor heavily subsidised, and the villages were compelled to earn their keep through reasonably fair competition with the industrial areas.

Furthermore, while labour costs are the major factor in determining whether to use larger or smaller amounts of equipment per worker, the relationship between wages and machinery is not a smooth one. Wages may rise for some time before the substitution of machines for men becomes imperative (A.K. Sen, *Choice of Techniques*, 56.) Thus Mao could afford to postpone a final decision on income levels until he had resolved other vital problems, such as the reorganisation of agriculture through the co-operatives and the communes.

In addition, L. Pasinetti has pointed out that the rate of investment — and hence the ratio of consumption to national income — is easier to work out in socialist countries than in capitalist economies. He observes how in capitalist societies, no guarantee exists that investment will meet the growth needs of the economy. Individuals and firms are free to decide not to invest their savings. Under socialism, once full employment has been reached (which the co-operatives made possible in China), the ideal amount of investment depends on technical progress and population growth. Money needs to be spent on only that new equipment required to raise output through exploiting technological advances and to create new jobs for new workers. If the state wants to prevent labour or equipment from standing idle, the profit rate fixed by the government must equal the economy's natural rate of growth. (*Growth Economics,* 110.) On this analysis, the correct policies for investment and profits, and therefore earnings and prices as well, are in a sense self-evident in a socialist country, provided the authorities behave rationally. Mao, perhaps unconsciously, felt that this area of economic policy, although important, need not claim too much attention in his initial creation of a development strategy for China.

Mao obviously understood the link between living standards and increased output. What then distinguished his approach from the 'material incentives' bitterly denounced by the Chinese as a Soviet 'revisionist' phenomenon, 'turning all human relations into money relations and encouraging individualism and selfishness'? (*On Khrushchov's Phoney Communism and Its Historical Lessons for the World,* 53.) Mao drew a boundary line between reasonable incentives and an incomes policy which would create a privileged caste. He maintained: 'The gap between the income of the working personnel of the party, the government, the enterprises and the people's communes, on the one hand, and the incomes of the mass of the people, on the other, should be rationally and gradually narrowed and not widened. All working personnel [cadres] must be prevented from abusing their power and enjoying special privileges.' (*ibid.,* 69.) In addition, Mao felt convinced of the peasants' natural enthusiasm for socialism, which was heightened, he believed, by industrial progress. (AC, 16-18.)

He also believed that ideological education would awaken the latent energies of his nation. 'Political work is the life-blood of all economic work. This is particularly true at a time when the economic system of a society is undergoing a fundamental change.' (SU, 302.) One writer explained Mao's belief quite forcefully: 'Until communist ideology is placed in command, the masses' revolutionary vigour is given full play, the communist spirit of daring to think and act is promoted, overall interests are taken into account, full co-operation is implemented and favourable factors mobilised, there will be no hope of applying socialist principles and accelerating socialist construction.' The author admitted, however, that disagreement existed on this question. A minority regarded 'material incentives' and 'special consideration for the interests of individuals and small groups of people' as the best means of increasing the population's enthusiasm for greater output. (*Li-lun Hsueh-hsi*, 18/1959.)

In effect, Mao Tse-tung put his trust in the ordinary people of China. 'A decisive factor is our population of 600 million [in 1958]. More people mean a greater ferment of ideas, more enthusiasm and more energy ... the outstanding thing about China's 600 million people is that they are "poor and blank". This may seem a bad thing, but in reality it is a good thing. Poverty gives rise to the desire for change, the desire for action and the desire for revolution.' (SR, 403.) In many ways, this assertion was true. Life for the ordinary Chinese could not have been more desperate when Mao won power. How soon the masses would reach a point at which their past gains from communism made them unwilling to make further sacrifices for uncertain improvements in their personal standard of living was a question which did not trouble him in 1958.

Mao Tse-tung added: 'On a blank sheet of paper free from any mark, the freshest and most beautiful characters can be written, the freshest and most beautiful pictures can be painted.' (*ibid.*) The economic strategy outlined by Mao between 1956 and 1958 was both new and attractive. His economic thinking was novel by either Chinese or European communist standards. Its essential validity was patent when tested against general Asian experience or evaluated on the criteria of Western economics. Mao's policies offered as high a growth rate as China's resources would permit but without the dreadful cost in human suppression and exploitation of Soviet-type industrialisation. The difference between Mao and old-fashioned Russian economists in devising a strategy to create a prosperous nation came through in a single sentence: 'Some price we will have to pay, but we hope it will not be as high as that paid during the period of revolution.' (PE, 130.) Mao had only his people to employ in the fight against China's poverty, and he was not prepared to add blood and tears to the sweat he knew would pour out of them in toiling to build a new China.

Chapter Five

'The Masses are the Real Heroes'

Mao Tse-tung's claim to be remembered as a leader must rest not on the structural changes he introduced into Chinese agriculture and industry, nor on his success in laying the foundations for communism through methods which were moderate and bloodless compared with East European socialist countries. His place in history will be determined by his view of human nature. His onslaught against destitution, illiteracy and the cruel dictates of nature was founded on an overwhelming conviction of man's ability to conquer a harsh economic environment. Mao's brand of social engineering to tap the energy and ability of the ordinary people should win him the respect which Marx has earned for refusing to accept the proletariat as the inevitable victim of immutable economic laws.

Marx forced his century to examine the rights of workers as human beings, formerly somewhat safeguarded by a Christian morality brushed aside by the birth of capitalism. Mao Tse-tung, in the era of Asian revolution against both poverty and colonialism, made the welfare of the masses and their aspirations the ultimate test of virtue in a government. The importance of the common people in Mao's eyes was expressed most dramatically in his declaration: 'Our God is none other than the masses of the Chinese people.' (SW III, 272.)

The association of economic development with social change has been widely recognised. Sir Arthur Lewis strewed his chief contribution to development theory with references to social factors which stunt growth: 'Convention and taboo may restrict opportunity in various ways ... Probably the most important prejudices hampering economic development at the present time are the prejudices about livestock ... Next in importance are the taboos relating to family life, especially those relating to the sort of work which women may do and those relating to birth control ... When we come to social institutions, the role of religion is almost always restrictive.' (*The Theory of Economic*

Growth, 43, 103.) Gunnar Myrdal attacks the ossification of under-developed nations' social institutions: 'As the inherited social stratifi-cation in these countries has been shaped by the impact of long periods of economic stagnation and is very uneven and very stale, this will in most cases imply preserving social chasms inimical to the strengthening of those centrifugal spread effects which are necessary for sustained economic development ... Underdeveloped countries thus need real democracy even at this early stage to break down the existing impediments to economic development.' (*Economic Theory and Under-developed Regions,* 83.) Almost every work on poor societies contains a section couched in similar language.

Most authors differ little in sentiment from Mao Tse-tung. Since he tried to inculcate respect for the masses among the élites ('Revolu-tionary statesmen ... are simply the leaders of millions upon millions of statesmen − the masses.' SW III, 87), Mao was more tactful in describing the barriers to progress raised by popular attitudes. Nonethe-less, he asserted: 'A cultural revolution is the ideological reflection of the political and economic revolution.' (SW II, 373.) This remark shows an understanding of the need to transform society's ideas in the process of development. 'The masses too,' he said, 'have shortcomings, which should be overcome by criticism and self-criticism within the people's own ranks ... the question is basically one of education and of raising their level.' (SW III, 91-92.)

Mao Tse-tung also accepted Marx's description of the communist state springing from capitalism 'in every respect, economically, morally, and intellectually, still stamped with the birth marks of the old society from whose womb it emerges'. Mao's own dictum was: 'Before a brand-new social system can be built on the site of the old, the site must first be swept clean. Old ideas reflecting the old system invariably remain in people's minds for a long time.' (SU, 302.)

Few students of development even question the importance of social and mental obstacles to economic growth. One exception is Angus Maddison who makes the point that: 'The desire for material improvement is now overwhelmingly strong in poor countries and the motivation is powerful enough to reduce the importance of barriers which kept them back in the past. Anachronistic social arrangements still hamper growth, but there are no cases where they have stopped it from occurring.' (*Economic Progress and Policy in Developing Coun-tries,* 87.) The average Western economist tends to expect social bottlenecks impeding growth to be ended through the activities of the

96

entrepreneur – the innovator willing to risk his patrimony in a new business venture.

The importance of this figure seems exaggerated. Concentration on his ability to break down barriers to growth implies that social institutions are fragile in developing nations, a suggestion hardly true of China. A small social minority which rejects the bonds of tradition is seen by the typical economist as able to engineer radical changes in a community which formerly stagnated because of its attachment to custom. One theme repeated constantly is the all-round expertise of the entrepreneur in a developing society. He has to accept responsibility for 'innovation, capital provision and risk bearing, management, assembling materials and labour'. (Charles P. Kindleberger, *Economic Development*, 87.) But this wide range of activities is said to narrow drastically after development has accelerated.

Thus, the all-conquering entrepreneur is absent (by definition) from a primitive society; he is not needed in an advanced economy since the modern corporation and its professional managers have made the traditional entrepreneur obsolete. (Robin Marris, *The Economic Theory of 'Managerial' Capitalism*, Chapter one.) This special breed's sudden evolution and swift extinction (in a biological sense) is difficult to account for. Some writers find themselves trapped by the role they ascribe to the entrepreneur in modernising some communities and their explanation of his absence from other societies in terms of those backward attitudes he is supposed to kill off. (Meier and Baldwin, *Economic Development*, 357, 395-96.)

Irma Adelman brings out the lack of precision in defining the entrepreneur's nature in the work of Schumpeter – who made this figure a key category in economic theory. She shows Schumpeter's entrepreneur is portrayed as no more than an innovator whose actual functions may include management or not, according to circumstances. The entrepreneur, as Schumpeter saw him, emerges in response to prior changes in society's outlook. (*Theories of Economic Growth and Development*, 101-2.) Thus the entrepreneur is an instrument of change in a community, whose transformation however must be well advanced before he can flourish. Other authorities, notably McClelland and Winter, believe entrepreneurs need training to engineer economic transformation in a society fettered by tradition. (*Motivating Economic Achievement*.)

Perhaps the concept of the entrepreneur can be redefined in the light of these conflicting and often contradictory views as a man ready to break loose from the accepted norms of economic behaviour and thus able to act as a lever which prises open the community's mind to welcome more efficient methods of production than those passed down through history. Albert O. Hirschman has suggested that far from being a strong individualist, the ideal entrepreneur must be able to win the co-operation of others to work with him. The pioneering spirit of the entrepreneur is less important than his capacity to sell new ideas to the rest of society. (*The Strategy of Economic Development*, 16-17.) This approach is illuminating as it makes the entrepreneur a bridge between modern attitudes or techniques and the economy which must adopt them.

In the battle for China's development, Mao Tse-tung did not ignore the role of the human catalyst. His entrepreneurs were to be the communist cadres, an army of unselfish, brave and unprejudiced men, struggling to learn and eradicating stereotypes from the people's minds. The standards demanded of the cadres were analagous to qualities attributed to the entrepreneur in Western communities in the crucial stage of economic take-off. But Mao, like Hirschman, saw them always as linked to society, creating change through co-operation with the ordinary people. Communists, Mao Tse-tung proclaimed, must be 'the most far-sighted, the most self-sacrificing, the most resolute, and the least prejudiced in sizing up situations, and should rely on the majority of the masses and win their support ... They must be cadres and leaders versed in marxism-leninism, politically far-sighted, competent in work, full of the spirit of self-sacrifice, capable of tackling problems on their own ... It is on these cadres and leaders that the party relies for its links with the membership and the masses.' (SW I, 274, 291.) These sentences illustrate Mao's conception of communists as more than evangelists of marxist dogma. They were to be activists responsible for implementing reforms. A well-indoctrinated and loyal communist party was not a goal in itself, but a means to an end. Mao Tse-tung demanded cadres should be practical and devoted to study to mobilise 'the dynamic energy of the whole nation ... and build a new China'. (SW II, 198.)

However, Mao did not view the cadre as an isolated element in society. The virtues expected of the party member were also innate characteristics of the masses. Mao believed: 'The proletariat and the communist party are the ones most free from narrow-mindedness and selfishness, are politically the most far-sighted, the best organised and the readiest to learn with an open mind.' (MW, 90.) He refused to relegate the masses to a subservient status in the struggle for prosperity. 'The working people should master knowledge and the intellectuals should become habituated to manual labour . . . It is necessary to build up a large detachment of working-class intellectuals.' (*On Khrushchov's Phoney Communism and Its Historical Lessons for the World*, 68.) Any nation most of whose people have been denied a decent education must contain talented individuals who could contribute to development if their hidden abilities were discovered. As Mao observed: 'Such great inventors as Watt and Eddison were former workers. Franklin, who first invented the generation of electricity, sold newspapers as a boy. Many great men of learning and famous scientists never went to university.' (LL, 53.)

Mao's personal interpretation of the human factor in modernising society parallels a recent trend among non-communist economists. D.B. Keesing remarks: 'Economic theorists are coming to realise that the central process of economic growth is not so much accumulation of material resources as up-grading of human resources along with technology. People must acquire modern horizons, working habits and, above all, technical skills.' (*Economic Development: Challenge and Promise*, 279.) The United Nations publicised the same message in a review of Asia in 1965, stressing the quality of human resources as productive agents. (*Economic Survey of Asia and the Far East, 1965*, 19.

The distinction Mao Tse-tung drew between the intellectual élite with its modern professional skills and the hard-headed cadre at work on practical problems has considerable significance. Everett E. Hagen states the assumption that the élite in a backward society is less maimed by the sense of impotence before the overwhelming forces of nature which afflicts the average individual is false. Society sets constraints on the behaviour of the upper classes through the crippling influence of as authoritarian an upbringing as that of simple folk. The élite's sophistication, he argues, is often a veneer concealing a disbelief in the individual's ability to control his environment similar to the fatalism displayed by the peasant. (*Development of the Emerging Countries*, 12-13.) Mao believed intellectuals — even those recruited from the masses — were contaminated by their education which had not discarded the 'dross' of the old society. (PW, 8.) As Henry F. Dobyns states very accurately, the élites often derive their prestige from being money-lenders and landlords, making some form of 'rebellion' necessary for the creation of co-operative economic entreprises — a Mao formula for development. (*Agricultural Co-operatives and Markets in Developing Countries*, 171.)

Keesing delves deeper into this issue. He analyses the effect on a society's leadership when protected from overseas trade competition. His conclusions would apply, however, to any community in which officials, managers and technicians lead a sheltered life either because they are defended by tariffs from matching world standards or because their social positions put them beyond criticism. 'Skilled professionals such as engineers pick up the listless and careless ways of their fellows in a stifling bureaucracy and learn to avoid technical suggestions and decisions. There is little call for their expertise, and it would frequently prove more dangerous to their careers to point out what is being done wrong than to go along and say nothing. Workers learn lackadaisical ways, not being pressed to raise their productivity. Thus, the wrong skills are learned.' (*Economic Development: Challenge and Promise*, 282.)

This 'complacency' was a favourite target for Mao's invective. He was particulary bitter about the tendency to discourage new programmes. Mao, like Keesing, recognised that knowledge by itself was not enough to start society moving towards economic and social transformation. The leadership had to be ready to meet the challenges of ideas and policies which were completely novel. His sarcasm was acid: 'The people are filled with an immense enthusiasm for socialism. In a revolutionary period those who only know how to follow the routine paths cannot see this enthusiasm at all. They are blind. All is dark before them. At times they rant to a point of standing truth on its head and confusing black with white. Haven't we had enough of persons of that sort? ... Let something new appear and they invariably disapprove, they rush to oppose it. Later, they admit defeat and do a bit of self-criticism. But the next time something new appears, they do the same things again — and in the same sequence ... Someone always has to give him a poke in the back before he will move forward.' The remedy for this conservatism was to 'walk awhile among the people, learn what they are thinking, see what they are doing'. (SU, 44-45.) Again Mao's belief in the good sense of the ordinary people, in closer touch with reality than the party or educated élites, comes through strongly.

Mao resented another group, those people 'in leading positions' who, when faced with a problem, 'simply heave a sigh ... They lose patience and ask to be transferred'. Mao wrote off these defeatists as 'cowards' unwilling to look at the facts – even through a conference in their offices instead of meeting the masses on their own ground – before confessing failure. (SR, 34.) Other comrades he portrayed as 'content to leave things as they are'. Mao went on to describe their sloth: 'They eat their fill and sit dozing in their offices all day long without ever moving a step and going out among the masses to investigate. Whenever they open their mouths, their platitudes make people sick.' (*ibid.*, 39.)

In the search to understand why Mao Tse-tung felt so deeply that the masses could play as useful a part in development as the various Chinese élites, a review of the vices he thought were debilitating the party is essential. He spoke of individuals who 'abused their power and bullied the people, employed methods of coercion and commandism to get things done, thereby arousing discontent among the masses, or had indulged in corruption or encroached upon the interests of the masses'. (SW IV, 228.) 'Bureaucratic leadership', manifested as 'slacking at work due to indifference or perfunctoriness' or giving orders instead of winning the people's co-operation, should be 'thrown into the cesspit'. The party frequently weakened its popular appeal by 'closed-doorism, haughty sectarianism, and adventurism'. (SW I, 134, 275.) Straight political ignorance aroused his wrath. (SW II, 294.)

Another weakness was the group which 'still carry a great deal of the muck of the exploiting classes in their head'. 'Proletarian ideology?', they asked, 'the same old stuff!'. A cadre might sneer at his comrades because he came of the proper social class. The intellectuals and the unschooled held each other in mutual contempt. The young felt 'bright and capable'; the old, 'rich in experience'. Each found the other inferior. Those with poor work records lost heart; the veteran became opinionated. Cadres ought to free their minds of these 'encumbrances' and 'baggage', Mao stated. 'We must call on our party cadres to get rid of the baggage and start up the machinery.' (SW III, 94, 173.) Although Mao never stressed the fact, the reluctance of cadres to go to the war front compared with the valour of peasant troops, which he reported, must have contributed to his cynicism about the élites. (SW II, 222.)

Another factor in Mao's disillusionment was the behaviour of the party towards its own members. He had scant respect for those who could tolerate no mistakes among their comrades. He regarded malice as far more serious than errors in a speech. (Quotations, 162.) Of ideological heresies, he stated: 'I am not advocating the spread of such things, I only say "a few of them do not matter much".' (PW, 18.) His cadres, however, did not share this broad-minded outlook.

Mao listed a host of faults in the party's work style, including the tendency to indulge in 'personal attacks, pick quarrels, vent personal spite or seek revenge'. 'An old acquaintance, a fellow townsman, a schoolmate, a close friend, a loved one, an old colleague or an old subordinate' was treated by cadres with kid gloves — as Chinese custom demanded, whatever Mao thought. To sit silently at meetings but to gossip in private, to avoid responsibility and to play safe were other sins. Some cadres abused their party authority to work off private grudges. (SW II, 31-32, 441.) Fame and position were other pitfalls. Mao found cadres trying to 'draw some people in, push others out and resort to boasting, flattery and touting among the cadres'. Rural cadres were laughed at as 'clodhoppers'. Old cadres disliked raw recruits. Party members frequently lacked respect for non-communists. Mao was upset at the ruthlessness of internal party struggles. He hit out at those who demanded praise but could tolerate no criticism. (SW III, 43-49, 57-58, 159.) Then came those always out to protect their careers: 'Some people say they dare not write even when they have something to say, lest they should offend people and be criticised.' (PW, 14.)

Here Mao Tse-tung was battling against the entire system of Chinese social relations. Little research can be done on the conventions of modern China's bureaucracy in its daily operations, for the obvious reason that Peking does not permit social scientists to inquire into the secrets of its government departments. Mao Tse-tung's criticisms suggest the party's behaviour has not varied essentially from the typical game played in any Chinese hierarchical situation. Personal observation indicates the paramount importance of cultural factors in shaping the attitudes of Chinese working inside a formally-structured organisation. One obvious characteristic is insecurity. Few feel free enough of their traditional social obligations — friendship, clan, family and the others cited by Mao — to exert their full authority over subordinates or to speak out frankly to superiors. This phenomenon is not uniquely Chinese; its results, however, are more serious in China than in European or American communities in general. (For example, in Western business corporations, as R. Dahrendorf has observed, managers cannot act in complete disregard of their subordinates' wishes and interests. *Social Inequality*, 97-99.) The constraints on the exercise of authority seem far more unconscious and impersonal in the West than in China, where the influence of lower echelons upon their superiors' freedom to 'command' is very restricting by Western norms.

The links between individuals in Chinese society are so numerous (dialect, common school, kinship by blood, marriage or 'adoption') that the cadre can never be sure his juniors do not possess some personal connection with those above him. Such links can be used to monitor his performance. In addition, when aware of the social backing a subordinate enjoys, the cadre has to modify his treatment of the junior official to allow for his influential connections. Obligations in Chinese society extend far beyond the usual 'old-school-tie' system. An individual may have to pamper a colleague because he is linked to the superior of some fairly remote (by Western standards) relative of the cadre. Unhappy subordinates reporting adversely on an official are almost as bad as superiors who have uncovered genuine failings in his work. Life becomes a perpetual compromise to keep both those above and below on his side. Even his peers can be dangerous as they may get promoted and subsequently hold the cadre's prospects in their hands. Or they may fail to advance and feel envious of the cadre's success.

Partly as a result of this complex social system but also for other reasons, a higher value is place on having contacts in the right places than even in Western bureaucracies. Information on new policies in the offing, access to a superior's true opinion of the official's record, gossip on what is happening at the lower echelons are vital for survival. Intelligence on these subjects allows the cadre to protect himself against spiteful tittle-tattle, to adjust his work to policies in the pipeline and thus to avoid criticism for political backwardness, to know when a senior officer is planning to move against him. A network of informants can be built up safely only around the traditional ties which China has used over the centuries for coping with authority.

Voting in party meetings and public criticism by the masses were introduced by Mao into Chinese political life. Hence the need for solid alliances, able to muster claques during 'rectification' campaigns or to swing the requisite number of votes, has increased the value of every type of social connection. While personal experience of the attitudes and activities of cadres trained in China indicates they display greater frankness and less concern for the formalities of rank on the surface, rivalries, personal jealousies, inter-departmental envy and, above all, the continuing pull of personal relationships are still much in evidence. The crises of 1959 and 1966 were to show how little Mao had achieved in his effort to substitute objectivity and proper party discipline for personal considerations.

By comparison, the masses were straightforward, hard-working and reliable. Social factors pushed Mao towards the common people as a counter-balance to a bureaucracy which never seemed able to attain a decent level of communist purity for long. But economic factors were no less urgent in making Mao conscious of the masses' role in China's development. If the supply of entrepreneurs is as important as Western economists appear to believe — and given Mao's fear about the shortage of experienced cadres when he came to power — to have the government and the people marching in step towards common goals reduced the strain of supervising the people's economic transformation.

In addition, Henry J. Bruton, one of the few economists to offer a broad analysis of the social environment's impact on development, has stated: 'Traditionalism in the underdeveloped country is . . . both an impediment to the mobility of relevance to the development effort, and also a source of social stability that is essential to development.' (*Principles of Development Economics*, 243.) He argues that unless anarchy reigns, a society tends to resist the changes needed to allow the growth of a more efficient economic system because of its adaptation in the past to the demands of the traditional economy. He quotes a forceful example of the conflict between change and stability. The extended family, he says, may stifle enterprise but some alternative institution must be offered to replace its protection for the individual in an impoverished society before the disappearance of the extended family can be accepted by the community.

Mao Tse-tung set out to create a modern industrialised nation. Yet his philosophy represented a compromise rather than a break with the past. Nevertheless, some pots and pans had to be smashed, as he expressed it, in the process. If the masses could be convinced the communist party was leading them in the right direction, they would tolerate social changes with a minimum of resistance and without losing all sense of discipline as traditional restraints were discarded for modern behaviour patterns.

Mao's conception of the masses' contribution to the new China and his view of party and government relations with the public were topics which exercised his mind constantly. They were also issues on which his priorities shifted delicately with the exigencies of the moment. To get this aspect of Mao's philosophy into perspective, the best starting point is economic history, which (together with community development) is a field of social science long aware of the masses' place in an industrial revolution. David S. Landes, describing

Europe's technological revolution, quotes Newton's advice to 'learn not teach'. He sees the industrial revolution starting in the West because 'the will to mastery, the rational approach to problems which we call the scientific method, the competition for wealth and power' completely destroyed inherited values. 'Rationality in means and activist, as against quietist, ends' plus a degree of violence helped to give birth to an industrial society. He argues: 'Only the strongest incentives could have persuaded entrepreneurs to undertake and accept these changes; and only major advances could have overcome the dogged resistance of labour to the very principle of mechanisation.'

Landes states the industrial system not only seeks efficiency in combining machines and raw materials but tries to maximise its returns from wages 'by putting the right man in the right place'. He contrasts 'this "universalistic" standard of selection' with 'the so-called "particularistic" criteria of the pre-industrial society, dominated by agriculture, landed property, and an Establishment resting on interlaced family ties and hereditary privileges'. (*The Unbound Prometheus*, 33, 43, 546.) The essential elements in economic development uncovered by his analysis are the introduction of a rational outlook, encouragement of risk-taking, some social violence, the defeat of the masses' aversion to new-fangled machines and assessment on merit instead of family background. Mao's thoughts on economic progress were concerned with the same factors.

Sidney Pollard has examined the social structure which emerged with industrialisation from the management angle, a useful analysis here since this was Mao Tse-tung's standpoint as the nation's leader. Pollard sums up the transformation imposed on the worker: 'There was a whole new culture to be absorbed and an old one to be traduced and spurned, there were new surroundings, often in a different part of the country, new relations with employers and new uncertainties of livelihood, new friends and neighbours, new marriage patterns and behaviour patterns of children and adults within the family and without.' Discipline, regular hours and constant application to the job in hand were essential in the age of mechanisation. This unremitting and mechanical work pattern was repugnant to men used to the varied rhythm of farming or handicraft industries. Employers saw the moral qualities of their employees, their industry, ambition, sobriety and thrift, as factors in the efficiency of the labour force. Where a town or village was controlled by a single master, he attempted 'to reform the whole man' to create disciplined workers amenable to his management. (*The Genesis of Management,* 191, 216, 226-32.)

In the early days of the English industrial revolution, some employers handed over control of the workers to men drawn from the masses' own ranks. 'The discipline was to be the older form of that of the supervisor of a small face-to-face group, maintained by someone who usually worked himself or was in direct daily contact with the workers.' (*ibid.,* 222.) The picture offered here is of resistance by the masses to the social transformation made necessary by the mechanical revolution. Management sought to inculcate its own moral ideals in their employees to make their control easier and to build up the self-discipline demanded by the factory system. Some employers found it worthwhile to leave the masses to run their own affairs, with supervision placed in the hands of men involved in the workers' production situation. The problems confronting China were to be tackled by Mao along similar lines.

Mao Tse-tung believed the masses, led by communism, to be invincible. 'Of all things in the world, people are the most precious. Under the leadership of the communist party, as long as there are people, every kind of miracle can be performed.' (SW IV, 454.) 'We must have faith in the masses; we must have faith in the party . . . If we doubt these principles, we shall accomplish nothing.' (AC, 7.) However, Mao put the masses into a special category. He spoke of 'the inexhaustible creative power of the masses', and declared: 'The people, and the people alone, are the motive force of world history.' (SW III, 266, 207.) This sense of the strength of the people themselves arose from Mao's combat experience when poorly-armed peasant bands faced seasoned and well-equipped troops. 'Weapons are an important factor in war, but not the decisive factor; it is people, not things, that are decisive. The contest of strength is not only a contest of military and economic power, but also a contest of human power and morale.' Mao justified this contention on the grounds that military and economic power is 'necessarily wielded by people'. (MW, 217-18.)

At the same time, Mao obviously was expanding on Marx's aphorism: 'Of all the instruments of production, the greatest productive force is the revolutionary class itself.' He was echoing too the teaching of Mencius: 'The people are the most important [in society]; land and grain take second priority while the ruler comes last.' But a contradiction had to be resolved here: why had the masses suffered in bondage so long despite their numerous revolts? Mao's answer was that because of the lack of 'correct leadership such as the proletariat and the communist party . . . although some social progress was made after each great peasant revolutionary struggle, the feudal economic relations and political system remained basically unchanged'. (SW II, 309.)

Mao Tse-tung, therefore, needed an explosive force to breach the walls which held back the creative energies of the masses. This dynamic element was marxism-leninism. 'The wealth of society is created by the workers, the peasants, the working intellectuals. If they take their destiny into their own hands, use marxism-leninism as their guide, and energetically tackle problems instead of evading them, there is no difficulty in the world which they cannot overcome.' (SU, 14.) Here communist theory was depicted as a leaven within the class ranks even without the party's leadership. Yet marxist-leninist ideas do not 'drop from the skies' nor are they 'innate in the mind'. 'They come from social practice, and from it alone . . . the struggle for production, the class struggle and scientific experiment.'

Again the party was not regarded as the fount of communist truth. Neither did the party form the link between the 'correct ideas' derived from 'social practice' and the people. Mao traced the process of conveying communist wisdom to the masses who then employed this knowledge to unlock their own strength without mentioning the party. 'Once the correct ideas characteristic of the advanced classes are grasped by the masses, these ideas turn into a material force which changes society and changes the world.' Indeed, Mao went on in the same article to denigrate the average party member's inability to grasp this process. (PE, 134-36.) If Mao Tse-tung's remarks on the leadership role of the party are set in the context of his awareness of ordinary cadres' faults, he appeared to split the party into two parts: the 'advanced class' capable of bringing out the best in people and the rest, capable of only pedestrian performance.

Mao Tse-tung proceeded from the tenet that: 'A basic principle of marxism-leninism is to enable the masses to know their own interests and unite to fight for their own interests.' (SW IV, 241.) The problem was that, as Mao had stated, the communist party had to be trusted to undertake the work of bringing communism to the masses. This relationship between the party and the people involved considerable difficulties. Mao resolutely opposed those who 'one-sidedly propagated the view that the poor peasants and farm labourers conquer the country and should rule the country, or that the democratic government should be a government of the peasants only, or that the democratic government should listen only to the workers, poor peasants and farm labourers'. (*ibid.*, 197.) Mao had to adopt this line of some superior authority (the communist party) running affairs since he felt only under a communist government could the people enjoy the right conditions to shake off the old society's dust. (*ibid.*, 418.) Yet for Mao, the test of a policy's validity lay in its acceptance by the masses. (SW III, 88.) Mao came close to suggesting that policies only became correct when implemented by the masses: 'The only yardstick of truth is the revolutionary practice of millions of people.' (SW II, 339-40.) The covert qualification was the adjective 'revolutionary'. Someone had to light the fires of a rebellion before this criterion took effect. In a later period, Mao was compelled to admit: 'The forces representing the advanced class sometimes suffer defeat not because their ideas are incorrect but because ... they are not as powerful for the time being as the forces of reaction.' (PE, 135.) This confession was made in 1963 when Mao had learned that marxism-leninism did not flower of its own accord even in the red sunshine of the new China.

How to quarry concrete truth from the masses was another issue which Mao Tse-tung had to solve by a compromise between his lofty notion of the masses' talents and the crude realities of government. 'All correct leadership is necessarily "from the masses, to the masses". This means: take the ideas of the masses (scattered and unsystematic ideas) and concentrate them (through study turn them into concentrated and systematic ideas), then go to the masses and propagate and explain these ideas until the masses embrace them as their own, hold fast to them and translate them into action, and test the correctness of these ideas in such action ... the right task, policy and style of work invariably conform with the demands of the masses at a given time and place and invariably strengthen our ties with the masses.' Yet Mao admitted the masses could be oblivious of the need for change, and the only remedy was to wait in patience, 'otherwise we shall isolate ourselves from the masses'. 'Do everything as the masses want it done' was a slogan Mao scorned. 'The party must lead the masses to carry out all their correct ideas in the light of the circumstances and educate them to correct any wrong ideas they may entertain.'

Mao was attempting to steer a middle course between 'commandism' (demanding more from the people than they were ready to contribute) and the equally pernicious 'tailism' (the party lagging behind the masses' desire for reforms). The only sure way to keep the party in step with the masses was for the cadres to 'go out to face the world and brave the storm'. Throughout these mental gymnastics to strike the safest balance between party leadership and respect for public opinion, he was concerned to establish popular support for his policies: 'The motive of serving the masses is inseparably linked with the effect of winning their approval; the two must be united.' He was anxious lest the communists 'separate themselves from the majority of the people . . . by leading only a few progressive contingents in an isolated and rash advance'. (SW III, 119, 265, 186; IV, 232; III 266, 158, 88; II, 201.)

Although this analysis has concentrated on the political aspects of party-people relations, Mao Tse-tung's views on this subject were of profound economic importance. He desired to achieve consciously and deliberately that social transformation of China which had accompanied the industrial revolution in the West without any guiding hand. He was as interested in the total transformation of man's morals as any early Victorian capitalist in England. Marxism-leninism, he believed, led to rational comprehension of the world and opened men's eyes to scientific solutions. (SW III, 21, 23-24.) He was seeking to implant the same objective outlook towards the material environment which had made possible economic development in Western Europe. Mao had to abolish respect for social status in dealing with people for the same reasons which led to the birth of an industrial and commercial 'meritocracy' to challenge the European upper classes in the era of industrialisation.

Whereas profits and wages could be used to dull the danger and pains involved in the transformation of European society, Mao's nation was unable to afford 'material incentives' for long, financially or ideologically. China under Mao Tse-tung could not wait the decades which Britain, for example, spent in passing through the stages of machine-smashing, the campaign for a voice in industrial affairs for workers through their trade unions and the battle for extension of the suffrage until the arrival of a reasonably stable, urban, manufacturing society. To let new techniques induce gradual changes, filtering down to the masses via a small class of adventurous managers, would take longer than China's poverty could allow.

Mao's theoretical teachings on officials' treatment of the masses were accompanied by practical instructions. 'Every communist engaged in government work should set an example of absolute integrity, of freedom from favouritism in making appointments and of hard work for little remuneration. Every communist working among the masses should be their friend and not a boss over them, an indefatigable teacher and not a bureaucratic politician. At no time and in no circumstances should a communist place his personal interests first; he should subordinate them to the interests of the nation and of the masses.' (SW II, 198.) This set high standards. The cadres were to meet Mao's demands by personal involvement in the masses' problems. To issue orders without the active participation in physical labour of those in leading positions was likely to lead to poor results. 'In the financial and economic field, the party and government personnel at the county and district levels should devote nine-tenths of their energy to helping the peasants increase production, and only one-tenth to collecting taxes from them.' Mao condemned those who neglected to organise the masses and who concentrated instead on the personnel employed by economic organisations. 'While taking from the people we must at the same time help them to replenish and expand their economy.' (SW III, 117, 132, 155, 113.)

He was particularly anxious to ensure that the people and not just the bureaucrats were kept informed of government policy. (SW IV, 241-42.) Mao wanted the party to throw open its doors for the masses 'to discuss local ideological work and all related problems'. (PW, 20.) This directive was important because of the dominant position of the party in the affairs of a communist country. Mao was not thinking here solely of party propaganda: 'Ideological and political education is an arduous task. It must be based on the life and experience of the peasants and be conducted in a very practical manner, with careful attention to detail. Neither bluster nor over-simplification will do. It should be conducted not in isolation from our economic measures, but in conjunction with them.' (SU, 303.) He expected the party to listen to the people's voice: 'If you do not explain things to the cadres and the masses, bare your hearts to them and allow them to make known their own views, they will fear you and be too afraid to speak out. It will be impossible to mobilise their enthusiasm.' (LL, 38.)

Other Asian leaders besides Mao Tse-tung have tried to involve their nations in the process of creating economic policy. Gunnar Myrdal devotes a whole chapter of his *Asian Drama* to the abortive efforts to implement 'democratic planning' in South Asia. (II, Chapter 18.) He explains the resistance among the people to the ideology of planning imported from overseas by educated élites. Because of the persistence of paternalism and authoritarianism in South Asia, 'the masses are led to expect or demand that the government do more for them, without showing greater readiness to change their own ways'. (*ibid.*, 729-30.) This danger was what Mao's development strategy was designed to avoid. Unlike other Asian rulers, Mao Tse-tung challenged his élites' authoritarianism and fought to make a reality of popular participation in drawing up and executing economic programmes. His success varied, but the Cultural Revolution showed the lengths to which he was prepared to go in subjecting political authority to public criticism.

Consultation with peasants and workers was not a matter of informing them what Peking had decided. The pace and direction of economic programmes were to be harmonised, as already noted, with the people's enthusiasm for radical or novel policies. Colin Leys has shed considerable light on the value of popular participation in economic planning. He sees the process as having broader goals than permitting the public to feel they help to shape the programme and thus should identify themselves with its targets. Development calls for certain quantities of labour, materials and other resources. Their availability in any area may be less important than the inhabitants' willingness to supply the inputs needed for the plan. Consultation on economic problems at the grass roots becomes a forum for negotiations about the 'price' the people want for carrying out the plan. This bargaining process allows the authorities to estimate more precisely the chances of achieving national output goals. The government is given the opportunity to modify targets according to the public's own predictions (its favourable or adverse reactions to official proposals) about its future economic performance. (*Politics and Change in Developing Countries*, 273.)

Mao saw the process of popular participation in economic policy as a two-way communication, with the government and the people both influencing each other; hence the slogan 'from the masses, to the masses'. Mao's vision of economic leadership touched upon the same problem which concerned Leys. Mao defined the art of government as: 'To be good at translating the party's policy into action of the masses, to be good at getting not only the leading cadres but also the broad masses to understand and master every movement and every struggle we launch . . . It is also the dividing line that determines whether or not we make mistakes in our work.' (SW IV, 242-43.)

Mao Tse-tung sometimes appeared to demand political issues take precedence over all other considerations: 'Political work is the life-blood of all economic work. This is particularly true at a time when the economic system of a society is undergoing a fundamental change.' (SU, 302.) Another motto was: 'Put politics in command.' (PD, 12 November, 1966.) James Chieh Hsiung comments that 'politics takes command' conveys very little in English but implies in the original Chinese putting public interests first. (*Ideology and Practice,* 115-16.) In advancing this slogan, Mao added: 'Go to the masses and be one with them.' Mao's anxiety here was to achieve a transformation of mental attitudes through persuading the cadres and people to unite in looking to national horizons rather than the interests of their village or workshop, to public rather than to individual needs.

In discussing the impact of mechanisation on agriculture, the point was made that unlike production, farming does not degenerate into an occupation for automatons, forced by the factory to abandon their traditional skills and mental habits. Much the same was probably true of the small plants Mao Tse-tung advocated, in which machinery was scarce, skilful hands at a premium and little specialisation of labour possible in the absence of a proper assembly line. Peasants and workers in light in- dustry (intimately connected with agriculture) and the smaller enterprises faced little in the economic environment of the new China to compel them to abandon their family and clan customs or to adopt a new world outlook. The traditional pattern of life seemed valid. The philosophical inheritance preserved in everyday speech and even the popular (often semi-magical) view of the universe retained their usefulness. They gave an order and meaning to life, however much Mao Tse-tung urged the superiority of 'scientific' marxism-leninism on his people. (Gustav Jahoda, *The Psychology of Superstition,* 124.) Faced with this situation, Mao had no option but to hammer away unceasingly at the importance of putting politics – communism, for him, the rational, objective, unselfish world view – in control of life. Mao Tse-tung was not arguing that politics was all that mattered. He was fighting a battle on yet another front to effect the social changes he saw as the only way to open the floodgates which had dammed the creative energies of China's millions for so long.

Mao's acclaim for the masses as 'the real heroes' was tested brutally in 1958 and the lean years which followed. The Great Leap Forward and the switch from co-operatives to communes began in mid-1958. Mao Tse-tung had stated in February 1958: 'There has never been such an upsurge of enthusiasm and initiative among the masses of the people on the production front. The people of the whole country are inspired by the slogan of overtaking or surpassing Britain in the output of iron and steel and other major industrial products in fifteen years or a little longer.' (CS, 1.)

The peasants in particular were spurred throughout the year to incredible productive feats. Not only was agricultural production reorganised on a commune basis, but a network of rural industries sprang up to exploit local mineral deposits through 'backyard furnaces' and similar makeshift techniques. The goals of the 1958 Great Leap Forward were announced in May by Liu Shao-chi (who seven months later replaced Mao Tse-tung as head of state). The essence of the Great Leap was a massive acceleration in development. To critics who preferred a more cautious approach, Liu spelled out a harsh message: 'Surely one should be able to see that a really terrible tense situation would exist if more than 600 million people had to live in poverty and cultural backwardness for a prolonged period, had to exert their utmost efforts just to eke out a bare living, and were unable to resist natural calamities effectively.' The target was: 'While giving priority to the growth of heavy industry, we must make great efforts to develop agriculture, which means to get the greatest domestic market in the world to place immense orders for heavy and light industrial products, including farm machinery, chemical fertilisers, building materials, fuels, electric power and transport facilities; and to mobilise the biggest labour force in the world to increase the production of foodstuffs, meat, vegetables, etc., and the output of cotton and other industrial crops, to contribute its astonishing labour power to produce enormous wealth, accumulate large amounts of funds for national industrial construction, and itself to build small industrial enterprises in the villages.' (CC, 429-30.)

The tactics to achieve these vaulting ambitions were taken by Liu directly from Mao Tse-tung. Cadres were dropping their mandarin habits under the onslaught of mass criticism, Liu claimed, and officials were taking part in productive labour. An upsurge of volunteer work for national not personal gain had appeared. The wisdom of the common people was demonstrated in a host of technical innovations created by their own experiments. 'Conservative' attitudes had been defeated through ideological remoulding. The small-scale enterprises favoured by Mao were lauded, and economic authority transferred down to the lower echelons. In obedience to Mao's teachings, Liu called for the overhaul of regulations hindering production and a general streamlining of the government structure. Ideology and politics were described by Liu as 'always the soul and guide of every kind of work'. (ibid., 421-23, 425, 431, 435-36.)

In August 1958, the party central committee blessed the birth of the communes. 'In several places they are already widespread. They have developed very rapidly in some areas. It is highly probable that there will soon be an upsurge in setting up people's communes throughout the country and the development is irresistible ... The establishment of people's communes with all-round management of agriculture, forestry, animal husbandry, side-occupations and fishery, where industry (the worker), agriculture (the peasant), exchange (the trader), culture and education (the student) and military affairs (the militiaman) merge into one, is the fundamental policy to guide the peasants to accelerate socialist construction, complete the building of socialism ahead of time and carry out the gradual transition to communism.' (*ibid.*, 454.)

The glorious future held out to the nation soon turned sour. In August 1959, the central committee admitted output claims for 1958 had been 'a bit high', a monumental understatement of the chaos which had struck the economy. (*ibid.*, 534.) The committee called for readjustments in the allocation of labour and capital to obtain the fastest possible returns. The quality of backyard furnace production was to be raised forthwith. Supplies of consumption goods were to be increased, and the natural disasters threatening the harvest had to be dealt with before the year's production plan could be completed. (*ibid.*, 538.) In the same month Prime Minister Chou En-lai denied allegations that the 1958 drive to produce iron and steel locally had been a catastrophe when the costly inputs of men and money were compared with the poor results obtained. But he confessed of the communes: 'It is unthinkable that they were perfect and flawless from the very start and that there were no defects or difficulties.' The errors had been corrected, the prime minister insisted. He admitted too that the increased purchasing power following expansion of employment during the Great Leap had allowed demand to outstrip available supplies. But Chou asserted: 'The Great Leap Forward and the people's commune have registered great achievements, the present economic situation is favourable to us and our future is bright. This proves that the party's general line for socialist construction ... [is] entirely correct.' (*ibid.*, 542-45.)

Despite a spate of propaganda denouncing those who questioned the success of the Great Leap and the communes (e.g., *ibid.*, 556), 1958 saw the collapse of the steady improvement in economic performance China had enjoyed since 1949. Peking no longer bothers to conceal this fact and ascribes the slump to sabotage by Liu Shao-chi and his followers, the withdrawal of Soviet aid in 1960 and harvest failures.

The standard description for conditions from 1958 is 'temporary difficulties as a result of the Khruschov renegade clique's sabotage and three consecutive years of natural calamities'. (*The Struggle between the Two Roads in China's Countryside*, 15.) The reality was more cruel. The village steel campaign had resulted in colossal waste, diverting labour from the fields at the height of the harvest. (Jones and Poleman, *Communes and the Agricultural Crisis in Communist China*, 9.) Jan S. Prybyla highlights the desperate food shortages which faced the nation. (*The Political Economy of Communist China*, 294.) Minister of Defence Peng Teh-huai asserted at a closed session of the party central committee in 1959: 'If the Chinese workers and peasants were not as good as they are, a Hungarian incident would have occurred in China and it would have been necessary to invite Soviet troops in.' (*Peking Review*, 34/1967.)

The tragic results of the Great Leap Forward and the introduction of the communes are of more than historical interest. They raise questions about the extent to which 1958 witnessed a genuine experiment in the application of Mao Tse-tung's economic strategy. Clearly, a failure of the magnitude which occurred after 1958 would go far to discredit his policies if Mao could be shown to have initiated or supported fully the measures adopted during the Great Leap. Most of the evidence implicating Mao in the disaster comes from documents released during the Cultural Revolution by sources of varying credibility recounting the debates at the Lushan meeting of the central committee in 1959. Ironically, Lushan, a mountan so wrapped in cloud that its true shape is always disguised, forms the basis of a still current Chinese proverb on the difficulties of uncovering truth.

Mao Tse-tung, according to the speeches attributed to him at this conference, flayed the planning commission for abandoning control of the economy in August 1958. Previously, said Mao, economic mistakes could have been laid at the prime minister's door as Mao himself had not been concerned with production. However, the Great Leap Forward, the communes and the backyard furnaces, Mao took on his own shoulders. (*Chinese Law and Government*, Winter 1968-69, 39-41.) This admission seems to make Mao Tse-tung's part quite plain. Unfortunately, a bald narration of his remarks at the party conference obscures the undercurrents of Chinese polemic normal on such occasions. Mao Tse-tung's speeches give the impression he was trying to shelter colleagues, principally Chou En-lai, from attacks he regarded as unwarranted. He stated at Lushan he had no responsibility for economic developments before 1958. His listeners must have contrasted this claim with his written record. Mao had published three major works from 1955 to 1957 on the economy: the first, *Socialist Upsurge in China's Countryside;* the second on agricultural co-operatives; and the third, his famous essay, 'On the Correct Handling of Contradictions'. Mao's remarks were a challenge: if the Great Leap Forward's critics wanted to push their attack to extremes, let them try a showdown with Mao himself.

Assuming Mao Tse-tung was not speaking to defend himself but to shield others, what about the case of Peng Teh-huai, destroyed at this central committee session, according to Peking's subsequent account, for his savage opposition to the Great Leap Forward? (*Peking Review,* 34/1967.) Again, the truth is shrouded in Lushan's mists. A Red Guard document stated Peng openly expressed incredulity at a statement made by Mao Tse-tung at the meeting. (*The Case of Peng Teh-huai, 1959-1968,* 1.) Chinese are quite capable of denouncing a liar. However, at an official meeting, such bluntness would alienate other members present. The standard and highly effective technique for exposing an opponent's mendacity is sarcastic acceptance of his assertions and the patently insincere recital of some plausible reasons for the opponent's failure to uncover the facts. Peng could have said that as party chairman, Mao Tse-tung had been too busy to inspect the rural conditions which so badly worried Peng. The same *Peking Review* article accused Peng of penning a letter to Mao critical of the Great Leap Forward. This document seems no more outspoken than another missive on the same subject from a senior planner. Peng was attacked savagely for his memorandum; the planner was praised for his courage although criticised by Mao for pessimism. (*The Case of Peng Teh-huai, 1959-1968,* 7-13; *Chinese Law and Government,* Winter, 1968-69, 25-26, 47-51.)

Why then was Peng dismissed if not for opposing the Great Leap Forward? The simplest explanation lies in his reference (quoted already) to the danger of rebellion in China and the possibility of having to appeal to the Soviet Union for troops to crush an uprising. Any minister of defence unable to guarantee his own army's ability to handle internal security is too unreliable to keep in office. The danger of a Hungarian-type revolt was to be mentioned continually in the early stages of the Cultural Revolution in 1966. (For example, GSCR (1), 25; (3), 9.) The 1956 uprising in Budapest seems to have been a nightmare Mao could never shake off. Perhaps, too, the cut in the military budget proposed by Mao in 1956 and revealed as official policy by Liu Shao-chi in the same year was another consideration. (CS, 25; CC, 178.) Peng was denounced in the *People's Daily* (17 August, 1967) for 'placing military technique in the first place'. Under 'the pretext of regularisation and modernisation', he had resisted the dominant position of politics in army-building. Shortly after Peng was cashiered, Lin Piao, later nominated as Mao's heir till his disgrace in 1971, wrote a long article which put modern weapons firmly in second place to ideology in China's defence policy. (CC, 583.)

Peng almost certainly attacked the Great Leap Forward and the communes, and so did many others. Some pointed out the strains these policies were to create even before their official adoption. Liu Shao-chi dismissed all such 'conservative' notions. Liu derided what proved the most accurate forecast in the light of later events: 'Ideological and political work can produce neither grain nor coal or iron.' He preferred to trust the masses' enthusiasm rather than heed the cassandras. (*ibid.*, 429-31, 436-37.) Chen Po-ta, a close associate of Mao, in late 1959 devoted a long article to 'a small number of persons' inside the party who had the temerity to find fault with the Great Leap Forward. (RF, 22/1959.) The attention this 'small number' received from press and radio suggests their influence was disproportionate to their alleged size.

Thus Peng might have been broken not only for his failure to pledge the safety of China against serious disorder and for demanding more money for his troops but also to demonstrate the crisis of 1959 was no time to question the economic wisdom of the party leadership. Significantly, he was not attacked by name following the Lushan conference. The central committee had to worry about filling stomachs in the months ahead. Recriminations over responsibility for past blunders would only divide the administration when a united front was essential to promote economic recovery. A number of military officers and economic officials were discreetly removed at the same time as Peng. (*China under Mao,* 30.) In several cases, they had close personal connections with the disgraced minister of defence which apparently made them too risky to trust in high office – an interesting insight into the workings of Chinese officialdom.

The analysis of the Lushan central committee has been admittedly speculative and based on a personal view of Chinese behaviour patterns in groups under tension. But Mao Tse-tung's writings suggest that whoever invented the Great Leap Forward, its lack of balance cannot be ascribed to him. In 1957, he had stated: 'Government workers are not sufficiently experienced and have to undertake further study and exploration of specific policies. In other words, time is needed for our socialist system to become established and consolidated.' He also remarked: 'As most of our co-operatives are only a little over a year old, it would be unreasonable to ask too much of them. In my view, we will be doing well enough if the co-operatives can be consolidated during the second five-year plan [i.e. by 1962].' His emphasis in 1957 was on the country's economic bottlenecks. (PE, 95, 102, 127-28.) While Liu's speech outlining the Great Leap Forward in May 1958 was carefully phrased to demonstrate its harmony with Maoist principles, no Chinese leader has suggested Mao's relationship to the Great Leap Forward was that of midwife let alone parent. Godfather seems to sum up his role.

Mao's aphorism about 'achieving greater, quicker, better and more economical results in building socialism' was only the slogan used by the party central committee — not Mao alone — as the basic principle of the Great Leap programme in 1958. (*The Socialist Transformation of the National Economy in China*, 252.) Li Fu-chun, chairman of the state planning commission, traced the genealogy of the Great Leap thus: 'In the winter of 1955 . . . Comrade Mao Tse-tung scientifically foresaw the possibility for the national economy to develop at still higher speed . . . Afterwards, he put forward a series of programmatic proposals for the realisation of this objective possibility, including the draft twelve-year national programme for agricultural development (1956-1967) and the report on the "Ten major relationships". On the practical experience in socialist construction in 1956 and 1957 and the development of Mao Tse-tung's thinking, the second session of our party's eighth national congress formally laid down the [Great Leap's] general line.' (CC, 587.) Responsibility for economic decisions, by this account, was not Mao's directly. Needless to say, none of the documents to which Li referred called for anything resembling the reckless pace of advance sought by the Great Leap.

The commune's parentage has never been questioned: 'A great creation of the Chinese people evolved in accordance with actual needs.' (*National Programme for Agricultural Development, 1956-1967*, 32.) It was the masses' own invention, though doubtless multiplied by eager cadres. While the speed with which the commune movement embraced the whole nation has led Western observers to doubt its voluntary and spontaneous character, Ezra Vogel has provided an excellent account of how Peking creates high tides of popular

118

enthusiasm. He shows that the element of compulsion is generally subtle in the extreme and is derived from traditional Chinese social norms. Vogel's account makes clear the dividing line between persuasion and compulsion under Mao and sets out the communist rationale for claiming the masses created the communes. (*Soviet and Chinese Communism*, 170-73.)

Donald S. Zagoria believes Mao's role in the Great Leap Forward was 'adjudicator' between Liu who favoured the movement and Chou En-lai who would have preferred a more gradual approach. (*The Sino-Soviet Conflict, 1956-1961*, 70.) Lucian W. Pye, however, blames 'the whims of one man', Mao Tse-tung. He holds: 'Much of Peking's erratic behaviour suggests that decision making is responsive to individual ideas but not to the requirements of manipulating reality.' (*The Spirit of Chinese Politics*, 226-27.) The truth may be simpler. Premier Chou confessed in 1959 economic planning had been unrealistic while the statistical units lacked experience. He clearly implied a gap existed between what Peking thought was happening and actual developments in the vast countryside. (CC, 546, 548-49.)

Mao Tse-tung had harsh words in the same year on the subject, which are worth quoting fairly fully to test the implications of Pye's portrait of Mao and his officials as unwilling to face reality. 'When output quotas are fixed, we should make known the actual quotas we can guarantee ... We must not tell lies about various measures for increasing production ... Those who are honest and dare to tell the truth are, in the final analysis, beneficial to the people's cause and they themselves also have nothing to lose. Those who are fond of telling lies will do harm to the people as well as themselves. They are always at a disadvantage. It must be said that many lies are told because of pressure from the upper echelons. When these resort to trumpet blowing, applying pressure and making promises, it makes things difficult for their subordinates. Therefore while one must have drive, one must never tell lies.' (LL, 35.) Mao had cautioned in his 1955 blast against 'conservatism' that 'no-one should go off into wild flights of fancy, or make plans unwarranted by the objective situation, or insist on attempting the impossible'. In 1959 he referred to 'the high-flown talk that is in vogue at present'. (SU, 9-10; LL, 35.)

The contrast between promise and performance was tragic in the Great Leap Forward. One feature of this period which deserves more attention than it normally receives is the consistently cautious attitude of the party central committee indicating that the leadership was not in favour of the Great Leap Forward's abandonment of all restraint. This body was sufficiently under Mao's control for him to remove the minister of defence in 1959. While Mao relinquished his post as head of state at the end of 1958, he had the leading party position firmly in his hands in 1958 and 1959 (though the party communist rank and file made no urgent appeal for him to remain as head of state which may have impaired his prestige somewhat). Thus the committee's caution can be interpreted as having Mao's approval. The first decree on the communes (August 1958) ordered that they should be formed without endangering production. Their establishment should match the peasants' enthusiasm for the new institution, with experiments to test its feasibility. 'Compulsory or rash steps' were forbidden. The transfer of ownership of commune assets from the members to the state was discouraged. Members were to be paid on the principle of 'from each according to his ability and to each according to his work'. (CC, 455-56.)

The statement issued by the central committee in December, 1958 made very sober reading: 'There is as yet insufficient experience of successfully running and developing the people's communes.' The central committee chided those who believed short-cuts to prosperity and a full communist state were possible in China. The provision of free supplies to commune members instead of paying them according to their work was criticised. 'In every aspect of production and capital construction, thrift must be observed, careful plans worked out and manpower, material and financial resources used as rationally as possible; production costs must be reduced, expenditure cut down and income increased.' A vast improvement in farming methods was called for, and it was emphasised that industrialisation linked to the needs of agriculture should be accelerated. Adequate rest and recreation were to be given to the masses. The improvement of labour management was stressed. 'In the course of checking over the communes, it is necessary to carry out an overall and thorough check-up of the production plan, distribution, welfare facilities, management, financial work, organisation and leadership in the communes.' The committee's communiqué sounded as if a majority of its members had grave doubts as to the wisdom of breathless haste in setting up communes. (NCNA, 18 December, 1958.) And at this stage, the national government could not have possessed sufficient information to be able to predict the tragedy lying in wait for the economy in 1959. Thus a fall in grain procurement was explained in the autumn as due to the excessive strain imposed on the national transport system by the bumper harvest. (NCNA, 22 October, 1958.)

Po I-po, chairman of the national economic commission, while backing the Great Leap on the industrial front, stated: 'To carry out specific economic tasks requires not only a total revolutionary effort from the masses but proper preparation of the necessary material and technical conditions.' Politics were important but objective economic conditions could not be ignored, he continued. (RF, 1/1959.) The Lushan meting in August 1959 described the year's output targets as too high. Backyard furnaces could be dropped if local authorities found they lacked the labour to maintain both agricultural output and steel production. Inevitably in a communist nation, the central committee denounced sagging morale among the cadres and insisted mistakes in commune management because of inexperience were exaggerated and had been put right in any case. (CC, 534-35.) The reduction in output quotas at the Lushan meeting, where Mao Tse-tung's views had prevailed over Peng Teh-huai, hardly suggests that the Chairman had stuck pigheadedly to the Great Leap as his pet economic programme. Furthermore, Mao described the contest with Peng at Lushan as 'a class struggle, a continuation of the life-and-death struggle between two antagonistic contradictions – the bourgeoisie and the proletariat – which has gone on all through the socialist revolution in the last ten year'. (PD, 17 August, 1967.) If Mao did not agree with the need for the moderation and realism displayed in the meeting's communiqué, his tacit endorsement of the committee's public statement would imply he was not prepared to fight for his principles even though he had battled fiercely against the 'class enemies', Peng and his supporters.

A statement published in 1971 exonerated Mao from all responsibility for the mistakes of the Great Leap Forward. Liu Shao-chi was attacked for promoting excessive radicalism to sabotage Mao's policies in 1958 by urging the hasty nationalisation of the communes and abolition of wages based on the individual's work performance. (Canton RS, 22 April, 1971.) In other words the excesses of the Great Leap Forward and the initial defects of the communes were laid at Liu's door, while Mao was depicted as the moderate. While this account smacks of rewriting history to protect Mao's reputation, the accusations against Liu tally with the fact he introduced the Great Leap while in 1957 considerable caution on economic policy had been expressed by Mao personally, an attitude reflected in the 1958 and 1959 communiqués issued by the party central committee dominated by Mao Tse-tung.

If Mao Tse-tung was not a fervent believer in the Great Leap Forward and the hasty establishment of communes throughout China, why did the Cultural Revolution attack such leaders as Tao Chu for their caution after 1958 over excessive enthusiasm for these policies? Why were greater central control and supervision, after the Great Leap Forward began to falter, so widely condemned in the Cultural Revolution? Why too did the Cultural Revolution echo the catchphrases of the Great Leap Forward? (Yao Wen-yuan, *Comments on Tao Chu's Two Books,* 20-21, 26-27; RF, 3/1968; ID 61-62, 159.) The clue to the importance of the Great Leap Forward for Mao Tse-tung comes from James R. Townsend. He argues that as the economy ground to a halt, the emergency measures taken by the party cast doubt on three of Mao's most cherished assumptions. Firstly, a slump in living standards, however obviously the result of inclement weather, could only weaken popular faith in the ability of Mao's party to devise economic programmes to protect China from the periodic distress which had afflicted the nation in the past. Mao could no longer expect unquestioning reverence for party edicts. Secondly, the need to prevent free supplies taking the place of wages based on output meant the party lacked faith in its power to raise the production enthusiasm of the masses through ideological education. Thirdly, the Great Leap Forward's failure demonstrated the weakness of the basic-level cadres in linking the central government to the population. (*Political Participation in Communist China,* 100.)

Mao's contempt for the typical cadre implies the last point would be of least moment to him. The first two, however, were vital. His entire economic strategy hinged on the masses' creative energy, once inspired by marxism-leninism, to conquer every physical obstacle. Their eager response to a programme was, in Mao's view, a test of its validity. Their readiness to imbibe communist truths to rid themselves of poverty was also an article of faith with Mao Tse-tung. To argue the Great Leap Forward failed because of the people's inability to defy natural calamities and that policies had to be revised in 1959 and subsequent years because the enthusiasm of ordinary workers and peasants fluctuated with material rewards represented a direct repudiation of the most vital element in Mao's blueprint for prosperity. The blame had to be shifted to 'conspirators' such as Tao Chu who, with Peng Teh-huai, had been determined to 'foil' the masses' eagerness to strain every muscle to overtake Britain within fifteen years. The rehabilitation of the Great Leap Forward had useful political advantages in 1966, as an account of the Cultural Revolution will show. But the main aim was to prove it was turncoats, not the people, who lost heart in 1959.

After this review of the third and final strand in Mao Tse-tung's development strategy — his social engineering formula — the validity of his programme for economic growth seems plain. Various facets of his philosophy can be matched with the experience of other Asian nations seeking an escape from poverty. Mao, indeed, appears to have been more progressive and hard-headed in his approach than most of the region's leaders. Western economists ought to find much to approve of in Mao Tse-tung's prescriptions for prosperity. His tactics for defeating basic obstacles to progress have enough parallels in non-communist studies to testify to Mao's freedom from cant and to his willingness to seek a pragmatic road for the transformation of a primitive economy. Once he broke loose from the tutelage of Soviet economics, a new vigour was possible for China's economic planners. The weight of the available evidence exonerates Mao from direct involvement in the collapse which followed the Great Leap. Hence, this disaster does not discredit his theories.

The host of Western authorities from so many branches of social science whose works support the soundness of Mao's economics in no sense implies he consciously imitated the West, although his references to James Watt and other inventors demonstrate some familiarity with Western history. Mao Tse-tung, in fact, may have taken much of his thinking from a somewhat peculiar source, from Japan, still the symbol of bestial cruelty for the ordinary Chinese who recall the barbarities of Japan's invasion of their country. Chinese communists in private conversation on this topic state emphatically any similarity between the Chinese and the Japanese growth models is a coincidence arising from the common needs of economic evolution in Asia. Nothing in Chinese publications since 1949 even hints at such an imitation.

But the 'coincidences' are too numerous to be ignored. Japan was shackled by a feudalistic farming pattern which made improved techniques impossible until the Meiji restoration. Thereafter, imported techniques were used to raise agricultural productivity but these failed. The country turned to the wisdom of 'veteran farmers'. Backward districts began to learn from advanced areas' methods. (Klein and Ohkawa, *Economic Growth*, 144, 151.) Mao too relied on the peasants' wisdom and preached the need for emulation. R.P. Dore has noted how the Japanese at the time of the Meiji restoration were ready to absorb foreign knowledge. He describes officials as being in personal contact with the villages. Rural communities were tightly-integrated co-operative units. He remarks: 'The village is like nothing more than a Chinese commune.' The Japanese farmer was production rather than profit-orientated. The innovations which allowed him to improve his harvests were simple and virtually costless. (*Agrarian Change and Economic Development*, 96, 103, 104, 106, 117.) Mao more than most recognised the value of all three factors: absorbing useful foreign learning; cadres in touch with the masses; and rural co-operation. Mao's distaste for the profit motive also finds a striking parallel in the initial stage of Japan's take-off.

Even the slow movement towards rural progress encountered by Mao was observed in Japan. E.S. Crawcour claims: 'Technical change was not as rapid and spontaneous as it is sometimes represented. This should not surprise us, since experienced observers maintain that it takes something like thirty years for even a fairly minor change to become fully accepted by Japanese farmers of today.' He also comments on the slow growth of new consumption patterns in Japan, a trend Mao would have endorsed fully as he was in no hurry to encourage increases in consumer spending. (*Agricultural Development in Asia*, 16, 23.) The impoverishment of the samurai, a warrior class with a highly-disciplined, ideological framework, was balanced by the emergence of leaders of exceptional quality in this group. They overthrew the old régime and were responsible for political, military and economic advances under the Meiji restoration. (Allen and Donnithorne, *Western Enterprise in Far Eastern Economic Development*, 187-88.) These unusual Japanese entrepreneurs bear a striking resemblance to the men who fought beside Mao Tse-tung and then became his instruments for the transformation of China.

Kamekichi Takahashi has pointed out that while willing to import foreign technology, the Japanese soon discovered modern science needed 'digestion'. In particular, the lack of capital and the small scale of manufacturing operations made direct borrowing unprofitable. He notes two other key features of Japan's economic development. Respect for clan, family and social status shifted to prestige earned through merit. The high level of patriotism among Japanese businessmen made them regard profits as secondary to the national interest. (*The Rise and Development of Japan's Modern Economy*, 36-38, 68, 137-44.) This picture is somewhat romantic, and traditional social patterns persist today. However, Mao Tse-tung warned of the dangers of

124

trying to use imported techniques without modifying them to suit local conditions. An end to family and clan influences and priority for the common good were also on Mao's list of goals. William W. Lockwood has discussed another aspect of Japanese development which was to form part of Mao's development strategy – 'complex systems of production and marketing within which numerous small establishments came to perform highly specialised functions and were yet linked together in a flexible and far-reaching pattern of social co-operation'. (*From Underdevelopment to Affluence*, 280.) The list of 'coincidences' could be extended. (R.P. Dore's *Land Reform in Japan*, for example, presents three documents in Appendix IV which sound exactly like communist party branch edicts in rural China.)

Is it possible that Mao Tse-tung had analysed the lessons of Japanese economic growth and exploited them to China's advantage? Alfred Zauberman has commented on the relevance of the Japanese model to China and seems to teeter on the verge of suggesting some borrowing has occurred. (*The Chinese Communes*, 63, 71.) Wu Yu-chang, a prominent communist intellectual who studied in Japan, specifically denied China followed the Japanese road to development. But his argument was based on the different degrees of capitalist development in the two countries and referred to the pre-Mao period. (*The Revolution of 1911*, 33.) The outstanding element common to the two nations' economic growth models is the similar attitude towards social change, both in organisations and attitudes. Mao's solitary flattering reference to Japanese institutions was elicited by his admiration for the fighting spirit of Japan's troops inculcated by indoctrination. (MW, 250.) Edgar Snow recorded Mao's youthful pleasure at Japan's victory over Tsarist Russia. (*Red China Today*, 641.) Mao would have been acting out of character if he had not given careful study to the history of a foe who almost crushed him. Furthermore, despite Mao's insistence that marxism came to China by way of Russia, the first socialist notions were absorbed by Chinese intellectuals from their Japanese counterparts, and much of the political vocabulary of China today was borrowed from the Japanese language within the last century. (Li Yu-ning, *The Introduction of Socialism into China.*)

The opportunities for learning from Japan existed both when Mao Tse-tung was still a student and after he came to power. Jerome Ch'en maintains that the teacher who exerted the greatest influence on Mao had studied for six years in Japan. (*Mao and the Chinese Revolution*, 48.) Stuart Schram names two other men who moulded Mao's thinking after they returned from Japan. (*Mao Tse-tung*, 34, 42.) Liang Chi-chao, an important political figure in Chinese politics in the declining days of the Manchus and the early years of the Republic, was a prominent personality in Mao's home province of Hunan. Joseph R. Levenson records Liang's advocacy of Japan as the model which China must follow to recover its strength. (*Liang Ch'i-ch'ao and the Mind of Modern China*, 50, 79-80, 141.) Mao has an uncomplimentary footnote on Liang's political record, but this does not prove Liang's considerable standing among Chinese intellectuals left Mao untouched during his student days. (SW IV, 424.) Chinese economic historians since 1949 have published very few explicit comparisons between China and Japan. Albert Feuerwerker has examined one study on the subject which emphasises the differences between the two countries' economies at the end of the last century. (*The China Quarterly*, April-June, 1965, 49-51.) This Chinese article seems sound enough in its analysis, a fact less important than the availability within China of materials for detailed investigation of Japan's growth.

Finally, one of Mao Tse-tung's oldest and closest comrades, who played a central part in the Chinese government from 1949, was a former university student in Japan. This man, Prime Minister Chou En-lai, had a hand in every sphere of national politics, including economic policy. Is it conceivable that Chou learnt nothing about Japan's development techniques as an undergraduate, or failed to discuss his Japanese experiences with Mao over the years? Perhaps the cultural borrowings Japan had made from China in the centuries before embarking on industrialisation made it inevitable that China should follow a similar path to that travelled by Japan in modernising the nation under Mao Tse-tung. This type of historical 'accident' cannot be excluded. However, as a socialist state, Mao's China is supposed to have developed according to a set pattern and not to have been blown along at random by independent social and economic forces. Mao dropped the Soviet model between 1955 and 1957. To have synthesised an economic programme from his direct experience of China and his knowledge of Japanese history would have been a perfectly rational solution to the problem of working out his own strategy for Chinese growth.

Chapter Six
'Ghosts and Monsters'

The failure of the Great Leap Forward and the three disastrous harvests which followed brought the Chinese economy to a temporary halt. If the post-1966 accounts are to be trusted, the decision of the central government to suspend local industrial projects started in the 1958 burst of enthusiasm added to the waste caused by the primitive technology the peasants had adopted. Although the emergency was acute, its impact on China's long-term development can be exaggerated. Waste and failure are an inevitable part of the effort to turn peasants into industrial producers. As M. Friedman remarks: 'There is hardly an underdeveloped country that does not waste its substance on the symbol of a government-owned or government-subsidised international airline. And there is hardly one that does not want its own steel mill as yet another potent symbol.' (*Foreign Aid,* 68.) Dick Wilson cites several examples of mismanagement and fraud which devour Asia's precious investment funds. The two-year delay in commissioning the rolling plant at the Rourkela steel mills cost the Indian government some US$145 million according to West German estimates. Marshal Sarit, Thailand's 'relatively popular and efficient dictator', embezzled over $30 million in state funds between 1958 and 1963. President Sukarno of Indonesia was in the habit of writing out chits for millions of dollars to young actresses which the head of the Indonesian central bank admitted were honoured from the national exchequer. (*Asia Awakes,* 114, 343.) At least Peking could put its losses down to hunger for progress in 1958 compounded by crop failures rather than to the sloth, inefficiency and corruption typical of most underdeveloped countries. A sign of the ultimate realism of the government of the People's Republic was its willingness to swallow ideological pride. In the crisis to keep the economy alive, drastic measures were adopted, even when they ran counter to the tenets of Mao Tse-tung.

The years from 1958 to 1966 are a murky period with obscure and conflicting currents at work. The policies between the Great Leap Forward and the 1966 Cultural Revolution do not fall into neat patterns, with a hard-headed group opposed to Mao and espousing pragmatism ranged against zealots determined to resist any tinkering with Maoist purity. Confusion stems from the way the government as a whole — including those later denounced by the Red Guards as guilty of betraying Mao Tse-tung — seemed to have been in general agreement on a return to more radical plans once the immediate catastrophe of the Great Leap and its aftermath were overcome. Yet a number of groups grabbed the chance to impeach indirectly the validity of Mao's economic philosophy and to run the nation on a command basis through the communist party instead of through mass participation. Other elements simply coped with the day-to-day shortages which hampered output and met the dictates of Peking as best they could, only to find themselves branded as ideological heretics after 1966. And behind the scenes, certainly from 1962 and possibly even earlier, Mao Tse-tung was laying the ground for a political comeback. Thus Peking's accounts of misdeeds, heresies and inefficiency in various sectors of national life reveal a mixture of jumbled economic ideas, garbled Maoist and marxist politics and conflicting opinions on what was the correct road for China to follow. Reports on official policy and its implementation showed the country being tugged in several directions at the same time. At the risk of compounding the confusion about basic trends in this period, the situation in key sectors of the economy is described here as Peking itself painted the picture. The lack of clarity in so many intelligent people's minds was an important feature of the period in which Mao planned his return to unrivalled authority in national politics and helped to create the conditions for the chaotic Cultural Revolution in 1966.

The process of reversing the policies of the 1958 massive spurt forward which had paid scant regard to its cost in human energy and local resources was relatively slow. The rebuilding of the centre's economic control apparatus was tackled more urgently. The cautious nature of the shift away from the Great Leap Forward was illustrated vividly by a 1960 speech of Vice-Premier Tan Chen-lin (ousted during the Cultural Revolution). He gave an account of agricultural progress under the national development programme, paying handsome tributes to Mao Tse-tung's inspiration, the strength of the communes and rural industries' role in support of farming. For all his genuflections to such Maoist edicts as mobilisation of cadres to work in the fields and peasant control of their own research programmes, Tan's keynote was a plea for unified planning of the economy instead of local autonomy and the use of surplus funds in the countryside for capital construction rather than improved living standards. (NCNA, 6 April, 1960.)

Peking showed itself particularly anxious to restore respect for central policies and national planning. One writer explained that priority must be given to the faithful implementation of 'all guidelines and policies of the party and state and all unified national plans'. While he argued that the central authorities allowed sufficient leeway in their decrees for plans to be adjusted to meet local conditions, he ended by emphasising the need to put national interests foremost and to strengthen discipline. (*Worker's Daily*, 11 February, 1962.) Another article in the same vein allowed some freedom to industrial enterprises in managing their financial affairs. Yet the author underlined the 'chessboard' concept, with pawns moving in obedience to gambits worked out by the grand masters at the top. During the economic crisis, he stated, 'it is especially necessary to stress a high level of centralisation and unity'. Enterprises were ordered not to deviate from production directives. He denounced factories which disobeyed state planning targets and manufactured goods solely on the basis of their profitability. This situation apparently arose because, as the writer explained, the enterprise could use certain funds under its control to improve its staff's welfare. The factories thus had a strong incentive to chase profits. At the same time, industrial units which turned out the maximum volume of goods regardless of quality or cost were condemned. Waste through hoarding of supplies, misappropriation of surplus stocks and poor labour management was castigated. (*Southern Daily*, 7 April, 1962.)

An economist took up the same cry for more control of the most decentralised sectors of economic life, agriculture and light industry. He stuck to a Maoist line on the importance of light industry and saw agriculture as the basis for general progress because of the funds for investment the state could gather if light industry expanded through more prosperous farming. The author was concerned to encourage a greater flow of food to the cities by offering the villages more industrial goods. This point was of obvious importance when after three harvest disasters, the peasants' main concern would have been the amount of food available for their own families and not the demands of the urban areas. This commentator argued vigorously that efficiency in light industrial production depended on 'planned economic co-operation' between factories and farmers. He suggested higher prices for crops used by industry and called for greater attention to finding synthetic substitutes for raw materials to avoid fluctuations in supply due to the weather.

Waste of every kind had to be overcome, with the author listing the potential for re-using even the materials in which goods were packed. (ER, 6/1962.) Stricter observance of output targets was an obvious priority when Peking had to allocate both consumer and industrial supplies whose output had slumped badly. Any reasonable system of rationing meant tight regulation from the centre. These calls for Peking to take charge led eventually to articles which contradicted virtually outright Mao Tse-tung's economic strategy. Thus two economists writing on transport problems in 1965 stated almost bluntly that self-sufficiency at the grass roots was nonsense and decentralisation of economic activities so much verbiage. (*ibid.*, 2/1965.)

In January 1961, the party central committee laid down the goals which tighter central direction should achieve. Agriculture was described as 'the foundation of the national economy'. The communes were to be strengthened and every effort made to produce a successful harvest and protect the peasants against the effects of the natural calamities which had paralysed the nation. Light industry was urged to struggle against the lack of supplies and to ensure that the population was not deprived of basic necessities. To save face a little, the central committee reduced capital investment on the grounds that heavy industry had done so well. The new policy was summed up as 'consolidating, filling out and raising standards'. Quality, skilful husbanding of resources, lower costs of production, technological progress and improved labour productivity were the committee's watchwords. Output of consumer goods and industrial raw materials was to be raised by promoting the use of peasants' free time to work for their own reward; rural fairs were given the party's blessing. The central committee revealed a rectification campaign was under way to weed out the ten per cent of the lower-level cadres in the pay of landlord and bourgeois elements or who had 'degenerated due to influence and corrosion' by the 'reactionary' class. The central committee stated, in effect, the party was not responsible for the hardships suffered by the masses. The blame was put on cadres who 'infringe laws and violate discipline in the villages and cities to the detriment of the interests of the people'. (NCNA, 20 January, 1961.)

In the following year, Premier Chou En-lai expounded more

details of the party's policy. Agricultural production had to be boosted. Light and heavy industry should be regulated on a rational basis with the maximum possible output of basic consumer goods. Capital investment was to be kept down, and development resources employed only on essential projects. Workers and cadres who had fled to the cities should be sent back to the countryside. Each enterprise's stocks and funds should be carefully scrutinised. Domestic and foreign trade were to be improved. The standards of various cultural and health services were to be raised. Expenditure was to be slashed and revenue expanded. He ended with an explanation of the special importance of planning 'to ensure an all-round balance between the branches of the economy'. (NCNA, 16 April, 1962.) In September 1962, the prime minister's statement was endorsed by the central committee.

At this point, Mao Tse-tung's bid to reimpose his authority began to emerge. The communiqué issued after the central committee meeting spoke of steady improvements in the economy which seemingly emboldened Mao to fire his first salvo. The committee attacked officials at a somewhat higher level than in 1961 for the nation's misfortunes: 'Because of the incompetence of the leading cadres, some production teams, some factories and some business establishments have produced less or become unwelcome to the masses.' The communiqué included a passage later officially ascribed to Mao although in a rewritten form. It warned of constant plots by 'the reactionary ruling classes' to stage a comeback. Even more significant was the next sentence: 'There still exist in society bourgeois influences, the force of habits of the old society and the spontaneous tendency towards capitalism among part of the small producers.' The party was ordered to be vigilant against the stratagems of the class enemy. All this amounted to a broad hint that the Chairman was uneasy about the long-term implications of the post-Leap policies. (NCNA, 28 September, 1962; ID, 20-21.)

The risks to communist purity had been recognised by many from the first steps taken to use every weapon to defeat the threat to China's economic future from 1959 to 1962. At that time, Peking had no alternative but to resist all unnecessary or unprofitable demands from the lower levels on the nation's straitened resources. The government also had to use every device to drain the last ounce of energy out of the peasants and workers. The authorities were forced to attempt to control assets which technically were at the free disposal of factories and communes as they represented these enterprises' savings. The principle was enunciated that even if a project were necessary and could be financed by local funds, work must not begin until the official planners had granted permission. The central committee had issued a directive forbidding any project to be started unless formally included in the unified national plan and had ordered work to cease on all capital construction begun on local initiative outside the plan. But money was still devoted to 'unofficial' projects and spent on such non-productive undertakings as skating rinks. (*Southern Daily,* 15 May, 1962.)

The policy of cutting down on every item of expenditure not absolutely vital to China's economic survival seems to have caused highly unpopular losses to the local undertakings so strongly urged in 1958 to move forward under their own steam. Thus Liaoning province has claimed construction of small coal pits advocated during the Great Leap Forward was brought to a halt in the austerity campaign at the beginning of the 1960s when they were half finished. The veto on bringing these collieries into production meant writing off the capital already spent on them. The loss was borne apparently by the local levels which thus had good cause for complaint at the reversal of the Great Leap Forward. (NCNA, 9 June, 1970.) Similarly, the equipment acquired for backyard furnaces was widely dismissed as unprofitable but the furnaces were erected with the labour and funds of the communes. Some of this crude plant was capable of turning out iron and steel quite efficiently, according to Honan province, which in 1970 said sixty per cent of the equipment in one district's blast furnaces dated back to 1958 and had been renovated. (RS, 11 July, 1970.) The ordinary population must have felt considerable frustration at being ordered to abandon industrial operations they had paid for, even though the paramount need to concentrate all available forces on agriculture was surely clear enough after the harvest failures.

The government found it impossible to avoid using material incentives to boost production in both industry and agriculture during the economic crisis. The *People's Daily,* for instance, stated that only by linking pay packets to worker's output 'could greater activism be stimulated among the masses encouraging them to create more wealth for the community'. (5 July, 1961.) The paper later commented: 'The more precisely a man's output is reflected in his wages, the more material interest will persuade him to take greater interest in what he produces, and in his own productivity and efficiency.' The article reflected the confused thinking typical of the period. After a sophisticated discussion of the way wage and bonus systems should be operated, the writer ended by returning to the basic Maoist position that ideology should dominate all economic activities. The article insisted on 'putting political education in the first position' with material incentives second. (PD, 28 October, 1961.) Another commentator on this subject confessed frankly the reason for wage differentials and relating payment to output was 'traces of the capitalist outlook still lingering in the minds of the people' and the demands of general industrial efficiency. While quoting Mao Tse-tung to refute the argument that all wage rates should be identical, the author demanded proper allowance for the effect of political motivation on the worker's willingness to increase efficiency. (*Chung-kuo Ching-nien Pao,* 8 November, 1961.)

Communist writers in this period faced a conflict between Mao Tse-tung's view of the masses as invincible when armed with marxism-leninism and the positive response of the labour force to greater rewards. This dilemma showed up in another typical article which declared workers were still poisoned by the former capitalist society and were unwilling to labour purely in the interests of society. Thus incentive bonuses were indispensable. However, the author felt moved to warn that material incentives did nothing to beget a proper communist view of work, and hence bonuses and wage incentives were not the ultimate solution to China's production problems. Political remoulding was the only permanent answer. (TKP, 14 May, 1962.) One economist maintained that while wages had to be linked to output, the advance towards full communism, with income based on need rather than work, would be retarded if too much stress were laid on material incentives. (ER, 4/1962.)

In the countryside, the problem of encouraging increased output through greater material rewards was more complex. Firstly, the rural industries established by the communes played an important role as subsidiaries to large-scale factories. Secondly, they contributed directly to agricultural efficiency through their output of implements and the repairs they undertook of farm machinery. Thirdly, much of their output consisted of light industrial goods needed to maintain and improve rural living standards. But in 1961, the serious difficulties caused by the over-rapid development of commune factories had to be resolved. 'Consolidation' rather than expansion became the slogan, and particular importance was attached to allocation of resources to plants capable of making the best use of scarce raw materials. This policy implied a drop in the quantity left in commune hands for their own industries. The essential need was to ensure no less than eighty per cent of available manpower in the countryside was employed directly in the fields. Siphoning off workers for industrial activities could not be allowed to endanger food production when yields had slumped because of adverse weather. (RF, 8/1961.) The conflict between the useful work carried on by commune factories and the dependence of the harvest on a combination of good weather and human energy was illustrated in a review of farm productivity. Its author saw the eventual answer to low productivity and the slow increase of farm yields in the adoption of machines and modern cultivation techniques – which rural industry would make possible. Technical reform would take time, so manual labour still governed harvest levels. Furthermore, immediate improvements in farming methods such as better ploughing and planting practices, for example, demanded greater inputs of labour. (PD, 15 December, 1960.)

The bait held out to the peasantry for better performance was the 'three guarantees and one reward', a system denounced from mid-1966 as a symbol of treason to Mao Tse-tung. The 'three guarantees' were a pledge by the villagers to meet production targets, to provide all the labour required under the local farm plan and to keep within the limits set for production costs by the plan. For overfulfilling quotas, the peasants got their 'one reward'. In an authoritative explanation of this technique for stimulating peasant enthusiasm, two commentators traced its origins to the early agricultural co-operatives when time was wasted in allocating daily work to members. By handing out specific responsibility for different jobs to individuals and groups, farm organisation was rationalised and the peasants could anticipate how much they would earn. The authors analysed the various problems which arose under the system, particularly the demands it made on management skills and the necessity for the 'guarantees' to be acceptable to the peasants. The masses, they stated, should be in control of establishing and implementing the 'guarantees' through full consultations.

The difference between the rural and the urban scenes was apparent from the peculiar role ascribed to political education in making a success of the 'three guarantees and one reward'. In the factories, economists could see greater ideological awareness leading industrial workers to the stage where they would work for the state and not for personal gain. This aim was mentioned as a rural objective, but more essential was to demonstrate the connection between beating output targets and extra personal income. (RF, 15-16/1961.)

While this approach was to prove blasphemous in the eyes of the Maoists during the Cultural Revolution, its justification emerges from the campaign to get industrial workers to grow as much of their own food as possible from any waste plots of land. (*Worker's Daily*, 11 January, 1962.) In addition, agriculture during this period was responsible directly and indirectly for half the state's revenue. Poor harvests meant not only hunger, shortages of raw material and a drop in industrial production but also a threat to national investment plans. (*Shih-shih Shou-tse*, 9/1962.)

Just as Mao Tse-tung's desire to exploit all potential talent in the earliest period of the People's Republic had allowed the resurrection of the middle classes and their influence, so the policies adopted to overcome the desperate shortage following the Great Leap opened the door once more to tendencies which were, in Mao's view, totally hostile to his ambitions for the new China. Those responsible for the emergency programmes were fully aware of the political risks they ran but felt they had no alternative. One writer made a valiant attempt to resolve the contradiction between Maoist orthodoxy and economic reality by arguing China must remain a 'pre-communist' society as long as material shortages prevailed and while differences continued between agricultural and industrial conditions, between mental and manual labour and between town and country. The party's current task was to promote education in communist principles rather than seek their immediate application. Thus the spirit of putting the common good before personal interests should be encouraged against the day when an abundance of supplies made possible a completely communist society with income determined solely in accordance with needs. (PD, 30 March, 1961.)

But the damage was done. In 1958, the central committee had foreseen a fairly short interval between the establishment of communes, still owned by their members, and their nationalisation 'by the whole people'. This prediction was an encouragement to the idealists who looked for a speedy birth of a communist Utopia unsullied by any remnants of private ownership. Many believed, apparently, that the foundation of the communes meant the final step towards this vision was just around the corner. By the end of 1958, the central committee was showing itself far less optimistic about the possibility of abolishing incentives for peasants in the form of higher incomes and was quite reserved on prospects for nationalising the communes. (CC, 462, 479, 492-95.) At the beginning of 1959, one analyst explained the very stringent conditions to be met before communes became the country-side's equivalent of state industry – rural enterprises fully owned and controlled by the central government. Commune output would have to increase so that it met not only members' needs but provided a sizeable proportion of national production. The surplus set aside for investment by the communes would have to grow so large that commune capital had a significant impact on China's overall development. The com-munes would have to be free from dependence on the weather, for once nationalised, the state would be responsible for their losses during natural calamities. The various communes would have to achieve roughly equal standards of income, otherwise state ownership, and the unified pay scales it implied, would remove any incentive for the poorer communes to improve their performance. If they were nationalised before commune incomes rose substantially, the state would be under a moral obligation to provide the peasants with 'a bountiful life and a constantly rising income'. A hint was given that premature nationalis-ation would reduce the funds available from the countryside for investment because the peasants' relatively low consumption standards would have to be raised through cuts in savings. In addition, the villagers would have to learn to put public before private gain. (*Tsai-ching Yen-chiu*, 1/1959.)

The weight of the article was on the economic barriers to the eradication of the last forms of private (in fact, communal) property in the countryside and hence the conquest of the final obstacle to a fully state-owned economy in China. Commentaries couched in such terms must have dampened enthusiasm for marxism-leninism as expounded by Mao Tse-tung. As in the early 1950s, so in the first years of the 1960s, Maoism seemed open to compromise and adulteration when conditions demanded. Ideological rectitude could be sacrificed to expediency.

No evidence exists to prove Mao himself objected to such pragmatism after the Great Leap's demise. But by 1962, as the passage quoted from the central committee of that year indicates so strongly, Mao had woken up to the betrayal of his principles for pure economic advantage by significant elements within the party. Franz Schurmann brilliantly perceived well before the revelations of the Cultural Revolution the significance of the post-Great Leap policies which removed the masses from management in the name of rationality and put profits before production. Schurmann commented: 'Concern over money somehow seems to be a conservative attitude in almost any society.' He suggested – correctly, as the Cultural Revolution showed – a debate was in progress among the leadership between two schools of thought. In their extreme forms, Schurmann felt, one faction would have followed the Yugoslav economic model; while the other would have returned to a centralised bureaucratic system. (*China Under Mao*, 232, 236-37.) In fact, Yugoslavia's example (or Soviet 'revisionism') was being used as a basis by one group, in Mao's opinion. This tendency he was determined to resist. He was also bent on trying out his own development strategy which was neither bureaucratic nor centralised but, rather, based on appeals to man's idealism instead of to his baser instincts.

The political atmosphere which sprang up after the retreat from the Great Leap was a threat to all Mao Tse-tung cherished as vital to the creation of a new society. The prevailing mood can be captured from revelations about the lack of political idealism among key groups published in lengthy series of newspaper and magazine articles in the period preceding the 1966 Cultural Revolution. Perhaps the biggest blow to Mao's dreams came from the young educated class reared by the new China. Many intellectuals believed in the motto 'politically passable, professionally proficient and living well'. The notion of self-sacrifice for the nation no longer gripped them. They argued that during the war and the communist revolution, political goals had to come first. But China's need was now economic development. The intellectuals' attitude was, 'politics is empty, professional work solid'; only technical accomplishments could make a genuine contribution to the construction of a socialist state. Since income was based on work, the more skilled the individual, the higher his standard of living and social status. One young technician confessed he had been seduced by remembering the affluence of the old Shanghai middle class. While anxious to serve socialism, unless a project were 'grand and magnificent' offering him the chance to create an 'outstanding masterpiece', he gave perfunctory attention to his jobs.

An engineering student argued for a division of labour. Technologists could not be expected to specialise in their own fields and 'have a good knowledge of marxism-leninism as well'. Since 'man's time and energy are limited', intensive political study would reduce the effectiveness of professional training courses and harm China's progress, he claimed. Another technician, a member of the Young Communist League, looked upon his professional expertise as 'an iron rice bowl' which guaranteed a comfortable career. He disliked maintenance and repair work and preferred assignments which challenged his creative abilities. A musician described how before 'seeing the light' ideologically, he had believed: 'Political proficiency cannot contribute to solving the technical problems of singing, playing the violin or blowing the horn. The audience comes to listen to a performance not to judge political proficiency.' A university lecturer felt forced to attack the view that as long as technical cadres were not opposed to the party or socialism, they should be left alone. A teacher in an agricultural middle school admitted her disappointment at being sent to teach in the countryside after failing to enter a university. A doctor stated some of his colleagues wanted to work on obscure diseases and undertake scientific research instead of concentrating on the common ailments which afflicted the masses. (*Chung-kuo Ching-nien Pao,* 24 December, 1964, 7, 16, 23 January, 1965.)

Young men and women who viewed their future in these terms were hardly the standard-bearers to whom Mao could pass on his revolutionary torch. Even allowing for a certain colour added to give punch to the propaganda, the amount of space devoted to the political diseases infecting the cream of China's youth was testimony to a serious situation. (This deduction is based on the theory that Peking's propaganda machine acts rationally and its limited resources are not wasted on matters of no account.)

In the technical field, the position was particularly menacing. Not only were ideological heresies rampant but development resources were being frittered away on useless undertakings. Ironically, one technician complained in 1962 that despite his colleagues' efforts to remould their thinking, they were always portrayed in novels, films and plays as politically backward, remote from the masses and inhabitants of ivory towers. (*Worker's Daily,* 5 August, 1962.) Such parodies of the typical technician seem well justified from confessions made by scientific personnel in later years. One draughtsman described the process of designing a waterworks to employ a staff of twenty-six. A simple project was requested. Instead the designers decided 'to erect a monument to ourselves. We made it as grand and magnificent as possible'. A two-storey office block complete with six bathrooms was recommended. Avoidable waste of official funds spent on this scheme was Yuan 200,000. (*Chung-kuo Ching-nien Pao,* 16 January, 1965.)

One group of construction workers found the procedures for assembling equipment laid down by official blueprints completely impractical. They felt mistakes in plans for construction projects arose from the unwillingness of engineers to leave their offices and investigate conditions on the site. A rubber worker complained that machines were designed without any regard for the need to service them. Even screws were badly machined and almost impossible to remove. Overhaul of various parts of a machine often meant dismantling most of the equipment. Another worker related how the labourers on one project unsuccessfully urged the architects to reduce ornamental decorations to cut costs. However, false economies were sometimes made. A coking plant denounced engineers for using cast-iron where steel was essential. This sort of practice reduced the machine's price but added considerably to maintenance expenses. Pure stupidity was much in evidence. One factory's power department needed coal trolleys. These were built on so cumbersome a scale that the workers preferred to carry coal on their shoulders rather than break their backs wrestling with the monster wagons. Architects constructed army barracks facing directly into the winter wind. In the manufacture of screws, standards were lowered after investigation proved that – untypically – an unnecessarily high quality had been specified and maintained, raising productivity some two hundred per cent. (PD, 15 December, 1964.)

An economist showed how baffled individuals could become when ideology and reality clashed. He narrated how up to 1957, the trend was to imitate both foreign and traditional models. During the Great Leap Forward, the masses were encouraged to play an active part in technical design. This change was healthy but brought in its train the defects of 'insufficient respect for truth and an inadequately scientific attitude'. (Such practices Mao would have expected competent officials to eradicate by effective education of the masses.) The writer listed technical draughtsmen's current faults as 'seeking the large-scale and perfection, the unnecessary pursuit of high standards and attractive designs, sticking to old-fashioned techniques, over-confidence in textbooks, worship of foreign designs and adoration of traditional models'. The solution lay in modifying the design of equipment and plants to meet Chinese conditions, the economist concluded. Here he found he had to ignore his opening remarks. Technicians could discover what was required only by mixing with the workers and sharing their practical experience of the nation's needs. (ER, 9/1965.) The contradiction, nevertheless, was a surface one, for integrating cadres and masses had never meant officials should abandon their leadership role.

The efficiency and realism of those who guided the construction of new industrial facilities directly affected the rate of return from every yuan of investment. But another sector, trade and finance, was of equal importance if Mao Tse-tung's development strategy was to have any chance of being implemented. In this area of the economy, his ideas were pushed out of their commanding position in the drive to recover from the post-1958 economic depression. The commercial and financial departments were the link between towns and villages, between industry and agriculture and between individual provinces. The loyalty of workers in this sector to Maoism had considerable potential impact on the degree to which the economy as a whole responded to Mao's guidelines. One retail company in Shantung province recorded the common opinion among commercial staff that if business flourished, they must be on the right political track. They argued state plans embodied political goals. By implementing these plans, they would achieve Peking's political aims simultaneously. A Shanghai bank official complained of colleagues whose ideological 'slackness' was illustrated by their propensity to chat when customers were few. 'As a result wrong entries were made' — ordinary incompetence was equated with political ignorance. But ideology was shrugged off quite frequently. An accountant noted the attitude that a balance sheet was drawn up correctly through a grasp of book-keeping rather than political principles.

The harm done by not putting 'politics in command' was outlined in simple terms by the spokesmen of a Honan province wholesale unit. They explained how they had forgotten that 'man is the decisive factor'. In consequence, the unit had assumed that so long as supplies could be obtained, sales would take care of themselves — a reflection presumably of market shortages in the early 1960s. It had also worked on the principle that good-quality goods would be snapped up by the public. 'Making purchases blindly' without examining demand resulted in overstocking and losses to the state. Human error added to their problems when a clerk inadvertently added a zero to a cable ordering ten thousand pairs of shoes. The manager of a store in Liaoning province found sales were running well below target. His remedy, which he insisted was ideologically correct, was to stock up with high-quality merchandise. The manager stated goods of this sort allowed him to over-fulfil his plan even if his shop's service to its customers was indifferent. A similar point was made by another representative of the same province. He claimed no matter what the salesmen's efforts, unpopular goods were a drag on the market. Another shop decided to cut down the range of goods it sold to avoid a surplus at stock-taking time for which it might be criticised. As a result, its business dwindled away.

A communication and electrical supplies company in one central province related how it surpassed its targets by refusing to supply small customers (a policy very much at odds with Mao's doctrines). It concentrated on the needs of large purchasers, pushing lines which sold fastest and brought in the largest profits. One food store thought political work could be neglected in the busy season but confessed this led to a breakdown in managerial efficiency, ineffective storing of vegetables and large losses through spoilage.

Szechwan province's school for finance and trade cadres told of arguments among its students to the effect that a barber satisfied his customers with a good haircut not political orthodoxy and that with the best will in the world and an ideological campaign to boot, a defective elevator could not be brought into operation without a qualified electrician. An accountant gave his concept of putting politics first which amounted to ensuring marketing targets had been met through cash not credit sales and that profit quotas were reached in accordance with the state's guidelines. Not everyone took such a profit-and-loss view of ideology. A study group in one bank branch saw the slogan 'politics in command' as implying the encouragement of savings by the public not for their own benefit but for 'the glorious tradition of hard struggle in support of socialist construction'. This statement was one of the few indicating a true grasp of Mao's principles. One Peking worker set his priorities in terms which left little doubt about the drift of this sector of the economy away from Mao's philosophy: 'It is necessary to see how business targets are met, regardless of whether Mao Tse-tung's thought has been put in command, the party's directives and policies have been implemented or whether we have carried on ideological work among the masses and raised their class consciousness.' (TKP, 25, 30 May, 3, 8, 11, 15, 18, 25, 29 June, 2, 6, 10, 13, 16, 20 July, 1965.)

Another difficulty was the low social status attached to commercial work — a throwback to the traditional contempt in which the merchant class was held. (Anxiety about position and rank betrayed a very non-communist outlook.) Employees in the commercial sector were said to be infected by 'bourgeois notions of luxury and wastefulness' — presumably a denunciation of pandering to public demands for attractive articles instead of popularising cheap 'proletarian wares. (PD, 20 February, 1964.) One odd feature of the long debate on the role of politics in the nation's business life conducted in the columns of the *Ta-kung Pao* in mid-1965 was the editor's failure to close the discussion on a firm Maoist note. The paper, in fact, seemed eager to provoke the maximum freedom of opinion on the relationship between politics and economics, a matter which should have been beyond dispute to any sound marxist-leninist. (TKP, 24 July, 1965.) The flood of articles from trade and finance staff was more writing on the wall for Mao Tse-tung.

The cadres were also a thorn in Peking's side. A 'socialist education campaign' — the 'four clean-ups' — was launched personally by Mao Tse-tung in 1962 to improve the quality of low-level rural leadership. In the four years which followed, the movement was controlled by Liu Shao-chi, and it attacked with increasing venom nepotism, corruption, embezzlement and general malpractices by rural officials. Despite the valuable researches by Richard Baum and Frederick C. Teiwes, the full ramifications of this campaign remain obscure, and it is even possible to regard the affair as a trap into which Liu Shao-chi and his allies among the top party leadership were drawn deliberately. (*Ssu-Ch'ing: The Socialist Education Movement of 1962-1966.*) Is it inconceivable that Liu and his associates were persuaded to intensify a rectification movement which smashed the morale of the rural party and undermined their own popularity in the countryside until Mao produced a more lenient policy in 1965 and reaped the consequent political advantages of mollifying rural officials on the eve of the Cultural Revolution?

Whatever the truth about the socialist education campaign, Peking published several accounts showing the bureaucracy at the grass roots completely at odds with the standards set by Mao Tse-tung for cadres. 'Communes, it is claimed, are basic-level organisations directly in contact with the masses.' However, cadres were badgered by constant demands from their superiors for statistics, meetings and telephone conferences. One commune reported seven administrative units requested reports in a single day, four of them on the same subject — a local drought. The amount of paperwork and formalities meant the average cadre had no time to go out and work with the peasants on the crops. A deputy party secretary in a Shantung commune explained he had worried unnecessarily about organising routine agricultural work before the socialist education movement although the peasants were perfectly competent to decide their own cultivation routine. But he complained two problems remained unsettled. When people were criticised for mistakes, they never dared take responsibility again. Alternatively, if praised, they came back repeatedly for the official's advice. The masses had reached the point of feeling unable to act independently of the local party. So much for Mao's plan to put the masses in direct contact with their leaders. And where was the decentralisation he had urged?

A Shensi province rural political department elucidated its failure to make progress in agriculture. No long-term plans had been drawn up concerning overall development of the district's economy. The cadres relied on orders passed down from their superiors. Officials tended to concentrate on production, neglecting the political work which would have inspired the masses to a bigger effort to conquer natural obstacles to progress. Land reclamation, irrigation projects and exploitation of better seeds and new crops never seemed to make headway despite a steady flow of ideas on what improvements were necessary. A party secretary in Heilungkiang province recounted how the cadres' advice was not welcomed by the peasants who felt more competent than their county officials. The animosity was mutual. The county party secretary was overworked and his committee unwilling to delegate responsibility. In consequence, apparently, the views of the masses were ignored, contrary to Mao's instructions.

A report from Shansi province suggests the memory of retribution for the failure of the Great Leap had burnt into the souls of county and commune cadres. They stated: 'There was trouble some years ago because . . . we aimed too high . . . we must make no more errors.' The principle of self-reliance so popular in 1958 was undermined. One commune admitted to borrowing from the state to buy farm equipment and to relying on state relief when the harvest was insufficient. The peasants described this unit as 'nationalised'. Other places were content to record a little advance every year instead of exerting all their efforts to boosting output to the maximum. Shensi province reported one county committee split into two groups. The first mingled with the masses. The other blamed the peasants whenever things went wrong and derided their comrades who mixed with the peasants on equal terms. Another area confessed it had neglected to discuss the national five-year plan with the masses to show them how much they still had to accomplish to meet the targets set by the central government. The practice of adhering to traditional farming practices instead of adapting cultivation patterns to the needs of modern agriculture was another complaint. In Kansu province, a county party committee apparently closed its ranks successfully to resist criticism, although Mao had repeatedly explained why public discussion of cadres' performance was essential.

At the root of the cadres' defects was the feeling: 'Since the principal purpose of building socialism is to develop production, there ought not to be any class struggle.' In other words, officials wanted to abandon the problems of inquiring into the state of people's political souls as long as their bodies were willing beasts of burden carrying China towards the promised land. (PD, 12, 13, 18, 22, 25, 29 October, 5, 8, 11, 12 November, 1965.) Oddly enough, despite these horrid tales of sinister heresies flourishing the length and breadth of the country, Mao Tse-tung, on Baum and Teiwes' reading of the socialist education campaign, was disinclined to excommunicate the cadres at the bottom. This attitude comes through in another campaign, very close to Mao's heart, which led up to the Cultural Revolution: the drive to learn from the People's Liberation Army. (LL, 48.) One side of this movement was to foster good relations between the troops and the ordinary civilians. The soldiers were ordered 'to study the local cadres' fine style of waging arduous struggle' without any obvious embarrassment by Peking at the contrast between this tribute and the long lists of officials' misdeeds it regularly published. (PD, 3 February, 1964.) The Cultural Revolution was to demonstrate Mao's anger was reserved for the top men in the party and government, not their low-level minions.

Another facet of Chinese life which reveals a considerable gap between Mao Tse-tung's expectations and actual respect for his philosophy was academic economics. Professional economists enjoyed great freedom of expression during the first half of the 1960s. They could have used this opportunity either to research in depth the implications of Mao's development strategy or to build their own growth models. The majority took neither course. The bulk of economists' articles during this period were usually sterile debates, devoid of any direct relevance to the country's industrial and agricultural struggles. When their discussions touched on specific issues, economists often proved highly confused about the meaning of official policies. Behind the scenes, another debate was in progress, in which Liu Shao-chi was personally involved, according to allegations made during the Cultural Revolution, backed up theoretically by Sun Yeh-fang, director of the economic research institute, Chinese Academy of Sciences. This 'underground' school of economics was to become the symbol of all the elements in national economic policy most repugnant to the true Maoist.

The flood of articles by economists during their years of unrestricted comment precludes more than a brief sketch of their deliberations. Academic confusion on the proper nature of economics under Mao Tse-tung was revealed at a forum on agriculture held jointly by five provinces in 1961. With the food crisis threatening the nation at the time, the participants naturally urged the utmost rationality in managing farm workers. However, they did not share Mao's belief that the country possessed no labour surplus, and they expressed peculiar notions on the function of the worker in a socialist state. The economists present seem to have been weak on the crucial marxist and Maoist concepts of the difference between a peasant's productive capacity as an individual worker and his performance in the context of such 'reformed' economic organisations as the communes. (KMD, 25 December, 1961.)

An odd debate took place in 1963 in Nanking. The city's economics association gave the impression that no improvements were likely in the organisation of agricultural production through the communes because of the peasants' desire for some property rights even if confined to collective ownership of commune assets. Nationalisation of the communes – the last obstacle to a socialist economy – was viewed as a distant, hazy prospect. Much time was devoted for some reason to defining 'agriculture'. Some argued in favour of restricting 'agriculture' to the cultivation of crops. Some wanted the term to include animal husbandry. Others felt all industries exploiting natural resources came into the agricultural category, possibly even coal-mining. The economists' ranks contained several who patently had not grasped why Mao Tse-tung saw agriculture as the foundation of the national economy. (Indeed the lack of explicit references in so many economic articles to Mao's works is astonishing.) One economist discussing industry insisted little could be expected from improving production techniques; factory output would expand more or less in direct ratio to the capital invested in plant and equipment. This view would not have been endorsed by Mao Tse-tung who demanded constant technical innovations from the workers to modify existing machinery and raise its efficiency. (ER, 7/1962.)

A round-up of economic studies in the following year showed a higher level of awareness of China's basic agricultural needs, but no well-defined set of priorities for a farming revolution. Mechanisation was held to have a double importance. Machines directly raised the peasants' productivity and created surplus labour for other occupations.

Some economists went further, maintaining that without mechanisation, improved irrigation and the use of more fertilisers would be impossible. This opinion Mao would not have accepted without qualification for he saw man as capable of anything a machine could accomplish given the right political climate. But mechanisation, as noted already, was one of his goals.

The importance to be attached to machinery was disputed. Irrigation was considered the basic need by some economists because modern farming — high-yield seeds plus chemical fertilisers — required vast quantities of water. In addition, irrigation schemes would be easier to achieve than extra inputs of machines and fertilisers which depended on costly industrial expansion rather than on the cheaper mobilisation of human labour to build dams and dikes. Better water control would end the dangers of both drought and water-logging. Another group felt fertilisers were the key to development. Irrigation was a once-for-all improvement; mechanisation only raised labour productivity; but chemical fertilisers meant the potential of the soil could be substantially increased. However, another school favoured popularisation of better farming methods as its only expense was teaching new techniques while it offered an immediate return in improved yields. (*ibid.*, 12/1963.)

The shifting balance of opinion about how China should move forward was well illustrated shortly afterwards when a call went out to forget mechanisation and to use instead better irrigation, advanced cultivation methods and additional fertilisers which would employ more labour. This new round of national discussions seemed to swing right back to the view expressed in 1961 that the country had plenty of hands but no spare capacity to manufacture machines to replace rural manpower. (RF, 2-3/1964.) One economist shed some light on the background to this un-Maoist pessimism about population. He explained China's underdeveloped economy was incapable of producing the modern inputs required by agriculture on an adequate scale. While mechanisation was desirable, its advent must inevitably be delayed. He went on to discuss the conflict between efforts to raise the yield of land and the output per peasant. He appeared to be warning delicately against plans to treat agriculture as if it could be operated on factory lines. The state had to strike the right balance between techniques which got more out of the soil in a China acutely short of arable and fertile land and those which would help to equalise rural and urban productivity. This issue could not be ignored as the gap between worker and peasant output was responsible for the difference in their living standards. (ER, 2/1964.) The argument sounded eminently sensible. However, the reader of this and similar articles might remark on the small impact of Mao Tse-tung upon these intellectuals and their curious air of remoteness from the world they discussed in such abstract and, for a poor nation, almost dehumanised terms.

Perhaps the nadir of economic debate by any standards was the pathetic attempt to explain away seasonal changes in the price of farm products. This exercise quoted Marx to argue that the value of goods varied with the labour used in their production. Price fluctuations for crops therefore reflected this marxist truth, an assertion unimpressive to anyone aware that supplies of different types of fruit, vegetables, fish and, most important, grain vary with the seasons, an objective factor requiring no further comment except that the price changes pointed to the existence of free market forces in Mao's China. (*ibid.*, 9/1965.)

Another controversial issue was price policy. The difficulty for economists was the conflict between the marxist principle of fixing an item's value (the direct and indirect labour required to produce it) and actual practice in China. The value of an article was determined not by the labour used in the factory which manufactured the particular item but by the average for the whole industry. This average concealed wide differences in productivity, capital resources and quality of output from factory to factory. These variations meant some enterprises made handsome profits, while others were lucky to avoid a loss. The claim was made that differences between factories would be marginal, a proposition of doubtful validity in an economy which contained primitive workshops started in the Great Leap Forward, sophisticated Shanghai plants, and factories in Tientsin equipped before the Pacific War with imported machines. The willingness of the state to subsidise the production of certain essential commodities caused confusion as their prices were out of line with the value of the labour they incorporated. Prices also reflected the patterns set in the pre-communist era but the government preferred to stabilise prices rather than reduce them. (KMD, 15 May, 1961.)

The headaches facing the Chinese economist on this score were related in a lengthy study. In times of acute shortage (the post-Leap period), prices had to rise somewhat. In addition, the rural fairs at which peasants sold the produce of their private plots and the goods made in their spare time were essentially free markets. If prices showed a general upward trend, speculation would start — a deep anxiety after the shattering inflation before the successful price stabilisation programme of the infant People's Republic. But if prices were set too low or allowed to fall, enterprises would make losses because costs of buying raw materials, for example, at the beginning of the manufacturing process would not be covered by the price of the finished product. Customers would hold off the market until assured that prices had dropped to their lowest point.

Yet price changes were necessary for several reasons. A major factor was the depressed prices paid to farmers by previous régimes, creating an excessive differential between industry and agriculture. While high prices for factory goods used by the peasants could bring in bigger profits for the state, and thus more finance for national investment, agriculture would be unable to employ these expensive products and thus fail to progress at a satisfactory rate. Efficiency of factory production changed over time, cutting costs of production and justifying lower prices to consumers. But the author warned if price levels were too low, the rewards for production would be unattractive and the labour force's morale would slump. When prices were too high, enterprises made a profit so easily that they could forget about efficient management. The author went into the effect of price policies in balancing relations between provinces short of some goods but with surpluses of other commodities. Foreign trade also entered into his calculations. This economist at least remembered to get in a Mao quotation. But as usual in these bewildered years, orthodoxy slipped when he suggested prices should be used to control market demand for commodities according to whether they were necessities or such luxuries as wine and tobacco. The writer's proposal implied a right to cater for those on higher incomes who could afford to buy a more gracious standard of living. On Maoist criteria, this analysis amounted to an encouragement of bourgeois patterns of behaviour, however reasonable this economist sounds from a purely Western point of view. (ER, 7/1965.)

Time was wasted on debating the nature of China's currency and its effect on the economy. A discussion took place on whether the yuan's value was based on gold, a meaningless controversy to the non-marxist since the gold standard has long been abandoned for internal purposes with little heartburn even by the United States. Indeed, this particular set of articles is almost impossible to translate into a working economic language, marxist or capitalist. (For example,

ER, 5/1965; 2/1966.) Two attempts to examine the importance of the supply of currency are worth noting. The first understood the significance of questioning the flow of currency between various sectors of the economy and its effect on their relations, but the debate held on the topic failed to produce any clear answers. The second article seemed to assume control of currency issued to the public was the most potent economic weapon in the government's hands. This theory has its American advocates but strikes an odd note in a country with socialist planning. (ER, 10/1962; 1/1965; Harry G. Johnson, *Essays in Monetary Economics*, 40-41, 101-3.) An arid essay inquired into the marxist concept of surplus labour, and an uninspired article tried to make sense of the balance between rural and urban population changes. (PD, 14 November, 1961; KMD, 7 October, 1963.)

Gregory Grossman's essay on Soviet market influences indicates the inspiration of large numbers of Chinese economists during this period — the debates which were flowering in Moscow on similar issues. (*Industrialization in Two Systems.*) Alec Nove's portrayal of the post-Stalin revival of Soviet economics also illustrates the parallels between Chinese and Russian thinking. (*The Soviet Economy*, 305-24.) Indeed, imitation was overt. China's leading ideological magazine lavished praise in 1959 on a Russian economics textbook: 'It describes comprehensively socialist productive relations and the role of economic principles in a socialist society.' (RF, 15/1959.) An article on the development of economic accounting explained how China had been helped in setting up a financial management system by Soviet lessons. (TKP, 1 June, 1962.) In 1961, Liu Shao-chi said Mao Tse-tung and the central committee of the communist party had borrowed from 'the experiences of the Soviet Union and other socialist countries' in the economic field. (NCNA, 30 June, 1961.) Agricultural mechanisation in its initial stage 'was copied from the Soviet Union'. This policy was reversed in 1958 but the former system based on the Russian model was reinstated in 1962. (*Nung-yeh Chi-Chieh Chi-shu*, 6/1967.)

For economists to be affected by the 'revisionist' Soviet Union was bad enough, especially after the Russians withdrew their technical assistance in July 1960. (PD, 4 December, 1963.) But even without this alien influence, the economists' writings and debates were anti-Maoist in style as well as content. To ignore Mao's philosophy to such a degree was almost a deliberate insult to the Chairman. But worse still was the inability to make economic discussions relevant to ordinary people. This error was condemned colourfully by a student: 'Some of our "theoreticians" ... hold discussions for the sake of "academic" discussion. Their long essays are difficult even for us students to grasp ... they certainly could not attract workers or peasants ... We do not want these puerile studies which are full of childish airs nor do we want scholasticism which takes several turns and adds some definitions without clarifying an issue.' (ER, 2/1966.)

The condition of economic studies in China before 1966 helps to explain the venom with which every trace of non-Maoist development thinking was tracked down from the Cultural Revolution onwards. The evil geniuses seducing China from its duty to Mao Tse-tung were named as Liu Shao-chi and Sun Yeh-fang. By 1970, the two had become almost inseparable in public denunciations, making it difficult to untangle who bore responsibility for any particular heresy. Sun Yeh-fang is the more important figure from the economist's standpoint since he has been depicted as inventor (or importer) of a set of development doctrines totally hostile to Maoism.

Sun was accused of working 'hand in glove with Soviet revisionist economists', paying several visits to the Soviet Union for consultations with his Russian friends. (PD, 24 February, 1970.) 'He shamelessly said that his "basic views" were taken from "Soviet comrades". Sun Yeh-fang is China's Lieberman ... the notorious revisionist economist of the Soviet Union.' (RF, 10/1966.) Sun's chief offence was to pay overwhelming attention to profits. He saw increased productivity and improved technology as directed to making money. Sun argued the state should regard profits as the main index of economic health at national level and in each enterprise. 'Total profits achieved should be regarded as the most sensitive indicator of technological advances and successful management of an undertaking ... The state should pay attention only to the profit quota and ... give free rein to an enterprise in other respects and let it be its own master.' (RF, 2/1970.) He compared the existing techniques for running China's economy to those of a primitive commune, adding: 'The unified and centralised planning department takes the place of the primitive clan economy's leaders ... and binds the hands and feet of our enterprises, restricting their initiative.' He showed a fine turn of phrase when it came to the party's economic management: 'As soon as the party lays hold of the economy, the economy dies, the party worries. When it gets anxious, the party loosens its grip; when control is relaxed, disorder overtakes the economy. When the economy is in confusion, the party lays tight hold on it again ... now one thing, now another.' (*ibid.,*

10/1966.)

Sun wanted enterprises to solve their own problems of acquiring equipment and raw materials, with freedom to dispose of both their assets and their output without supervision. (KMD, 11 February, 1970.) He argued: 'Workshops which make money will be rewarded, but no wages will be paid to those which lose money.' (*ibid.*, 23 January, 1970.) Sun saw the aim of production as the maximum output from the minimum resources in labour, raw materials and equipment. (PD, 16 April, 1970.) Sun, in short, wanted to buy the masses' enthusiasm for harder work; forget about class struggle and ideological purification; concentrate on production; base priorities on pure profitability; let economic undertakings solve problems through their own initiative; and abolish bureaucratic regulation of the economy. (RF, 2/1970.)

Sun is never mentioned without some insulting epithet attached to his name. His significance as monarch of the anti-Maoist underworld is indisputable. The non-communist social scientist may well feel a certain sympathy for Sun. His ideas are not so different from the concepts preached by standard Western textbooks. Japan, North America and Western Europe comprise most of the nations which have outgrown poverty, and their economic philosophy thus commands a certain respect for sheer efficiency – however distasteful this truth may be to the marxist. But Sun Yeh-fang's notions could not be implemented in China without dangerous consequences which had nothing to do with the ideological sovereignty of Maoism. One article noted that to make profits the sole criterion of investment meant abandoning defence industries and undertakings which the nation needed for strategic, social or other purposes unconnected with economic development. (*ibid.*, 2/1970.) Yet the issue was more fundamental than taking Sun's prescriptions to this logical but absurd extreme. (After all, capitalist countries do not neglect national defence even though armaments are a drain on resources which could be devoted to more productive investments.)

The case against Sun is so simple that despite his importance, he can be disposed of very shortly. Before any open attacks were made on Sun, a long article discussed the vital role of profits in regulating the economy. The author saw various problems in setting prices and thus profits (which represented the difference between sales price and costs of production). His argument basically sided with profits as the yardstick of efficiency but with profit quotas fluctuating from one industry to another because of the different conditions prevailing in various sectors of the economy. A rational profit policy, he declared, 'will guarantee to a large extent the soundness of our economic accounting'. (ER, 5/1964.) His position was not far removed from Sun's. A brilliant riposte was published to all who thought along these lines. The counterblast explained profits were not determined by an enterprise's efficiency. Investment funds were allocated to factories by the government; their production targets were fixed by the state. Some undertakings were called on to manufacture new products which promised little return. In other cases, the authorities looked for long-term dividends even though in the immediate future, an industry's expansion promised small rewards. While the superior efficiency of a planned economy is not self-evident except to a socialist, a communist must accept the value of economic planning. Mao Tse-tung himself had underlined the crucial importance of plans in China's development. Those who argued in favour of making profits the ultimate goal or regulator of China's economy were calling, whether or not they realised the fact, for Peking to dismantle central state control not only of production but of investment as well. Otherwise, profits would represent not individual achievements alone but the 'accidental' consequences of official planning decisions. (*ibid.,* 16/1964.) Ideologically, the abolition of state controls was impossible. The appeal by Mao for decentralisation of economic authority did not help to rescue the Sun school of economics, for Mao Tse-tung advocated regard for the national interest even at the expense of local advantages and thus represented an entirely different outlook.

Liu Shao-chi's economic shortcomings are embarrassing to dissect. The former head of state became the whipping boy for every mistake and heresy committed in China. Attacks on him are often childishly naïve. One article describing Liu as 'a running dog of imperialism' was based on a piece he wrote in 1924. (RF, 12/1970.) Another denunciation accused Liu of selling out to the capitalists in 1949. (*ibid.,* 3/1971.) Yet another indicated he attacked the Great Leap Forward and the communes in 1958. (PD, 29 December, 1970.) If these crass indictments alone were the case against him, Liu's rehabilitation would take little more than a quick browse through Mao's published works to find suitable quotations for the origins of these particular policies and statements by Liu. His book, *Self-Cultivation,* was also flayed for departing from Mao Tse-tung's thought and nowhere calling 'on people to be good pupils of Chairman Mao'. (PD, 8 May, 1967.) This literary evidence of an anti-Mao plot cuts no ice. A long review article on

Self-Cultivation in 1964 not only showed how a Chinese audience saw Liu's work as leading naturally back to a study of Mao's essay but Liu's book was invoked to denounce the very deviations from Maoism – an end to class struggle inside the communist party, for instance – later alleged to have been propagated by Liu Shao-chi. (RF, 2-3/1964.)

Instead of the rigmarole of laying at Liu's door every possible crime, why not offer the simplest and most convincing explanation for his removal? He was responsible in a special way for the health of the party. His book was its instruction manual. (PD, 21 July, 1971.) During the agricultural co-operative movement, the Great Leap Forward and the first half of the 1960s, the party disappointed Mao. It did not support the co-operatives; its rashness ruined the Great Leap Forward; and the socialist education campaign from 1962 to 1966 revealed a corrupt bureaucracy. The disgrace of the man who should have ensured a well-oiled state and party machine, totally loyal to Mao's ideals, was easily justified on this record. Liu could not handle his job. Mao must have calculated Liu was not able to cope with the Cultural Revolution, and with a fine touch of irony, Liu proved his unfitness for office by his political demise at the hands of the brash Red Guards.

Nevertheless, the major economic policies ascribed to Liu Shao-chi need some review to illustrate what became anathema after 1966 to Mao Tse-tung and his supporters. Liu was alleged to have 'slandered the broad masses as "not telling the truth" and as "failing to tell the true facts".' (RF, 10/1970.) This statement was used to prove his mistrust of the ordinary people. After the false figures produced during the Great Leap Forward and Mao's subsequent insistence on truthful reporting, a certain scepticism about information from the basic levels seems sensible enough. Indeed, the importance of accurate data from the grass roots was explained in an impressive article on statistical problems in 1962, and the difficulties of getting ill-educated peasants to fill in forms honestly were also discussed. (TKP, 7 May, 1962; ER, 6/1965.) These facts illustrate the difficulty of estimating precisely the value – or even the meaning – of many charges made against Liu.

The most serious attack concerned his wage policy. In his mouth have been put words almost identical to those of Sun Yeh-fang: 'Factories must make money otherwise they should close down and payment of wages should cease.' (KMD, 26 February, 1970.) Liu had upheld the principle: 'Enthusiasm for work can come from material incentives . . . If you do not give them a rise, they . . . will not produce successfully for you . . . With money, one can make a ghost turn the millstone.' The range of incentive payments was enormous: quarterly awards, monthly awards, safety awards, technical innovation awards, consolation awards. (*ibid.*, 25 November, 1969.)

This materialistic attitude was also expressed in Liu's belief that 'productive forces decide everything'. This slogan meant Liu believed development depended on technical resources and the level of national technology rather than human endeavour. This approach was explained as pernicious on two counts. It contradicted Mao's trust in the masses' ability to work economic miracles. It led to the ruthless exploitation of machinery and natural resources and to exclusive concern with the short term in a drive to make as much money as possible through boosting output. This charge is reasonable in view of the emergency policies China was compelled to adopt after 1958 to keep afloat. In the long run, China would have died, literally, without desperate efforts to raise production in every sector. But Liu was running counter to Mao's idealistic approach which depended on the population's ready understanding of the sacrifices demanded of them.

Liu Shao-chi was attacked for stating: 'We should learn from the West. As soon as we do that we shall make progress.' The slogan 'learn, imitate, import' was attributed to him. (*ibid.*, 3 March, 1970.) Again, this charge probably had a basis in fact. It would have needed the kind of faith which few except Mao possessed to believe the peasants ever again could be trusted to turn their hands to industrial production of any efficiency after the backyard furnaces of 1958. Furthermore, as the quarrel with the Soviet Union intensified during the 1960s, advanced technology — even minimal amounts of equipment for copying — had to come from the West. Again, was China during the post-Leap crisis in any position to divert managerial talent, even at foreman level, to develop indigenous technology when machines, though not always ideal for Chinese conditions, could be obtained from the West?

Perhaps Liu's real fault on this score lay in not recognising when the time had come to abandon completely the emergency policies adopted after 1958 by the central committee. While Liu probably had little difficulty in persuading his colleagues that concentration on production management by technicians instead of workers and more scope for the enterprise's officials made sense immediately after the Great Leap Forward, he was giving hostages to fortune for these measures were against the main tide of Mao's published comments on economic administration. (PD, 24 February, 1970.) Liu was denounced too for encouraging 'trusts', state concerns run on completely autonomous lines to escape from bureaucracy. He urged: 'Turn departments and ministries into corporations, ministers into managers.' The trusts were to be given blanket permission to 'consider doing whatever is profitable'. Liu's motives may have been of the best, but when attacked during the Cultural Revolution, these remarks were interpreted as propagating dangerous Soviet and Yugoslav notions. (KMD, 9 May, 1967.)

More important was Liu Shao-chi's approach to rural problems, Mao's special domain. Liu was held responsible for the 'san-tzu i-pao' — the 'three freedoms and one contract'. (This slogan meant: 'The extension of plots for private use, the extension of free markets, the increase in the number of small enterprises with sole responsibility for their own profits or losses, and the fixing of output quotas on the basis of individual households.') In 1961 and 1962, Liu was reported to have said: 'The peasants have gained nothing from the collective economy in the last few years . . . Don't be afraid of capitalism running amok . . . We must fall back [i.e. retreat from socialism] as far as necessary both in industry and agriculture, even to the extent of fixing output quotas based on the individual households and allowing individual farming.' (*The Struggle between the Two Roads in China's Countryside*, 15-16.)

He allegedly sabotaged Mao Tse-tung's plans for the mechanisation of agriculture. The picture here is not clear in all its details. But the main accusations are that Liu originally was opposed to creating agricultural collectives until industry had the capacity to produce the modern inputs large-scale farming needed. He was against handing over to the communes new machines on the grounds that the peasant was too clumsy to use them properly. Liu then undid Mao's efforts to establish a special ministry for tractors and similar equipment. Liu also fought against giving tractors directly to the peasants because maintenance was easier when tractor service stations were in control. This last policy allegedly created waste and extortion since the station personnel were interested only in making the fattest pay packets and avoiding difficult jobs. (*Nung-yeh Chi-chieh Chi-shu*, 5/1967.) The narrative contains obvious contradictions but gives a picture of Liu in a constant battle to safeguard the government's investments in the countryside. He is shown too as unwilling to trust the peasants' good sense.

The most significant criticism of Liu's rural policy is its encouragement of consumption by putting more money ('material incentives') into the hands of the peasantry instead of giving priority to savings for investment. This point follows naturally from the policy of increasing incomes to boost production in a period of shortages. The 'three freedoms' also meant the peasant had good reason to save his strength for spare-time activities since these were favoured and he had a local market in which to dispose of his wares at a profit. Industry, allegedly under Liu's influence, also rejected the obligation laid on factories by Mao to support agriculture. They produced not what the peasant needed but what commanded the best market. Such a consequence must have been hard to avoid when management of heavy equipment was separated from the agricultural production units — the commune and its production brigades and teams. (Shanghai RS, 31 October, 1969; Chinghai RS, 18 April, 1970.)

Liu Shao-chi seems to have seen the danger of inflation in an economy short of commodities because of natural disasters. Instead of the Maoist solution of appealing to the idealism of the nation, he proposed apparently that commodity prices should be raised by fifty per cent in 1963. Paradoxically he was also an advocate of increasing the volume of currency in circulation. (KMD, 14 March, 1970.) To try to deduce the logic behind these suggestions (which Liu never implemented) is dangerous, for Peking has offered no guidance as to what Liu's motives were apart from their general baseness. A rise in the selling price of commodities would have drained off from the factories and urban consumers a greater volume of cash. Part of this sum the state could then have used to raise output in the villages through higher purchase prices for commodities. Rural living standards would have risen at the expense of the towns' real incomes. Since Liu allegedly was not in favour of putting more machines into the communes, increased industrial prices (because of the factories' higher costs) would not have affected farm output significantly especially since bigger personal earnings would take care of morale. But 1963 was a bad year to make such a proposal. China's agriculture had turned the corner; the economy was on the road to recovery. Material incentives for peasants, with an indirect tax on the increased urban wages through a rise in commodity prices, were unnecessary.

The currency question relates to public behaviour in a period of shortages. Transactions in China, apart from consumer markets, are supposed to be settled by bank transfer. The demand for cash is mainly a multiple of prices and the volume of goods sold to individual consumers. Prices rose during the post-Leap shortages, and private trading increased as rural fairs were allowed greater freedom to operate.

Thus more cash was needed to pay for transactions which could not be settled through the banking system (despite the fall in supplies). However, the call for more bank notes, though probably based on objective needs, ignored the deep-rooted fear of inflation among Chinese. In addition, to refrain from putting more currency into circulation hindered to some extent the volume of private business which could be conducted since the notes to cover transactions were not available. This assisted the suppression of public demand for goods when the country was suffering from serious shortages. In other nations, the public would have overcome this obstacle by ensuring a greater turnover of the available currency. In China, with a rural, dispersed population, the physical difficulty of accelerating the exchange of currency notes from one individual to another must be considerable.

To pass a final verdict on Liu Shao-chi is distasteful on Mao's principle of 'no investigation, no right to speak'. The outside world has yet to be given the opportunity to examine in detail the evidence against Liu. At the same time, his obvious failing as a party leader would have justified his downfall in any government. All the economic policies for which he has been blamed may not have been his personal responsibility, although some of them clearly were. Mao's antipathy to them was inevitable once the immediate danger of China's economic collapse had been averted. Other economic policies were not wrong when first adopted but continued after ample signs had been given of Mao's growing uneasiness at the political climate developing in China, particularly his warning, already mentioned, at the 1962 central committee meeting.

The liberty with which the country's economists strayed from marxist truth, innocently imitating their Soviet counterparts and blithely ignorant of Mao Tse-tung's teachings, suggests their ideas were not out of favour with at least some of the nation's most powerful leaders. Mao could hardly have condoned their heretical analyses, which leaves only Liu Shao-chi and his associates as the obvious culprits protecting economists whose comments were so dangerously at variance with the teachings of China's ideological master. The whole band — Liu Shao-chi, Sun Yeh-fang, their political allies and attendant intellectuals — were the 'ghosts and monsters' the Cultural Revolution was to exorcize. Mao's justification for mobilising the Red Guard hordes in 1966 was simple. As the review of attitudes among young intellectuals, technicians, financial and commercial staff, rural cadres and professional economists has indicated, Mao Tse-tung had ample evidence that his struggle to persuade the groups who counted most in economic life to adopt his development philosophy had failed. Mao felt obliged to make revolution once again, this time on the 'cultural' front, against all the ideas which prevented China from following what he considered the correct road to prosperity.

Chapter Seven

'Preserve Oneself and Destroy the Enemy'

In the summer of 1966, China stunned the world once more. A colossal political upsurge under the banner of the 'Great Proletarian Cultural Revolution' engulfed the nation's cities. The movement was to leave battered or ruined almost all China's senior party and government leaders. The affair was so peculiar in its nature and development that it had no apparent precedent in history. The head of a ruling communist party, Chairman Mao, called on the people to rebel not only against the administration but against his own political organisation. The masses were urged in the name of Mao to seize power from the party and the bureaucracy. Veteran communist officials in both China and Hongkong have confessed their initial shock at the young and violent Red Guards who began the saga in 1966. These experienced cadres were as baffled by the first three years of the Cultural Revolution as foreign observers, although by the spring of 1966 news was already filtering out to Hong Kong that most Chinese had realised they should bar their doors and shutter their windows against an impending political whirlwind.

Peking has been frank about Mao's long-term plans for the 1966 upheaval and has spoken of 'several years of preparation'. (RF, 7/1967.) The first moves came in the cultural field in 1963 (GSCR (9), 4), presumably because of Mao's 1962 dictum: 'To overthrow a political power, it is always necessary first of all to create public opinion, to do work in the ideological sphere.' (ID, 28.) Chiang Ching, Mao's wife, implied the Cultural Revolution should have begun earlier and that it was delayed for perhaps as much as a year. (*ibid.*, 203, 210.) Her hints pointed to a definite strategy behind the event.

The party central committee announced in August 1966 that Mao had been responsible for revisions in economic policy from 1962 and declared: 'The series of questions advanced by Comrade Mao Tse-tung over the past four years concerning socialist revolution and socialist construction have greatly accelerated the development and success of

159

the socialist cause in our country.' (*ibid.,* 158, 162-63, 165) This declaration was further evidence that Mao had been seeking drastic changes in development programmes for a considerable period of time before issuing a public call to change the face of China through the Cultural Revolution. The central committee also made plain the movement's economic objectives: 'The aim of the Great Proletarian Cultural Revolution is to revolutionise people's ideology and as a consequence to achieve greater, faster, better and more economical results in all fields of work.' The committee described the campaign as 'a powerful motive force for the development of the social productive forces in our country'. (*ibid.,* 153.) Mao's management of the drama and its economic objectives are thus clear enough.

'Trust the masses, rely on them and respect their initiative. Cast out fear. Don't be afraid of disturbances. Chairman Mao has often told us that revolution cannot be so very refined, so gentle, so temperate, kind, courteous, restrained and magnanimous.' (*ibid.,* 138.) These were the battle orders for the start of the Cultural Revolution. The turmoil they provoked has been described so extensively by an army of observers that only two issues are of real concern here. The first is why Mao Tse-tung employed such destructive tactics to defeat his opponents. Secondly, what were the Cultural Revolution's economic implications? To try to answer these questions, special attention will be focussed on events at the end of 1967, the mid-point of the tumult, when economic conflicts and political rivalries were at their sharpest.

Mao's tactics in 1966 were designed first of all to bring him victory. The big contrast between the Cultural Revolution and earlier power struggles — the removal of Minister of Defence Peng Teh-huai in 1959, for instance — was the publicity which in 1966 accompanied the display of party and government dirty linen for China's inspection. The façade of total unity and sublimation of personal ambitions for the national good was shattered. Mao explained quite freely his reasons for rending the veil of secrecy which hitherto had enveloped the party central committee and the state council (China's twin over-sized cabinets). He remarked: 'You must never take it for granted that all things written in decisions will be carried out by all party committees and comrades. There are always some who are unwilling to carry them out. But this time things may be better than in the past, because formerly decisions were not made public.' (LL, 64.) In other words, when disputed issues were resolved by the party behind closed doors, opponents of the official line had been able to sabotage party policies with impunity because the people and the ordinary cadres were not informed of the latest decisions and hence could not complain to Peking of a leader's disregard of central committee directives. Mao repeated this point in explaining the failure to remove those guilty of political deviations in the past: 'We did not find a form, a method to arouse the broad masses to expose our dark aspect openly.' (ID, 25.) Mao was angered by the refusal of the party to heed his 1962 warning that the country was in danger of betraying true marxism and drifting towards the diluted socialism embraced by the Soviet Union. He had put his cards on the table in 1965: 'The main target of the present movement is those party persons in power taking the capitalist road.' But his admonitions fell on deaf ears. (*ibid.,* 20-23.) In 1966, Mao was no longer prepared to trust to the party's discipline or its sense of loyalty. He appealed over its head to the whole nation.

A Stalinist purge of all top officials he suspected of less than utter devotion to his ideology would in one sense have been more efficient than the turbulent Cultural Revolution, as the country could have gone about its normal life almost untouched by the cleansing of official stables. Several Western observers seem to imagine the Cultural Revolution bore a direct resemblance to the Russian blood-baths and that a mad Stalin was matched by a demented – or senile – Mao. Maurice Latey makes an explicit comparison between the two men, while Robert Jay Lifton sees the Cultural Revolution as a bid by Mao Tse-tung to prove age had not diminished his political potency. (*Tyranny,* 175; *Revolutionary Immortality,* 93-94.) Chalmers Johnson talks of the fight with Liu Shao-chi as the outcome of a 'gerontological comedy' caused by an argument over a film in 1950. (*Asian Survey,* January 1968, 8-9.) Richard Lowenthal describes the Cultural Revolution as: 'A desperate attempt to prevent a . . . triumph of economic rationality over ideological doctrine.' (*Issues in the Future of Asia,* 21.)

Such interpretations are attractive. They render unnecessary any further search for a clear pattern in the chaos of 1966 and the years which followed, since, on these analyses, the upsurge was produced by a mind deranged. Dementia, however, is an unsatisfactory explanation. Men such as Liu Shao-chi, the head of state, Teng Hsiao-ping, party general secretary, Lo Jui-ching, vice-minister of defence – to mention but three of the most distinguished leaders to fall from office – were hardbitten individuals, steeled in war and revolution, and well versed in the arts of political intrigue. If Mao had been senile (and not mad as Stalin was, possessed of a blood lust), these political warriors could have out-manœuvred Mao. The astonishing phenomenon is the relative ease with which they crumbled. They faded away with minimal resistance, rather like the men pressed into the Roman arena as gladiators' prey who turned in salute to the emperor for whose amusement they were about to perish.

The rationale for the disgrace of Liu Shao-chi has already been suggested: the poor state of the party and the cadres whose political health was his responsibility. The same reason seems to apply to many provincial leaders who were thrown out of office. The impetus of the Cultural Revolution was directed mainly against the party itself. Donald W. Klein has shown that members of the central administration who had never formally become communists survived to a remarkable degree, while party members disappeared in batches into political oblivion. (*Party Leadership and Revolutionary Power in China*, 362.) As far as Mao Tse-tung's ideological hatchetmen were concerned, another useful criterion was the relationship of a political 'suspect' to Liu Shao-chi and his principal 'counter-revolutionary' accomplices. A neat set of diagrams was drawn by one band of Red Guards, tracing personal connections with Liu right through the provincial administrative networks as well as the central government. (*Selections from China Mainland Magazines*, No. 651, 22 April, 1969.) The old principle of building up a personal following in any heirarchical organisation was clearly understood by the Red Guards, and they followed the scent of personal ties to sniff out potential traitors. They were encouraged to believe in 'guilt by association' by Maoist denunciations of secret cliques, 'watertight and impenetrable independent kingdoms', military factions and underground manipulation of organisations. (*Great Victory for Chairman Mao's Revolutionary Line*, 6, 42-43; GSCR (9), 10-11; RF, 12/1967.)

For the first time since 1949, indiscriminate violence was not discouraged. Red Guards smashed their way into private homes, government offices and diplomatic missions, assaulted individuals, destroyed property and dragged out for humiliation the mightiest in the land. These acts were distasteful to many Chinese leaders. Chen Yi, China's foreign minister in 1967, displayed visible embarrassment when questioned at a Western embassy reception about the assault on British diplomatic staff in Shanghai. Premier Chou En-lai informed the British Chargé d'Affaires in 1971 that the British mission was burnt down in 1967 despite his appeals to the mob. Whatever the personal feelings of such men, licence to use extreme measures had been granted implicitly to the student Red Guards in 1966. (ID, 144.) Indeed, for a nation attempting to rid itself of the past as China was, violence had a special value in 1966. As Bernard Crick explains: 'Precisely because thought and action are so determined by the superstructure of traditional society, and because the elements of this structure are so inter-dependent and interlocked, society can only, with very few exceptions – entirely tactical – be smashed, broken, overturned, shattered, seldom if ever converted or persuaded peacefully.' (*In Defence of Politics*, 43.) The Cultural Revolution, from its inception, anticipated resistance not just from its eminent targets but also 'from the force of habits from the old society'. (ID, 132.)

The communist party itself could not liberate society from the bonds of tradition as Mao desired. Nor could it expel the men hindering the implementation of Mao's policies, for, as he stated, 'representatives of the bourgeoisie . . . have sneaked into the party, the government, the army and all spheres of culture'. In any case, the party under Liu Shao-chi and his associates had proved disloyal to Mao's programme too often in the past to be trusted again. Mao Tse-tung fell back on the theory he had propounded in 1957: 'The working class remoulds the whole of society in class struggle and in the struggle against nature [in production], and at the same time remoulds itself.' (PE, 106.) Furthermore, Mao did not believe rebellion against the established order was a peaceful process: 'A revolution is not a dinner party, or writing an essay, or painting a picture, or doing embroidery.' (SW I, 28.) He had remarked of the more cautious and popular movement to set up rural co-operatives: 'The birth of a new social system is always accompanied by a great uproar and outcry, proclaiming the superiority of the new system and criticising the backwardness of the old. To bring our more than 500 million peasants through socialist transformation is a project of earth-rocking, heaven-shaking dimensions which cannot possibly be achieved in an atmosphere of calm seas and gentle breezes.' (SU, 253.) How much more 'heaven-shaking' was the attempt to accomplish the socialist transformation of the entire nation at one stroke. Violence as such did not frighten Mao Tse-tung. To be fair to his record, 'any method of forcing a minority holding different views to submit is impermissible' was an official decree from the very start of the upheavals. Such slogans as 'killing none and not arresting most' were repeated regularly, though the ban on coercion was widely disregarded. (ID, 141, 56.)

The use of the young generation (from school children to

undergraduates), recruited into Red Guard bands, showed considerable acumen. The employment of intellectuals as the vanguard of the upheaval paid conscious respect to tradition: 'All cultural revolution movements in contemporary Chinese history began with student movements and led to the worker and peasant movements, to the integration of the revolutionary intellectuals with the worker-peasant masses.' (GSCR (9), 20.) The Red Guards could imagine themselves as heirs to the traditions of the student agitation against the Manchus and against the betrayal of Chinese interests by the Treaty of Versailles, glowing pages in the history of Chinese youth movements. But the intellectuals were clearly a temporary phase, to be replaced by the masses into whose ranks the students would be incorporated.

Another factor was student discontent and disillusionment with the party which had first surfaced in the storm of invective against the communists in 1957 when the students were called on to express their views with total frankness during the 'Hundred Flowers' campaign. The continuity was remarkable between their contempt for the party in 1957 (which was quickly stifled) and their physical assault on its officials a decade later with Mao's encouragement. (A pamphlet on 1957 undergraduate opinion translated in *Union Research Service,* Vol. 29, Nos. 12 & 13, 1962 is a striking review of the goals which the students failed to accomplish in 1957 but achieved in the Cultural Revolution.) In 1957 Mao himself had not been safe from criticism; he cleverly exploited the latent grievances of the young in 1966 to mobilise them for battle on his behalf.

The Red Guards were important because they represented a contemptuous method of dealing with those whom Mao wished to remove. Mere boys and girls were able to humble men who had seen more blood spilled and endured more physical torment in the fight for communism than most revolutionaries. Yet these giants suddenly shrivelled before the relentless questioning and denunciations of the Red Guards. Apart from Premier Chou and Chen Yi, the majority of these veterans of the most brutal era in modern Chinese history gave up the ghost virtually without a struggle as far as can be judged from the outside. Certainly, few if any of those under attack lived up to the battle honour Mao had urged upon the Chinese communist: 'He who is not afraid of death by a thousand cuts dares to unhorse the emperor — this is the indomitable spirit needed in our struggle to build socialism and communism.' (PW, 11.) The men disgraced proved themselves unable to outwit callow youths and unwilling to defy their tormentors and so were self-condemned as unworthy to lead the new China. They lacked courage, the virtue most essential to conquer internal obstacles to progress and external threats to national independence. To allow children to break his foes was a masterstroke by Mao, far more effective than the forced confessions and rigged trials preferred by Stalin. Mao was left with no blood on his hands – the most famous victims of the Cultural Revolution were kept alive except for a few suicides – and the more eminent who fell 'bowed their heads' to children, a humiliation from which they could hardly hope to recover with any real prestige whatever honorific posts they might be granted in the future. Had Mao Tse-tung broken his own taboo against bloodshed and conducted a purge, the Chinese nation would probably have been revolted by a reminder of the old régimes. The Red Guards enabled Mao to win on handsome terms.

Mao Tse-tung's blessing of the Culutural Revolution involved certain ideological difficulties. His *Selected Works* contained a section denouncing 'excessive and sectarian inter-party struggles' and those 'who unduly or improperly stressed the importance of the leading cadres being exclusively of working-class origin'. It condemned the 'sectarian organisational policy of attacking comrades'; 'factional activities against the central leadership'; those who acted 'as if they were dealing with criminals and enemies'; and those who 'did not regard veteran cadres as valuable assets of the party; instead they attacked, punished and dismissed from the central and local organisations large numbers of veteran cadres'. (SW III, 181, 182, 187, 209, 1965 ed.) This section was deleted from the post-1965 editions, partly because the Red Guards employed precisely these tactics and partly because these pages contained several flattering references to Liu Shao-chi. Again, Mao had stated in 1957: 'The large-scale and turbulent class struggles of the masses characteristic of the previous revolutionary periods have in the main ended.' (PE, 95.)

The upsurge of the Cultural Revolution must have shocked those familiar with Mao's writings. The *Liberation Army Daily* on 6 October, 1966, attempted to give the violence of the Cultural Revolution an ideological justification by holding up as the model for the Maoist revolutionaries the Chairman's 1927 essay, 'Report on an Investigation of the Peasant Movement in Hunan'. This study contained one of Mao's rare endorsements of physical violence (apart from warfare) and lauded the peasants' attacks on the landlord class, their destruction of temples, the summary justice they meted out and the humiliation of their enemies led through the streets tied with ropes, wearing dunces caps and accompanied by gongs and drums. (However, Mao reported that only the worst local tyrants were executed, so the essay did not justify bloodshed. (SW I, 29, 36-38, 45.) These practices were reintroduced by the Red Guards.

Interestingly, Mao Tse-tung tried to avoid the impression of having assumed personal power. Decrees on the conduct of the Cultural Revolution were issued in the name of the central committee and spoke of setting up 'new forms of organisation whereby under the leadership of the communist party the masses themselves are rising to make the cultural revolution'. (ID, 107, 127; GSCR (7), 13.) Mao's trusted lieutenant, Yao Wen-yuan, condemned one leading communist for preaching: 'You can oppose anyone.' (Comment on Tao Chu's Two Books, 30.) Most cadres in all branches of government, economic, military and cultural, were depicted as offering 'support for the party and Chairman Mao'. (GSCR (7), 24.) Senior officials were permitted some reassurance by amnesty offers: 'As for some of the leading functionaries in our party organisations at all levels, so long as they are not anti-party and anti-socialist, they should come to the battlefront without any mental burdens. They should be courageous in self-examination of their shortcomings and mistakes and open mindedly accept criticism from the masses. They should not become disgruntled and disheartened just because the masses post a few big-character posters and voice some criticisms.' (ibid., (6), 9-10.) Unhappily, the Cultural Revolution's denunciations of party leaders were not played in such a minor key.

Mao Tse-tung stated at two central committee meetings in 1966 that he had not realised the Cultural Revolution would be so tempestuous and argued mistakes had been made through acting too hurriedly. He also implied the violence had been exaggerated, and a few months of disturbances would do no great harm. (LL, 68, 70.) He probably had not anticipated the momentum of the Cultural Revolution nor the way anarchy would spread like wildfire across the country as normal authority broke down. But to win, he could not allow an early restoration of conventional government organisations. Part of his strategy was to focus attention on himself as the only source of truth and security. Of the enemy within the party, he said, 'Some of them we have already seen through, others we have not. Some are still trusted by us and are being trained as our successors.' (ID, 127.) This statement left no-one free from suspicion of anti-Maoism. Ever since a campaign launched in 1960 to complete the publication of his works and to study them assiduously, he had been the front of ideological rectitude, with his philosophy an ever-increasing object of veneration. (*Chung-kuo Ching-nien,* 19/1960; PD, 14-15 November, 1960.) A check on two hundred major articles published between 1959 and 1966 shows only thirteen contained favourable references to Liu Shao-chi while Mao's name cropped up too often to be worth a precise count. Thus when treason was denounced in the councils of state, with the conspirators still masked by a spurious Maoism, the people of China dared not trust anyone except Mao himself and those he chose personally to endorse. No rival ideology existed; no alternative standard of political judgment had been allowed to develop. Anthony Downs has explored the uses of ideology in times of political uncertainty. His analysis indicates China had to 'vote' for Mao Tse-tung because the benefits his still-concealed rivals could promise in return for public support were totally unknown. (*An Economic Theory of Democracy,* 98-100.)

Mao Tse-tung needed an element of confusion to add drama to his movement. The Cultural Revolution was 'to hold aloft the great red banner of Mao Tse-tung Thought' and put the study of his works in command of the nation. (ID, 154, 173-74.) This call had been made before, but a problem which faces politicians in all societies is general ignorance and a lack of public willingness to participate in political life. Moore and Studdert-Kennedy have illustrated the woeful misinformation and apathy among Western electorates. (*Opinions, Publics and Pressure Groups,* 20-22.) The Chinese seem to have been no different. Yet Mao could not afford an apolitical society. The people had to be induced to dedicate themselves completely to his economic strategy if his ideas were to shape the country's future. The masses were the key ingredient in his growth model; they could achieve nothing unless aware of what was demanded of them. One way of making the public concern itself with ideological affairs was to dramatise politics through a movement such as the Cultural Revolution.

An orderly change to Maoist policies would not have affected the masses. He could have persuaded the central committee by sheer force of personality to remove the tainted elements within its ranks. But such tranquil reshuffles at the top would not have sufficed, Peking asserted later. (NCNA, 30 June, 1971.) Almost two years earlier, from 4 January, 1965, the *New China News Agency* had released details of the considerable changes in ministerial appointments announced by Chou En-lai to the National People's Congress (China's parliament). Among those promoted were Tao Chu to a deputy premiership, and Lu Ting-yi as minister of culture. The overthrow of these two men in 1966 illustrates the failure of attempts to make the administrative machine more amenable to Mao through discreet switches in personnel. By 1966, Mao believed literally in his slogan: 'The working class must exercise leadership in everything.' (ID, 50.) In any case, by testing the ability of senior cadres to survive the buffeting of the Cultural Revolution, Mao Tse-tung was able to assess the popularity and mass links of the leadership. In a sense, the Cultural Revolution was 'trial by ordeal', a substitute for the more placid popular selection of administrations in the West.

Another important issue is why Mao chose to strike at the cities and not the larger population in the countryside. A partial answer is probably that the rural areas could learn as onlookers from the dramatic events in the cities because the fall of the powerful and the anarchy of the Red Guards (and their successors, the 'revolutionary rebel' workers) were not matters anyone could ignore. By concentrating on the urban centres, Mao limited the attack and tried to avoid spreading the conflagration into every village with the risks this would have entailed regarding food supplies. In addition, the Chinese city-dweller enjoyed traditional social institutions to guard him from totalitarian authority, making urban life potentially as fluid and anonymous when it came to ideology as the average Western city. Louis Wirth observes of the urban inhabitant: 'He finds it difficult to determine what is to his own "best interests" and to decide between the issues and leaders presented to him by the agencies of mass suggestion.'(On Cities and Social Life, 76.) This ability to 'hide' from political involvement in the cities — in contrast to communes where, in theory, a zealous cadre could supervise more firmly political campaigns — made the urban population of special importance in Mao's effort to rally the whole nation behind him.

One puzzle is the survival of such individuals as Chou En-lai. On the published record, China's prime minister had generally been no more radical than Liu Shao-chi. A possible explanation for the premier's charmed life lies in Chou's role as a bureaucrat totally dedicated to the implementation of national policy. Apart from his charm and national repute, Chou had no popular political base to make others in the seats of power apprehensive about his ambitions. Liu had the party; Peng Chen, the city of Peking; Tao Chu, the whole of southern China. Chou En-lai also seems to have known in advance which direction the struggle would take. In 1964, the prime minister made a long speech, virtually every part of which foreshadowed the slogans and policies of the Cultural Revolution. The document reads almost as if Chou had been given a blueprint of the developments which would take place after the summer of 1966. His one 'lapse' was a courteous reference to Liu Shao-chi as the author of the 'half-work, half-study' educational system, which, the cynic might suggest, was hedging a bet in a small way. (NCNA, 30 December, 1964.) Mao Tse-tung, on this performance, knew Chou En-lai would place his considerable talents at the Chairman's disposal in a fight over the adoption of Mao's policies.

The Cultural Revolution was not a campaign to use 'violence and elimination of certain status groups [as a] substitute for change directed at economic growth or alterations in group commitments, social composition, and belief systems'. (Henry Bienen, *Violence and Social Change*, 97.) On the contrary, new attitudes and dedication to economic progress were the objectives of the violence. The monotonous economic theme of the Cultural Revolution was to abolish material incentives and outlaw the practice of 'putting profits in command'. These moves were not popular everywhere for they called on workers to sacrifice their bonuses. Various devices were used to prove the injustice of material incentives. Denunciations of cash rewards for hard work as 'political poison' were spiced with allegations that technical staff got larger bonuses than ordinary workers. This charge may also have been designed to provoke the labour force to take over the factories from the managements alleged to have profited so well from the system in the past. (NCNA, 12 December, 1967.) The clumsiness of the work point system when used to calculate peasant earnings in communes with incompetent administrators was used to discredit the idea of working for personal gain in the form of higher wages. (*Peking Daily*, 17 July, 1968.) Nevertheless, one report indicated considerable support for a call from rural 'counter-revolutionaries' for higher official prices for grain purchased in excess of the state production quota, and the authorities were worried lest peasants and rusticated students used the mounting chaos to slip away secretly to the better-paid city jobs. (PD, 1 February, 1967.) A tractor unit joined in to explain how material incentives encouraged personnel to chase after quantity regardless of the quality of their work. (*Nung-yeh Chi-chieh Chi-shu*, 4/1967.) However, the arguments produced in the campaign against material incentives were rather anaemic although its momentum continued to dominate almost every report on the economy.

For their part, those attacked in the Cultural Revolution exploited material incentives as their major weapon. In Shansi province, 'to save themselves from destruction, this handful of gangsters resorted to still more sinister means, that is economic warfare. They vied with one another in supplying some organisations with houses and motor cars and unlimited funds, gravely damaging Shansi's finance and economy and corrupting revolutionary organisations.' Cash was a powerful magnet. Under its influence, 'big crowds of people who did not know the truth attacked revolutionary rebels'. The province had to freeze funds in all organisations and impound vehicles. (NCNA, 25 January, 1967.) Shanghai, China's major port and chief manufacturing centre, was gravely affected by the desire for material incentives and by 'economism' — the willingness of cadres to buy off trouble. Workers were paid to leave the city and create friction elsewhere. Money was handed out lavishly to induce various groups to concentrate on the cash they were making — for keeping factory production going apparently — instead of concerning themselves with political struggle. The city's funds were frozen in January 1967, and the workers who had been allowed to leave the municipality ordered to return. (NCNA, 8 & 11 January, 1967.) But the public's appetite for hard cash rather than lofty ideals was hard to appease. Almost a year later, the city had to denounce excessively liberal loans to workers from factory funds, and calls for the traditional payment of double wages at the end of the year were attacked. (Wen-hui Pao, 20 December, 1967.) Outbreaks of violence were alarming. Workers split into rival factions and took time off to fight each other, with all involved claiming to be the true followers of Mao. In Kweichow province, the local radio station related how a Red Guard youth had been driving a lorry to a construction site to rescue fellow 'revolutionaries' wounded by their opponents. The youth was kidnapped and then murdered by members of a 'workers' alliance' who supported the old administrative set-up and had fought to the death against pro-Maoists during the summer. The army, by now on the scene, was apparently unable to restore order by direct action. As armed clashes continued in the province, a cotton mill was assaulted, with the counter-Maoists engaged in 'such fascist acts as cutting off water, food and the power supply, arson, poisoning and flooding' to force their adversaries to capitulate. A detachment of troops went to the mill to 'support the left'. A squad marched out of the premises to get food and were run down by a lorry. One soldier was killed. The troops seem to have been sent to put down the battle at the mill without arms of any kind. (RS, 10 & 28 November, 1967.) How much industrial plant and equipment was destroyed in such incidents, no-one can estimate.

Production undoubtedly slumped with the wave of anarchy. The vital communications sector was not immune to disorder. According to local broadcasts, the transport authorities in grain-rich Szechwan province tried to bring the railways to a halt, presumably as blackmail, to save themselves. They used railway regulations to buttress their authority and encouraged 'unreasonable wages and welfare benefits' to win supporters in their campaign to stop the trains. They managed to create considerable confusion, apparently, as some workers were induced to demand bigger pay packets while others were persuaded to leave their jobs in Szechwan to spread the revolution elsewhere. The army then took over the railways. Orders were issued for all staff to report back for work; Red Guards and various Maoist groups were told to keep their hands off the railways; funds were frozen: wage increases rescinded; policemen and workers from other industries instructed to leave the railway bureaux and go back to their own jobs. Dire retribution was promised for acts of violence, theft and sabotage. (RS, 12 December, 1967.) The confusion in China was such that an editorial in the *Szechwan Daily* saw nothing incongruous in referring to railway conditions as 'excellent' on the very day these military commands were published.

'Making revolution' became a valid excuse for skipping work. Many in the labour force stopped accepting orders on the principle 'whatever the masses say counts'. They downed tools whenever they pleased, quoting the slogan 'temper labour with rest'. If criticised, they claimed to be 'old rebels ... meritorious statesmen'. They quarrelled with decisions of the majority, crying 'no slave mentality' – an allegation that their colleagues were imitating 'scab' Liu Shao-chi. (*Wen-hui Pao,* 6 February, 1968.) In the summer of 1967, fresh resistance to the Cultural Revolution had to be crushed in Shanghai. By the winter, political struggles had been replaced by outright crime. The local daily reported women were insulted; robberies were frequent; attempts to get the Red Guards off the streets and back to school hindered; and state property damaged. More serious were the rash of illegal factories and the appearance of speculators who established black markets for goods in short supply. (*ibid.,* 21 December, 1967.)

Kwangtung province illustrated how the problem of restoring order was to be solved. The army brought warring groups of workers together in 'revolutionary great alliances', and the various factions were forced to substitute study of Mao's works for their own political debates. Slowly, unity was restored to the work force, first among the seamen, then among employees of electronics, textile, machinery, chemical, iron and steel, torch, pharmaceutical and printing factories together with workers in the transport and construction industries. To celebrate the first solid step back to normality through a military takeover of virtually every branch of the economy, the army commander, Huang Yung-sheng (later promoted chief of the general staff despite criticism of his use of armed troops to enforce law and order), attended a rally of 5,000 people. General Huang claimed agriculture and industry were flourishing — a highly optimistic remark — but added: 'Many people still do not have a correct understanding of the Great Proletarian Cultural Revolution.' (RS, 14 December, 1967.) At the same time, the army was touring even the remotest villages of the nearby border province of Yunnan to show the flag. (RS, 6 January, 1968.)

The extent and gravity of the threat to the economy can be gauged from these moves in Kwangtung and clearly belied the 1966 assertion: 'If the masses are fully aroused and proper arrangements are made, it is possible to carry on both the Cultural Revolution and production without one hampering the other.' (ID, 153.) In practice, the masses proved too fiery, while in many places no-one survived with the authority to make 'proper arrangements'. Ironically, the drastic fall in output can be measured by the massive increases in production reported by various enterprises from the autumn of 1967. These were meant to paint a reassuring picture. But the only way they can be interpreted sensibly is by taking them as an indication that output had dwindled so low that as life settled down, enormous leaps could be recorded in monthly production figures. The *Hunan Daily* wrote of one colliery which pushed the coal mined eleven per cent above target in October and twenty per cent in November — by which month, the miners were somewhat above the pre-1966 production norms. (15 December, 1967.)

Once the new administrative organisations, the revolutionary committees, had been brought into the world by the army after prolonged labour pains, many of their members fell into the same bad habits as their predecessors dismissed in the Cultural Revolution. Thus the revolutionary committee in charge of a power supply unit in the strategic petrochemical complex of Lanchow was reminded of its duty to practise democracy and not allow individuals to arrogate power to themselves. Its members were to maintain close ties with the masses, reduce the number of officials, 'oppose economism, oppose spending money freely to buy this and that . . . and oppose the lordly style of ostentation and extravagance'. (Kansu RS, 21 November, 1967.)

The *Wen-hui Pao* of Shanghai highlighted the difficulty of rebuilding the government structure by publishing a Mao instruction calling for old cadres to work in harmony with the officials newly recruited from the revolutionaries' ranks. (10 November, 1967.) Experienced officials could not be ejected totally from the scene; someone had to get on with the business of running the country. In Yunnan province, about forty per cent of the cadres retained their jobs in one county (RS, 22 November, 1967), while in a Szechwan county, the figure was ninety per cent. Here the former first secretary of the party committee had to be retained in the administration because of his local power base. (RS, 1 January, 1968.) This protection for individuals of talent who were alleged supporters of Liu Shao-chi provoked fresh trouble. Shanghai's *Liberation Daily* complained bitterly that some party organisations retained all their old members and made no effort to 'get rid of the stale and take in the fresh'. (24 October, 1968.) Peking was still fighting against the bureaucratic mentality two years after the start of the Cultural Revolution. (RF, 4/1968.) Either veteran junior cadres proved better at weathering the storm than their masters in the central government and party apparatus, or every recruit to the Chinese official hierarchy was infected instantly by the germs of the old mandarin class. Attempts to employ new methods of training cadres by exposing them to mass criticism made the average official 'unwilling to serve as a cadre for fear he may suffer, offend others or get purged'. (*Nung-yeh Chi-shu*, 11/1967.) Bureaucratic self-confidence was not fostered by commending officials to their constituents' tender mercies for 're-education'.

The downfall of various provincial leaders is highly illuminating. One interesting example, though not a very well-known personality outside China, was Li Ching-chuan, top-ranking communist official in southwest China with the military rank of political commissar. He had spent time in personal attendance on Mao and had good revolutionary, war and administrative records. The first accusation against him was persecution of local cadres, suggesting that in the political crisis, provincial and district loyalties had come to the surface. He was also attacked bitterly for his economic policies. In 1964, Li had gone personally to assist a production brigade, which showed a fine Maoist spirit. However, he soon revealed his 'treachery' when he asked young people: 'Do you want new clothes? Do you want to plant cotton? If you do not know how to plant, you can learn. I can transfer an expert and he will teach you how to plant cotton.' Thus instead of 'self-reliance', professionals were employed, and the area got special treatment in the allocation of fertilisers and other agricultural supplies. Rather than encourage the study of Mao at political education forums, Li turned these occasions into 'production mobilisation rallies' and stressed technical not ideological training. Worse still, Li was accused of silencing Mao's voice by refusing to give space in local newspapers to a major article by Mao's aide, Yao Wen-yuan.

Once the Cultural Revolution began, according to the official indictment, Li directed the attack against the ordinary cadres and tried to enact ordinances for the conduct of the revolution designed to prevent the masses from seizing power. He also wasted state funds stating: 'For such a great campaign, it is impossible not to spend some money . . . Don't keep too close a hand on the purse strings, loosen up a bit.' Li allowed former urban inhabitants sent to farming communes to return to the cities and make 'unreasonable economic demands'. He used his rural associates to rehabilitate persons denounced for 'rightism' in the 1950s, engineering through his cronies at district level a fraudulent mail campaign in support of these 'counter-revolutionaries'. Li's final undoing was not just his lack of native roots in Szechwan province where his headquarters were located and where he had served so long, but his onslaught against the minor cadres in the socialist education campaign during the four years prior to the Cultural Revolution. Li said in 1964: 'Of the cadres, forty to fifty per cent can be basically trusted. The majority cannot.' Office-bearers in the humbler outposts of the party and the administration were not powerful as individuals but they could rally popular support on a massive scale if united by a single goal. Li's non-Maoist economic policies, his political 'corruption' of workers, peasants and young people, his attempt to win friends with cash and bonuses in 1966 were all reprehensible. Yet the impression remains that, in the last resort, Li was ousted because the Cultural Revolution gave too many insignificant officials the excuse to band together against an outsider. Li had trampled on them for his own political ambitions through pretended loyalty to Peking in the socialist education campaign. (Kweichow RS, 4, 29 November, 1967; Szechwan RS, 4, 7, 8, 19, 20, 25 December, 1967.)

The Cultural Revolution appears to have been a carefully contrived exercise, not only to remove those unconvinced of the practicability of Mao's economic plans but to awaken the nation's mind by enacting a violent power struggle in public for the first time in the history of the People's Republic. The upsurge was not always under Mao's control, and many of the incidents which took place contravened his instructions against violence. Undoubtedly, China sat up and took note of ideological issues which in many instances became a veritable matter of life or death. The manner of Mao's victory – the abasement by the young of every source of opposition to his economic strategy – was an impressive display of political skill which placed Mao's authority beyond challenge. The costs of the Cultural Revolution were high. Production faltered. A reasonably efficient administrative machine (it had led the country safely through the dangers of collapse after the Great Leap) was smashed. To these must be added the breakdown of labour discipline, the upsurge of factional hatreds and the resurgence of district loyalties and illegal economic activities.

On the credit side, the Cultural Revolution and its evidence of strong undercurrents of demand for higher living standards – played on by those in peril from the Red Guards – successfully exposed 'the old ideas, culture, customs and habits of the exploiting classes to corrupt the masses'. (ID, 130.) Without the Cultural Revolution and the outbreak of demands made and met for better wages and bonuses in the initial stage and then crushed as patent anti-Maoist stratagems, how long could pressure for a big increase in incomes and a consequent reduction in the money available for investment have been resisted by the central government? After the Cultural Revolution, such instincts became incriminating evidence of secret sympathy for 'scab' Liu Shao-chi and thus controllable.

A refusal to use rising incomes as a spur to greater development efforts strikes an odd note to the Western economist, despite his acknowledgement of the need to drain off as large a surplus as possible to pay for new equipment, factories, fertilisers and roads. Baran and Sweezy make the point that if market demand is dominated by popular fashions and the influence of consumer incomes, machinery becomes obsolete not because it functions inefficiently but because its output no longer satisfies public whims. (*Monopoly Capital*, 107.) This sort of obsolescence is a luxury an underdeveloped nation cannot afford. Adolph Lowe has argued cogently that modern economists by sticking to their concept of the 'economically rational man' fail to explain the

175

frequent instances of individuals who do not buy when prices fall and who fail to invest in the 'scientific' manner ordained by economic textbooks. He has insisted that a consensus has to be created in society about the ambitions it seeks to satisfy through economic activity if a stable business machine is to be created. (*On Economic Knowledge,* Part Four; Robert L. Heilbroner, ed., *Economic Means and Social Ends,* 26-36.) Lowe, who is not a Maoist, has come close to saying that profits and incomes are not the final determinants of economic behaviour even in a capitalist society. His views resemble Mao Tse-tung's belief that man could strive after development even if his body were not comforted with material rewards. This was the ultimate message of the Cultural Revolution.

Chapter Eight

'No Construction without Destruction'

The Cultural Revolution swept away so many communist heroes and wrecked so completely the administrative and political machinery constructed with such care since 1949 that the summer of 1966 seemed to mark the start of a new period in modern Chinese history. From the outside, Mao appeared to be trying to return his people and the communist party to the revolutionary womb so that they might be reborn unsullied by the stain of 'original sin' inherited from the old régimes through the weakness or 'sabotage' of the leadership which had come to power with the creation of the People's Republic. Mao, however, regarded the Cultural Revolution in a different light. It was another stage in a protracted battle to eradicate the legacy of 'feudalism' and 'capitalism'. In 1966, the *Liberation Army Daily* illustrated this attitude with a quotation from a 1962 speech by Mao: 'The next fifty or a hundred years will be a great era in which the social system in the world will change completely, an earth-shaking era unrivalled by any historical period in the past.' (5 May, 1966.) Certainly, the Chinese public was not allowed to think that the Cultural Revolution closed a chapter in its history since the press constantly republished statements made by Mao over the previous two decades.

In tracing the origins of the Cultural Revolution, a large number of writers, while interpreting events in terms of their own fields of study, have tended to show how trends visible for many years before 1966 had been brought to a climax by the Cultural Revolution. Personal quarrels, ideological conflicts, social institutions are among the many explanations offered for the Cultural Revolution. (For example, the essays by Ross Terrill, Victor C. Funnell, David E. Powell, Lloyd Eastman and Parris H. Chang in *Problems of Communism*, March-April, 1967; March-April, 1968; March-April, 1969; May-June, 1969; and Philip Bridgham's article in *Party Leadership and Revolutionary Power in China*.) A common theme in most evaluations of the period from 1966

177

to 1969 is an attempt to show how the Cultural Revolution was the result of the natural forces within China's political and social system under communism. Strangely, however, the economic roots of the upheaval have been generally neglected, although economic factors were of central importance. (Yuan-li Wu's study in *Asian Survey,* March 1968, is a notable exception.)

From the start, Mao's spokesmen pointed to the Cultural Revolution's specific development goals and the dynamic element it would introduce into agriculture and industry. Official party communiqués on the upsurge also referred to Mao's attempts to shift the economy on to a new path from 1962. But the story is hard to unravel because of the cross-currents at work. Widespread anti-Maoist ideas and practices were openly admitted before 1966, while simultaneously the emphasis in official policies shifted steadily though discreetly from 1962 towards concepts and programmes to be praised as truly Maoist after 1966. The political struggles of the Cultural Revolution can thus be seen as a bid to eliminate all traits inconsistent with the spirit of Mao's philosophy. But the triumph of Mao Tse-tung in the Cultural Revolution did not lead to new economic policies; rather it placed beyond all question the economic strategy whose implementation Mao had been urging since 1962. Mao had increased his pressure on economic policy in the four years prior to the mobilisation of the Red Guards partly to ensure the ground would be cleared for the adoption of his economic plans by the entire nation once he had recaptured political power. He also seems to have realised how careful preparations would guarantee him solid support from the most vital sectors of the economy and also enable agriculture and industry to continue to function once he let his followers loose upon party organisations and government departments. In a sense, Mao had won control of the economy before conquering the political apparatus despite the grossly anti-Maoist tendencies so evident in economic affairs before 1966. Open disregard for his teachings by economic personnel was in many ways an advantage because potential opponents lacked any camouflage to protect them from elimination.

However, a statement Mao made in October 1966 asserted that over the years he had been kept uninformed about major policy matters. (LL, 71.) If this speech has been reported accurately, how could Mao from 1962 have laid his hand as firmly on the economy as the central committee claimed in 1966? One answer might be that Mao had to offer some explanation for his failure to intervene earlier when, according to his followers, anti-marxist errors were rampant. Denunciation of a conspiracy to hide the truth from him had a plausible ring in this context. An incontestable fact, however, is that Mao Tse-tung was not denied access to all secret government documents in the years before 1966. Edgar Snow's 1964 interview with Mao showed the Chairman had an intimate knowledge of international affairs and followed the pronouncements of foreign statesmen with meticulous care. (*New Republic,* 27 February, 1965.) Needless to say, information of this sort is not freely accessible to the Chinese population, and Snow's account implies regular and exhaustive briefings of Mao Tse-tung by the ministry of foreign affairs. If Mao could keep abreast of world diplomacy, could anyone have prevented him from finding out what was happening in the domestic field?

Another accusation made in the Cultural Revolution was that before 1966, Mao's proposals were constantly sabotaged by other communist leaders. (ID, 121-22.) One reasonable explanation for this apparent contradiction of the central committee's description of Mao's sweeping economic powers is that the adoption of more Maoist economic attitudes after 1962 commanded the support of most, if not all, of the central government and party leaders. Then perhaps they realised with consternation in 1966 that they had unwittingly put their own heads on the block by attacking compromises with Maoist principles. For these leaders had watered down Mao's economic strategy in their struggle to overcome the post-1958 agricultural slump and its effects on industrial development. At the end of 1965 or in early 1966, they saw the trap they were in and started to fight for survival. The alternative possibity is that their main disagreement with the Chairman was over tactics for the gigantic reform campaign which they, no less than Mao, believed should be carried out through a 'Cultural Revolution'. This latter interpretation can be substantiated from the official case against one of the first leaders to tumble, Peng Chen, denounced as the self-proclaimed 'uncrowned king of Peking'. (He was the capital's senior administrator.) The essence of the charge against him was his bid to prevent the campaign from falling into the hands of radical elements and his 'plot' to keep the Cultural Revolution under party control. Peng was opposed to the call to let the public clean up the communist ranks. (*ibid.,* 107 *et seq.*) Confusion over the Cultural Revolution is thus compounded by the shifts in economic policy before 1966 whose full implications were not apparent until the Cultural Revolution. They seem to have been inspired if not actually masterminded by Mao Tse-tung. Yet these changes were implemented by men later dismissed from office as Mao's adversaries. It is irritating to be unable to state precisely what was Mao's own handiwork and what was merely hailed subsequently by his supporters as orthodox Maoism. But the most important task is to search for the origins of those economic policies regarded as official Maoist doctrine after the Cultural Revolution.

The key moves before 1966 towards more Maoist policies were: to overhaul all areas of industrial management; to strengthen Mao's influence in the financial sector; and to bolster rural administration by sending students and cadres to work on the farms. These policies resembled those of the Great Leap Forward. But the reminders of the heady spirit of 1958 are somewhat misleading. The Great Leap Forward's inspiration had been Mao Tse-tung's gospel that the masses could propel China willy-nilly into an industrial revolution (though he appeared to find the means adopted to reach this goal less than satisfactory). Mao took at least four years to complete his preparations for the Cultural Revolution which indicates he understood the importance of building solid foundations before putting his development strategy to the ultimate test.

While relying on the 1958 concept of man's powers, Mao chose more refined techniques than the Great Leap Forward tactics for the experiment in growth economics to be conducted after 1966 under his supervision. Furthermore, he could no longer entrust direction of China's future to Liu Shao-chi — who had failed him three times — or to the other leaders whose ability to raise the calibre of the cadres and inspire the masses' enthusiasm was in doubt. Mao's assessment was accurate. Most of the top party figures lacked the political strength in their own departments and provinces to resist the Red Guards and, later, the Maoist worker groups. Sheer survival is the first test of a politician's ability to arouse overwhelming support from his constituents!

The industrial front was the main battlefield in Mao's view for victory in the Cultural Revolution and thus for the implementation of his policies. In laying down the basic principles for conducting the Cultural Revolution, the party central committee under Mao's guidance made the large and medium cities the principal target for reform. It later spoke of building a reformed communist party through absorbing 'above all' industrial workers into its ranks. (*ibid.*, 151, 191.) In 1968, one of Mao Tse-tung's best-known allies, Yao Wen-yuan, spoke of the tidal wave which followed the rallying of 'the mighty army of industrial workers' behind Mao Tse-tung. Yao suggested the Cultural Revolution had only been possible because 'a solid socialist position in the countryside' had already been established, implying the villages were a secondary target. (RF, 2/1968.)

The strategy for a Maoist take-over in industry was straight-forward. During the Great Leap Forward, cadres had been actively engaged in factory production, and the labour force shared responsi-bility for managing plants. (CC, 421, 509.) The system for creating 'worker-managers' and 'cadre-workers' had been termed the 'two participations, one reform and three co-ordinations'. This clumsy slogan meant: cadres involved in manual labour; worker participation in management; the reform of inefficient rules and regulations; and joint groups of managers, technicians and workers to superintend an enterprise's operations. (PD, 27 November, 1958.) The experiment was abandoned probably because of the lack of workers who could meet professional managers on anything like equal terms. (CC, 311.) While praising the concept of workers' involvement in management, one accountant pointed to the system's defects: 'Some enterprise and factory managements delegated too much power to the workshops, shifts and work teams, and weakened the centralised leadership of the factory managers.' The writer complained that worker activism, though a worthy goal, was no substitute for professional skills. (TKP, 1, 4, 6, 8 June, 1962.)

In the retreat from the Great Leap forward, authority reverted to the cadres. 'A director is the administrative leader accredited to an enterprise by the state. As such, he must take full responsibility for the administration of the undertaking. The director and the administrative organisation he heads are the commander and general headquarters for the unified organisation and direction of the administration.' The factory's party committee was given the right to discuss all major problems confronting the enterprise. The management was responsible for carrying out the 'collective decisions' of the committee, which, in turn, was ordered to pay special attention to the views of the masses because they were the group most familiar with production conditions. However, the workers' advisory function seemed more token than real, and the management and the party committee between them could insist on absolute obedience from their employees, (TKP, 20 November, 1961.)

The professionals had put the working man firmly in his place.

Mao tried to reverse the tide in March 1962 with his 'Constitution of the Anshan Iron and Steel Company'. This document instructed officials to become ordinary labourers and to offer workers a genuine place in running affairs. (NCNA, 19 September, 1969.) His recommendations ran into opposition from those who believed management could not be left to unlettered men. The main villain responsible for undermining Mao's attempts to promote the workers to positions of real authority was said to be Po I-po, the disgraced head of the state economic commission. Po was accused of defending professional managers as spiritually absorbed into the proletarian class. (Shanghai RS, 30 August, 1970.) Po's case is a good example of the difficulties of determining the truth when it comes to personalities condemned in the Cultural Revolution. His remarks were no more than a repetition of Premier Chou En-lai's 1956 observations on the same subject. (CC, 130.) The prime minister outlived the Red Guards; Po succumbed to their blows.

Nevertheless, Mao Tse-tung made some headway. The principle of total respect for orders from the central government, promulgated after the Great Leap Forward's failure, was modified considerably as an essay explicitly demonstrated in 1964. Man as the primary factor in production was recognised, but the role of discipline in creating factory efficiency was underlined. The question of how to combine centralised administration with a share in management for the masses was solved ingeniously. The author argued that many industrial officials failed to create effective administrations because cadres did not ensure everyone knew precisely what were their duties. The remedy was reform of factory regulations: 'We may then hand over a thousand and one problems to the masses for solution. This will free management from routine chores instead of involving them in red tape.' (RF, 12/1964.)

Another writer stressed the contribution to industrial efficiency of sensible rules setting out individual responsibilities. The masses, he reported, did not always respond to this approach because it seemed to add to their burdens. Management also often felt itself too busy with organising production to work on the assembly line in personal contact with the work force. Yet, said the author, exchange of functions between supervisors and employees was essential. The article stressed the importance of bringing the workers into the actual formulation of plans. It warned that if information and suggestions did not flow from the bottom upwards, the poor educational standards of the labour force would prevent them from understanding the factory's production targets and expansion programmes. The most important suggestion put forward by this article was for the practical training of the masses in management methods. 'In the process of drawing up and executing plans, the masses are to be mobilised to learn and popularise advanced experiences, and to undergo extensive training in basic skills.' The correct way to inspire the masses was not to work out targets behind closed office doors but to use the 'three-in-one' combination of cadres, technicians and workers in the planning process. (ER, 4/1965.)

Fushun colliery, one of China's biggest coal complexes with an annual output capacity of a million tons, announced in 1963 that twelve of its top twenty-five administrators were former miners, while some four thousand of its administrative personnel were staff promoted from the colliers' ranks.(NCNA, 14 October, 1963.) But recruitment of cadres from the proletariat was not sufficient for Mao Tse-tung. Even in 1962, the workers' congresses, an old institution for giving labour a voice in management, were lauded as of special importance in making the masses more willing to work harder and in supervising factory officials through 'mass criticism'. On paper the congresses had extensive rights: to scrutinise all data relating to the factory's performance, to demand the dismissal of unsatisfactory managers and to object to government directives. However, an exhaustive review of their history and functions hinted that the congresses were frequently replaced by meetings composed of all levels of management personnel. The minor supervisory staff apparently were invited to these discussions to give a spurious impression of rank-and-file participation. (RF, 2/1962.)

Another article defined the duties of workers' congresses in the same terms, adding: 'It is an important means by which all workers may participate in the enterprise's management.' The congresses could help to protect the workers' rights to object to policies which were politically incorrect and to denounce officials. They could assist the masses 'to participate in management of production, to combine mass participation with specialised management; to get workers to discuss output plans, key production problems and foster technical innovations ... to get the workers to take part in economic management ... in business accounting'. But this writer believed modern production was too complicated to be left to the ordinary worker. The party committee in the factory should gather employees' ideas and turn them into policy. However, the factory management could not abdicate its obligation to run business smoothly. At the same time, the writer described several techniques for bringing the workers into administration:

from allowing them control over the activities of the basic production unit to direct consultation with management. The workers' congress, the author stated, was only one means of consulting the masses. The long-term aim, however, was to end the division between masters and men: 'Through participation in management, the workers will be tempered, acquiring knowledge not only of production techniques but raising their class consciousness, improving their capacity for management, and learning how to run and superintend operations. In this way, the proletariat will be able to play a bigger part as masters of socialist construction, the life of the state and the administration of industry.' (PD, 23 November, 1964.)

The ideological inspiration for the inclusion of workers in industrial administration was plain from a number of articles which drew heavily on Mao Tse-tung's philosophy. The effect of material conditions — plant, tools, raw materials and machinery — was not disregarded. Yet one author stated: 'No matter how developed science and technology, no matter how advanced and complex the equipment of industrial units, the maximum development of the human factor must always be the precondition for a constant improvement of technical equipment and the fullest development of machinery's capacity ... the primary force for expanding production.' The writer insisted that 'unless the workers are the real masters not the slaves of modern technology', China's economy would slip back along the road to capitalism followed by the Soviet Union. The article stressed the Maoist concept of the human spirit as the biggest contribution to economic progress. (ER, 12/1964.)

Planning problems also came into this ideological approach to industrial management. The state set only the broad targets for an enterprise; the factory filled in the details for itself. A readiness among the labour force to strain after high efficiency and output could not be created by government decree but had to be stimulated by encouraging workers to regard as their own responsibility production targets initiated and approved by the masses. (*ibid.*, 7/1964.) A different aspect of the value of workers' enthusiasm for production was shown in a discussion of how to keep in perspective local and national needs when funds and supplies were scarce. The author believed the masses had a creative talent which could help to fill the gaps created by shortages of various kinds. (*ibid.*, 16/1964.)

Industrial management in a larger sense was also tackled in the years leading up to the Cultural Revolution. Co-ordination and emulation were fostered. A confectionery plant in Shanghai had guarded jealously its most popular recipe for twenty years, until the workers decided to teach it to any rival plants who wanted it. In Sian and Nanking, manufacture of bedding was stated in 1964 to have reached the standard of the most famous Shanghai brand. The movement to learn from advanced enterprises was said to have begun in 1958 but to have reached wide-scale proportions in 1964, with 30,000 people sent to learn Shanghai's manufacturing secrets and 200,000 individuals involved in a technical improvement campaign in Liaoning province alone. The main tool for raising technical standards was a 'three-in-one' combination, the usual team of cadres, technicians and workers. (*Peking Review*, 21/1964.) 'Noted specialists and experts brought out their "secrets" and opened their "treasure houses" for you to take anything you liked. Some old workers also brought out their cherished notebooks full of the practical lessons they had acquired over decades. Some of these were "heirlooms" obtained from master craftsmen during their apprenticeships.' This passage brings out the flavour of the campaign; the difficulties of promoting regard for national instead of local interests; and the 'mediæval' nature of an economy which guarded 'secret' techniques from one generation of artisans to the next. Advanced areas such as Shanghai had the most to offer but, to its surprise, Honan province taught the city how to solve a critical problem in making synthetic textiles. (PD, 24 February, 1964.)

Reports were published of the success of 'three-in-one' combinations in conquering serious 'contradictions' in production. An interesting example was a factory where quality had to be improved which meant reducing the working speed of the machines and thus total output. The management decided to consult the masses and learn from other plants. It experimented with its looms until the conflict between quantity and quality was resolved. A fascinating aspect of this account was the apparent inability of both managerial and technical cadres to handle the machinery in their plant. They had to learn how looms worked. (RF, 16/1964.) If such ignorance of technical matters were general in Chinese industry, Mao's demand that administrators and 'technicians' participate in manual labour was based on a genuine economic need. The implication was that cadres had been recruited not for their technical competence on the shop floor but for other qualities, either for administrative or for technical ability of a purely academic kind. Obviously, management's efficiency would rise if the administrative and technical personnel responsible for output had some idea of the nature and capacity of their equipment.

In discussing a 1957 central committee edict that officials should take part in production, the *People's Daily* referred to the usefulness of this experience in helping management to uncover obstacles and hinted that cadres were also acquiring technical skills. (22 September, 1964.) A major article on the same topic explained the merits of officials working as manual labourers partly in political terms, such as maintaining contact with the masses, learning their troubles, explaining party policy to the workers. But economic factors too were listed. Through manual labour, cadres could earn their salaries from production instead of being maintained out of tax revenues. The sight of cadres soiling their hands would be an inspiration to the masses. The article also stated: 'Functionaries at the basic level will know more about how production is accomplished. Those who do not have much knowledge of productive techniques . . . will learn and gain experience.' (NCNA, 10 July, 1963.) One author roundly declared that workers (and peasants) knew most about production and so the cadres should take the masses as their teachers. (*Che-hsueh Yen-chiu*, 5/1963.) The evidence suggests that the drive to integrate management and workers had a validity derived from the ignorance (or purely theoretical knowledge) of a factory's workings among leading industrial cadres.

Economic considerations were only part of the story nevertheless. Even where technical staff were dedicated and of high calibre, manual labour was prescribed to prevent management from becoming arrogant, corrupt, building lavish facilities for itself or indulging in such bourgeois recreations as parties and dancing. (ER, 4/1966.) Those familiar with Mao Tse-tung's analysis of social classes also feared the mentality left behind by the old régime. One commentator argued: 'Among the working class, state officials and industrial workers, degenerate or bourgeois elements may very well emerge.' While all were in danger of ideological corruption, the manual labourer was obviously less likely to absorb bourgeois ideas than the intellecutal with his better-paid job and higher standard of living. (*Hsin Chien-she*, 11/1963.)

Self-reliance allied to mutual co-operation was another slogan circulated during this period. Working only in the interests of a department or enterprise instead of for the nation came under fire. 'Worshipping foreign countries especially the United States' and excessive respect for technical conventions were vigorously refuted. The 1958 spirit of 'daring' in the field of technical advances was hailed, and China ordered to 'rely on our own efforts for salvation'. (RF, 19/1964.)

The nation was forced to consider the implications of its large number of small factories, many equipped with antique or primitive machines. They had to overcome this defect through their own innovations and modifying their own machinery. The country was told even modern enterprises needed to seek constant improvements in their technical efficiency by redesigning and adjusting their plant. Heavy capital equipment has a long life, the argument went, and machinery would soon become obsolete unless constantly improved. (*ibid.*, 7-8/1964.)

One economist reminded his readers of the communists' revolutionary tradition of relying on themselves and of Mao's belief in the 'hard work and the wisdom of our people'. Self-reliance meant arousing the idealism of the work force and 'full utilisation of all available resources within the country'. He added: 'The huge amount of capital needed for economic development can never be obtained from other countries through obtaining slavish loans at the expense of our sovereignty and independence. Nor can it be obtained through establishing colonies ... exploiting the labouring people of other countries in the imperialist style. Nor can it be obtained through wars of aggression and the indemnities demanded from defeated nations.' He saw only one solution: 'We can only rely on the people of the whole country to increase production and practise economy.' Careful state-planning would permit the efficient allocation of investment funds, the exploitation of China's vast natural wealth and of its huge market. Foreign methods should be studied but not copied blindly. (ER, 1/1965.) This was pure Mao.

Another article hinted that if foreign nations had found the resources to transform their backward economies, China could do likewise. The article attacked the 'passive' attitude of waiting for state assistance and regarding the funds allocated by the government as imposing a ceiling on production. An enterprise should exert itself to raise output from its own resources. The model Tachai peasants and Taching oilfield were quoted as examples of what workers could achieve through their own ingenuity. (*ibid.*, 7/1965.) (Both places were hailed constantly as paragons of self-generated growth.) Emulation drives and the careful study of advanced industrial units both domestic and foreign would 'raise quality, increase output, reduce inputs of raw and semi-processed materials, improve labour productivity and accomplish the tasks of increasing production and practising economy'. (*Chung-kuo Ching-kung-yeh*, 1/1965.) While the inventive talents of the workers were praised, an imaginative study outlined the obstacles to using home-made techniques in modern scientific undertakings. The author struck a neat balance between the value of drawing on all sources of technological expertise and the importance of continuing with China's own basic research. (NCNA, 11 May, 1963; *Hsin Chien-she*, 1-2/1966.)

During the Cultural Revolution Mao Tse-tung drew together the threads of these changes in industrial management in his description of how factories should be 'revolutionised' by 'establishing a three-in-one revolutionary committee ... changing irrational rules and regulations and sending office workers to the workshop'. (ID, 42-43.) A major policy editorial repeated Mao's command: 'The working class must exercise leadership in everything.' It called on engineering and technical personnel to take part in productive labour. The editorial denounced those who relied on specialists for progress, put material incentives or profits in command and neglected politics for production. Planning was stressed, together with the creation of new plants and the simultaneous exploitation of the potential of existing factories. Self-reliance, a mass movement for technical innovations and workers' participation in management were to be made standard practices. (PD, 21 February, 1969.) The editorial amounted to a summary of trends visible in China's industry well before the Cultural Revolution. The major innovation after 1966 was the installation of the 'three-in-one' combination — workers, 'revolutionary intellectuals and revolutionary cadres' — as the formal source of power in the enterprise to replace the former uneasy compromises for breaking down divisions between workers and administrators. (*ibid.*, 22 January, 1967.)

The financial world was the second target for reform. The reason for including this sector among the economic strongholds to be stormed in advance of 1966 was simple. Financial and accounting personnel (including bank staff) had a stranglehold on the economy. Their powers were virtually unlimited in checking accounts, verifying reports, examining production plans and controlling flows of money, materials, equipment and commodities. These employees were Peking's eyes and ears across the whole of China. If the financial cadres obeyed the 1962 code of conduct which defined their duties, no enterprise could violate instructions from the central authorities. (*ibid.*, 9 January, 1963.) The finance branches, for all their failings so roundly denounced in the press, seem to have been under steady pressure to take a broad view of their functions and make the 'chessboard' concept more than an empty slogan. Tax officials, for example, were told in 1962 to assist industrial and agricultural enterprises not only to strengthen financial management but also to solve production problems. Revenue officers were to avoid actual engagement in production but they should use their experience of financial trouble-shooting and their wide contacts with enterprises of all types to assist the communes and the factories under them. Tax officials were in touch with a great variety of different enterprises while tax receipts were a good index of how development was progressing. The fiscal authorities were thus ideally placed to contribute to the good management of the local economies. (TKP, 31 January, 1962.)

A later article gave more explicit instructions to financial workers: 'Cadres appointed . . . to enterprises must co-operate in strengthening their financial management and accounting . . . and solve concrete problems impeding production, supply and marketing.' (*ibid.,* 14 February, 1964.) But the main tool for vetting economic activities was the banks: 'The bank is a key instrument of supervision and one of the vital "meters" ' for monitoring economic activities and conditions. The banks controlled loans and advances to units under the state plan; checked applications for additional funds when enterprises ran into unexpected difficulties; scrutinised wage payments; and ensured enterprises' surplus funds were deposited in their vaults. Some eighty per cent of all transactions in 1963 were settled through the banking system. The banks also issued currency and performed the normal duties of banking institutions. But apart from their role as financial watchdogs, the banks were called on to intervene in management, to improve efficiency, to ensure co-ordination between enterprises, and to help to clear stocks. (RF, 1/1964.)

The attitude expected by Mao Tse-tung from such a powerful institution was explored in a review of the Agricultural Bank of China during 1964 (its first year of activity). The bank felt itself duty-bound to provide practical assistance to the peasants, with political motivation in the forefront of its work. Bank staff were to live under the same conditions as the peasants. They were to do their stint of manual labour and put themselves in the hands of the masses for investigation and criticism. Administration was streamlined as far as possible. Mao Thought was placed specifically in command of all the bank's activities. (*Nung-tsun Chin-jung,* 4-5/1965.) A branch of the bank in Kweichow province reported what these principles meant in practice. An oil press started in 1958 'not long afterwards ceased to operate for a variety of reasons' – the austerity campaign after the Great Leap Forward in all

189

probability. In 1962, the local credit co-operative suggested reopening the works but the building was in a poor state of repair and essential equipment was missing. The bank officials helped the peasants to gather timber to rebuild the plant. In 1964, when raw materials were in short supply, officials from the rural credit co-operative arranged a contract with a government department to start supplies moving again. (*ibid.*, 10/1965.)

In the industrial field, a similar spirit was supposed to prevail. A Kwangtung province bank branch helped to save a rope factory from losses when it was seeking new sources of raw materials after its old suppliers could no longer meet its needs. Bank officials went into an iron and steel factory in Canton city and took part in production before estimating what credit the plant needed to double its production. The idea that bank staff should confine themselves solely to considering loan facilities instead of getting together with a factory to solve production difficulties was attacked. Scrupulous regard for regulations instead of positive efforts to foster expansion of local industrial activities was condemned. Branches of the central bank — the People's Bank — were instructed to overhaul their regulations. (*Chung-kuo Chin-jung*, 9/1965.)

In December 1965, the eve of the Cultural Revolution, the People's Bank and the Agricultural Bank, perhaps like financiers everywhere with a keen nose for what was in the wind, held a joint conference. This meeting of branch directors claimed that in 1965: 'The work of the banks was further orientated towards production, the rural areas and the masses, and played a significant role in supporting the upsurge of industrial and agricultural production as well as in organising the economic life of the people.' The principle was laid down: 'Banks must operate in the interests of the revolution, put politics to the fore, direct themselves to the rural areas, support the movements to increase production and practise economy, do a good job of controlling stocks, settlement of accounts and other banking activities to support socialist construction and promote a sustained upsurge in industrial and farm output.' The manager of an agricultural machinery works lauded the new attitude of bank officials in his area. They had dropped their former practices of looking for irregularities and exercising strict financial control. Instead, the bank personnel became honorary members of the factory helping to raise the turnover of capital, rationalise inventories and showing the factory how to find the cash to buy new equipment. (*ibid.*, 1 & 2/1966.) The bankers put their house in order before the Red Guards broke upon the scene, which explains why it is difficult to uncover any serious examples of attacks on bank practices or dismissals of leading officials in the banking world during the Cultural Revolution.

The commercial workers were not overlooked. Their role was of paramount importance: 'Between industry and agriculture, production and consumption, the circulation of commodities is a vital bridge.' These personnel were instructed to assist in drawing up and adjusting state plans and to help the expansion of production as well as to carry out their ordinary commercial operations. Morale was not high in the profession: 'Some parents say, "After sending you to school for so many years, you still have to deal in sauce, oil and vinegar".' Young commercial workers were commanded to repudiate this sort of slur. The commercial front was told to devise new methods of running the national distribution system and to simplify irrational links between producers and consumers. Policies had to be discussed with the masses. The commercial sector was not to make profits the sole criterion of success. It was to encourage mutual co-operation between all branches of the economy, cut costs, supply goods and services useful to the masses and avoid arrogance. (*Worker's Daily*, 16, 17 February, 9, 13 March, 1965.)

Stores also had to be ready to experiment, transferring goods from city to country when sales in the urban areas were slow, and to take account of seasonal factors affecting demand. (ER, 7/1965.) In the villages, the commercial departments were responsible for assisting the development of spare-time production, the elimination of capitalist tendencies at country fairs, and for the establishment of price levels most suited to boosting output. Staff were to move to the communes despite the distaste of some workers for rural life and the fear that it was unprofitable. (*ibid.*, 12/1965.) Although the seasonal nature of farming made it difficult to put peasants into the management of trade and financial departments, peasants and workers had been taken on as financial and commercial staff on a part-time basis since 1963. (*Hsin Chien-she*, 1-2/1966.)

On the whole, while the trade organisations were not so well fortified as the banks against the upheavals of the Cultural Revolution, considerable steps had been taken to put Mao's philosophy in charge of commerce. The campaign to learn from the People's Liberation Army (which filled acres of newsprint in 1964) was an important part of the preparations for the Cultural Revolution. Since its objectives were

191

mainly political, it can be ignored here. Significantly, however, in 1963 'the party and government sent a large number of military cadres to work in basic-level commercial departments'. (PD, 20 February, 1964.) Mao Tse-tung was taking no chances on a total breakdown of supplies during the political storm which was brewing.

Mao Tse-tung's preparations in the financial and commercial fields were well rewarded, though rural commerce failed to reform itself sufficiently. (See PD, 18 January, 1969, for instance.) The trade and finance departments were 'among the first' in the country to proclaim their allegiance to Mao Tse-tung after the Cultural Revolution began, and they very quickly set up the 'three-in-one' combinations he favoured. (NCNA, 23 January, 1967.) When his opponents began to fight back on the economic front, courting popularity through bribing workers with higher wages or creating confusion by financing radicals to travel around China, Mao received vital intelligence with minimum delay. Some factory managers tried to defend their authority against 'revolutionary rebels' with 'financial baits to lure large numbers of workers . . . to leave their production posts. As a result, production was seriously affected'. In other cases, workers were eager to accept increased wages and bonuses, believed officials were shrewd managers and suspected the 'revolutionary rebels' of seizing power in Mao's name to get good jobs for themselves. (NCNA, 23 January, 1967.) The reaction of local and central authorities to attempts to bribe workers to forget the Cultural Revolution seemed surprisingly fast. The probable explanation for the speed with which the Maoists were able to crush 'economism' is that the banks and other finance departments, after putting themselves on a 'proletarian' basis before 1966 and then pledging loyalty to Mao Tse-tung, did their duty and supplied information against factories making excessive or abnormal payments to their workers.

The third prong of Mao's pre-1966 strategy was to shift large numbers of young students and cadres to the countryside. This movement was a two-sided campaign. Intellectuals and cadres were sent directly to engage in manual labour; at the same time, a bid was made to combine education with production in the schools. The motives behind the campaign to 'rusticate' intellectuals — anyone with a secondary education or better — were as much practical as ideological. Prime Minister Chou En-lai revealed in 1957 that previously those who had completed secondary school courses had gone automatically to institutes of higher education. He pointed out this situation could not continue once secondary education became universal. Yet the expectation of passing from a secondary school to a university or an equivalent establishment as a matter of course had been established. Chou felt compelled to state: 'We must explain very clearly to all students that our country has a bright future only because the working people have become the masters, that labour is the most glorious thing in our country and it is the workers and peasants who have the best future. Young persons and students should regard participation in industrial and agricultural production as the greatest of honours.' In the following years, 'half-work, half-study' schools were praised on three grounds. Firstly, the system reduced the costs of education. Secondly, working while still at school ensured students did not become intellectuals who disdained labour. Thirdly, China was preparing for the day when large numbers of people would have to move out of traditional occupations as a result of economic progress. To make such transfers possible, young people needed an all-round education. (CC, 311-12, 439, 444-45.) It is worth noting that 'half-work, half-study' schools were still regarded in 1970 as an important way of cutting educational costs. (Shansi RS, 17 October, 1970.)

Rural assignments and production work in the schools proved unpopular. As early as 1955, a young cadre who first left the city for the countryside in 1951 and had taken part in the land reform campaign — surely a joyful experience for a youthful idealist — complained he was suffering 'a living punishment', condemned to poor food, hard work and low cultural levels. (*Chung-kuo Ching-nien*, 20/1955.) A similar plaintive appeal came from a young man who watched with envy his fellow-students who remained in the cities or went to university instead of working all day with a hoe. (*ibid.*, 15/1960.) In 1957, over a million students were sent to work on the farms from just four provinces plus Peking. (*Chiao Shih Pao*, 13 August, 1957.)

The usefulness of these recruits to the peasantry was doubtful. A survey in Liaoning province showed most of those who had been sent from the city to work in one commune practised 'passive resistance', refusing to learn from the villagers. Some thirty-five per cent were reported to be unable to do general farm work, while only ten per cent could be termed skilled. (*Chung-kuo Ching-nien Pao*, 7 June, 1962.) After the failure of the Great Leap Forward, the movements to combine labour and study and to send intellectuals to the countryside abated. But by 1963, a bourgeois trend among the young was appearing once more. One report stated children found it hard to believe their elders' stories about past miseries compared with present joys and were jealous of their more affluent schoolmates. (*Southern Daily*, 4 July, 1963.) The failure to provide labour assignments for students over the previous two years was criticised. (KMD, 27 June, 1963.)

The situation for cadres was little different. Premier Chou, reporting on the Great Leap Forward, observed: 'Vast numbers of cadres have corrected ways of thinking and working which estrange them from the masses in varying degrees, and have overcome the bureaucratic, lifeless, spendthrift, haughty and finicky airs with which they were infected in the old society and now appear as ordinary labourers among the masses. Over a million cadres of state organs from the county level up have been sent to the countryside, to factories and mines to take part in manual labour and administrative work in basic units.' Chou had earlier remarked that the sight of cadres with soil on their hands made the peasants more willing to work. (CC, 509, 520.) This was an economic consideration. His reference to cadres becoming rural administrators was an indication of the need to improve lower-echelon management. But on the whole, the prime minister made manual labour sound like a *rite de passage,* an initiation ceremony which officials underwent to qualify as genuine revolutionaries.

The same impression is given about young intellectuals who, with their superior education, would eventually take over leadership positions. The new generation was described as having 'some cultural knowledge and class consciousness, yet the bulk of them have not suffered or personally witnessed the oppression and exploitation from which the masses formerly suffered at the hands of imperialists, landlords and capitalists'. (RF, 1/1964.) The role of manual labour seems to have assumed part of the function of the old imperial civil service examination, which had been a gruelling test of physical stamina as well as of mental ability for an ambitious youth. 'As to young comrades, many have grown up in a peaceful environment . . . They do not know what is class oppression or exploitation . . . Both young and old cadres . . . should go to the basic-level units for tempering. All cadres who have not gone through tempering at the basic level should pass this barrier successfully.' (*ibid.,* 17-18/1964.) This passage conveys the impression of officials being ritually ordained by society for their posts.

The movement of youngsters and officials to the villages had most significance in the economic realm. The marxist believes those who do not produce but merely administer are parasites. China, anyway, was keen to minimise administrative costs. These two factors justified the 'down to the country' campaign. But the transfer of large numbers to the countryside had another important consequence. Rural incomes were openly admitted to be lower than those in urban areas on several occasions. (For example, *Worker's Daily*, 3 August, 1961.) By removing the groups able to command the highest salaries from the cities (the educated class) consumption fell as officials and students were forced on to rural living standards. But the expected economic dividends were more direct, especially in the case of students. 'Educated youths . . . with their scientific and cultural education can quickly learn how to operate modern farm machines and implements, to apply chemical fertilisers and pesticides and manage modern farming equipment. Together with the veteran peasants they will become a powerful force in such fields as scientific experiments in agriculture.' (*Peking Review*, 29/1965.)

Some 40 million educated youths were estimated to be employed in the villages by 1963 when the peasant population was around 500 million. A review of the role of these youngsters emphasised their contribution to the modernisation of the countryside and to ending such traditions as 'farmers never go to school; scholars never farm'. (*Chung-kuo Ching-nien*, 23/1963.) Cadres were able to resist the rural draft to some extent. They had other duties to attend to, and the state had to devise special arrangements to free officials for manual labour. Szechwan province worked out a scheme to alternate office with physical work. It confessed: 'The broad masses of the cadres have not understood sufficiently the great revolutionary significance of this labour system. Most enterprises have still not made this system a regular practice.' (RF, 2/1965.) (This remark applied both to farm labour and to cadre participation in industrial production.) Cadres from all levels of the administration were said to have visited farms to investigate conditions and to offer moral support to the peasants rather than to work on the crops. (*Peking Review*, 16/1966.)

For all the political and social factors involved in transferring intellectuals and officials to the countryside, the potential gains were enormous from an educated élite sent to the villages to break the stifling grip of peasant conservatism. One backward village had a pond whose sediment could have been used with great advantage for cultivation. The water was regarded as 'sacred' by the local population, and a keen struggle took place over draining the pond to turn it into a field. The men laughed at the idea of women competing with them in the fields. Illiterate peasant girls had to take on the job of experimenting with new seeds, chemical fertilisers and pesticides, (*Shi-shih Shou-tse*, 5/1965.) The difference which even one person with a rudimentary education would have made in shortening their labours needs no elaboration.

The difficulty with introducing new agricultural techniques is that their suitability for local conditions has to be tested before widespread application. An effort was made to get cadres to study the experiences of advanced communes and then apply the lessons to other districts to overcome this problem. (PD, 19 March, 1964.) Only after the quality of the tractor stations' work was raised did the peasants respond positively to the idea of mechanisation. Management of farm equipment was difficult because of slipshod planning at the higher levels. Tractor station personnel were supposed to create contingents of rural technicians. How effectively this task was undertaken is hard to estimate, but the young, educated, tractor mechanics disliked the dirty and tiring conditions under which they worked. (*Chung-kuo Nung-pao*, 11/1963.) Only when officials and masses united solidly were impressive results achieved. Hence, it was reported: 'As the authorities monopolise affairs, some of the areas, cadres and masses do not see powered drainage and irrigation projects from which they are to benefit as their own business and thus fail to raise the necessary funds with any enthusiasm.' (*ibid.*, 8/1964.) One farm related how people who had returned from overseas – inevitably with broader horizons – supported agricultural experiments on inferior land. Local peasants, however, argued: 'It is simply a waste of money and energy to plant rice on such poor soil.' (*Chiao-wu Pao*, 1/1965.) The answer to this situation had been offered some years earlier: the linking of peasant wisdom to the skills of modern agronomists. (RF, 20/1962.) Clearly, by integrating the villager into the research team, he would be able to escape the bonds of custom through seeing whether his grandfather's techniques were more effective than those of the educated youngsters sent to help him.

The Cultural Revolution took the drive to get intellectuals and cadres on to the land further than ever before. The former practice of graduates walking straight into official positions after obtaining their degrees was condemned. They were first to engage in manual labour and obtain 'qualification certificates' from the peasants and workers before beginning their professional careers. (PD, 22 July, 1968.) One published collection of young people's experiences in rural labour

(*Take the Road of Integrating with the Workers, Peasants and Soldiers*) painted a somewhat mixed picture of commune life. They were told manual work would transform them into worthy heirs of Mao's revolution. They were supposed to spurn the idea of going to the countryside as ordinary labourers for a limited period and then becoming cadres. (Nevertheless, in Anhwei province, rusticated students and cadres were recruited in 1970 by the thousand for posts throughout the provincial hierarchy. RS, 27 October, 1970.) The collapse of initial enthusiasm among starry-eyed volunteers for rural assignments was depicted frankly. One group of students at first achieved good results from farming experiments conducted with the peasants' aid. They later became arrogant, rejected local advice and dejectedly watched their latest project fail. One point which came through was: 'Physical exertion was not enough in the battle against nature; we had also to use our brains.' But after 1966, brains were regarded as a collective asset and not the exclusive property of the educated.

Some students found themselves despised as failures who could not make a career in the cities. One girl was laughed at because she did not realise a ewe will only suckle her own lamb. The ignorance of peasants was equally astonishing. A production brigade had no-one who knew how to castrate animals. 'Every year a good deal of money had to be spent to get people from other villages to do the work.' A hint emerged that cadres and students sent to communes were not always welcomed with zest. This was not surprising, for the uninvited recruits had to be maintained by the commune. Even allowing for the work point system, by which output governed wages, the villages could not let the newcomers rot in dire penury whether or not they earned their keep through solid contributions to output. (*Take the Road of Integrating with the Workers, Peasants and Soldiers,* 2-3, 6-9, 12, 23-24, 28, 53-54, 79, 89-91.) Mao Tse-tung's interest in this campaign to inject an educated element into the stagnant world of the Chinese peasantry was displayed in his 1968 command: 'It is very necessary for educated young people to go to the countryside to be re-educated by the poor and lower-middle peasants ... Comrades throughout the countryside should welcome them.' (PD, 12 December, 1968.) The educational process, hopefully, was not completely one-sided.

On the school front, the Cultural Revolution began with the statement: 'A most important task is to transform the old educational system ... In every kind of school we must apply thoroughly the

197

policy advanced by Comrade Mao Tse-tung of ... education being combined with productive labour.' (ID, 148.) The Maoists refused to let schools carry out their own reforms; they had to place themselves under the supervision of workers and soldiers. (RF, 2/1968.) The 'college and secondary students who started work some time ago' were to be reformed to persuade them 'to integrate themselves with the peasants and workers'. Interestingly, adoption of proletarian habits was not the only test for a Maoist intellectual. Laurels could be won for 'inventions and innovations'. (RF, 3/1968.) This compromise between revolutionary zeal and the desire to encourage technical progress echoed an order issued at the start of the Cultural Revolution: 'Special care should be taken of those scientists ... who have made contributions.' (ID, 151.) However, Mao watered down the status of the pure intellectual. While universities were still essential – 'here I refer mainly to the colleges of science and engineering' – 'students should be selected from among workers and peasants with practical experience and they should return to production after a few years' study'. (PD, 22 July, 1968.)

Mao Tse-tung's edict on cadres was equally direct: 'Sending the cadres to do manual work gives them an excellent opportunity to study once again. This should be done by all cadres except those who are too old, weak, ill or disabled. Those who are now working as cadres also should go in groups to do manual work.' (*ibid.*, 5 October, 1968.) While the idea that farm labour was a punishment was denounced several times, work in the countryside was deemed most suitable for 'good people who committed the errors characteristic of the capitalist-roaders in power'. (ID, 54.) To ensure the cadres as a class were remoulded through labour, special 'May 7' schools were established throughout China to allow officials to combine agricultural work with political study. These schools were not attractive to all prospective students. Urban cadres insisted they had nothing to do with farming and would prefer to work in factories. (PD, 18 August, 1969.) Some officials argued: 'Those retained in the departments are one grade higher, while those sent to cadre schools are one grade lower.'

Manual labour in the countryside aimed at ending the division between the public and administrators. (*ibid.*, 17 October, 1969.) The schools were operated as separate units, largely isolated from the rest of the community. But peasants were brought in to share the running of the schools, and cadres went out to learn about life through working in communes. (*ibid.*, 27 October, 1969.) In a sense the cadre schools, by operating as special institutions, wasted much of the value of sending trained administrators to the countryside. However, some officials were transferred directly to agricultural units. Here they opposed such erroneous political trends as encouraging fresh production efforts from the peasants by promises of material reward. Cadres were often assigned to backward production teams and expected to play a significant part in accelerating rural development through their administrative talents. Yet, many officials resented the pressure to undertake manual labour and regarded it as a mark of their superiors' disfavour. Frequently they claimed the volume of work prevented them leaving their offices for the fields. The peasants, too, felt uneasy. They were intimidated by the important personages sent from government offices to the villages. The rural population complained of its inability to carry out the party's instructions to remould the thinking of these educated and accomplished officials. (Hupeh RS, 5 October, 1970; Anhwei RS, 10 April, 1970; Peking RS, 6 October, 1970; PD, 12 April, 1970.)

Mao's suspicions about the cadres' outlook on life seemed justified from these reports. What China clearly needed, and Mao wanted, was an integration of peasants and officials into a united force for development. To achieve this goal, cadres would have to get mud on their boots, and peasants cease to be ashamed of their poor educational standards and lack of sophistication. If the two groups could have established a working relationship in which the talents of both were harnessed to rural progress, conservatism, reluctance to change age-old techniques and the fear of exploiting modern science to master nature might have disappeared long ago.

While Mao Tse-tung put destruction before construction in his formula for social change, he paid scant attention to his own rule. The preparations for 1966 were elaborate. The sectors of the economy which determined the stability of industry and agriculture were brought closely into line with Mao's development philosophy well before he struck down all who doubted the wisdom or necessity of his economic prescriptions. Mao Tse-tung may not have been able to control every twist and turn of the power struggle from the summer of 1966. Yet he pulled off a remarkable feat in guiding events sufficiently to ensure the economic policies adopted during the Cultural Revolution avoided any compromise with his personal development programme. He did not have to sacrifice what he regarded as the catalysts for growth — especially self-sacrifice and ceaseless physical labour with no promise of material reward — to guarantee his triumph in the Cultural Revolution.

NO CONSTRUCTION WITHOUT DESTRUCTION

In bringing to a logical conclusion the policies put forward so carefully over the four years before 1966, Mao showed a political adroitness which would be hard to match. Premier Chou En-lai stated the cost of the Cultural Revolution had been calculated in advance and found reasonable. (NCNA, 10 October, 1967.) The evidence available casts no doubt on Chou's claim. And if the final result of the Cultural Revolution were to prove the permanent adoption of Mao Tse-tung's economic strategy, blending idealism and hard-headed analysis of the barriers to progress, then Mao's upheaval may be counted by China's future historians a cheap price to have paid for prosperity.

Chapter Nine

'Taught by Mistakes and Setbacks'

After recapturing the power to mould China's economy to his will, Mao Tse-tung began the arduous struggle to fashion solid programmes out of his abstract ideas. The first step towards translating Mao's economic philosophy from vague slogans into a coherent policy came on 30 September, 1969, the eve of the twentieth anniversary of the People's Republic. The new pattern for the nation's development was set out in 'The Road to China's Socialist Industrialisation'. (RF, 10/1969.) This essay began with a declaration of loyalty to the principles summed up in Mao Tse-tung's major economic works written in 1956 and 1957 — 'On Ten Major Relationships' and 'On the Correct Handling of Contradictions among the People'. Just under eighteen months later, the Chinese economy had chalked up a host of new production records. The Japanese foreign ministry in its review of the Chinese economy's performance during 1970 declared national income (gross national product) had reached US$75,000 million, a rise of ten per cent over the previous year. Cereal production was estimated to have risen by five to ten per cent, with 1970's industrial expansion at between fifteen and twenty per cent. (*Sankei,* Tokyo, 28 February, 1971.) Peking reported that total agricultural and industrial output in 1971 rose by ten per cent over the previous year; industrial production expanded by ten per cent in the same period; while the 1971 grain harvest totalled 246 million tons. This meant the grain harvest was only two and a half per cent above the figure given by Premier Chou En-lai to Edgar Snow in December 1970 for that year's grain output. On the basis of the Chinese figures, the farm sector as a whole grew by ten per cent in 1971. (NCNA, 31 December, 1971; PD, 1 January, 1972; *New Republic,* 27 March, 1971.) The 1970 momentum of development was thus sustained over the following twelve months. The question here is how far this burst of prosperity reflected the impact of Mao Tse-tung's development strategy and hence constituted a valid test of its efficiency.

The announcement of a Maoist economic programme in 1969 followed by a boom in 1970 and 1971 could be dismissed as mere coincidence unless China demonstrated that Mao's economic theories were implemented — and not given mere lip service — and in fact had produced these impressive results.

The 1969 essay began with a discussion of self-reliance as the means to achieve prosperity — mobilising the 'diligent labour and wisdom' of the people, 'full and planned use of all natural resources', moving forward at the greatest speed but at the lowest cost. To learn from abroad was permissible but straight imitation of foreign technology was not. 'Politics in command' was to be an absolute law. To forget ideology and 'one-sidedly stress material, machines and mechanisation' would mean, stated the essay, that the gains from progress would fall into the hands of a minority — the bourgeoisie — instead of the whole nation. This Maoist programme was summarised as: 'With heavy industry taking the lead, both industry and agriculture and both light and heavy industry are to develop simultaneously. Through centralised leadership, overall planning and division of work, both central and local industries are to be expanded at the same time and both foreign and indigenous production techniques employed together.' Officials united with the masses through manual labour were to reform rules and regulations and constantly to seek new ideas.

The correct road for the expansion of heavy industry was quoted (without acknowledgement) from Mao's 'On the Correct Handling of Contradictions'. Light industry and farming would have to expand first to satisfy the people's needs and raise the capital needed by the heavy sector. Only a prosperous agriculture could offer heavy industry outlets for its products. Agriculture and the peasants obtained the right to demand maximum support from all other branches of the economy. The essay rejected the idea that giving the countryside priority would prove unprofitable for the factories. Not only were large enterprises to aid the peasants, every county was instructed to set up an industrial network for the manufacture and repair of farm equipment. As a precaution against war (armed clashes had occurred on a serious scale along the Sino-Soviet border in spring 1969) each region, province and city should establish an independent industrial system. Local areas were to devise means of following suit, although mutual co-operation should not be forgotten. In short, a decentralised economy, built on agriculture and light industry, supported by a network of rural industries, was to act as the springboard for the leap towards a modern, advanced and balanced manufacturing economy.

After the Cultural Revolution, the country declared its adoration for Mao: 'As the nine planets revolve around the sun, so do the hearts of the people of all nationalities around the Red Sun, which is Chairman Mao and Mao Tse-tung Thought.' (Sinkiang RS, 16 January, 1971.) The Cultural Revolution gave Mao political power without which, he said, 'all is lost'. (*Liberation Army Daily*, 11 August, 1967.) It also achieved his object of 'liberating' the forces which could carry China's economic development to new heights. (*ibid.*, 3 August, 1967.) But the campaign failed to accomplish his dream of 'a great revolution that touches the people to their very souls'. (PD, 5 September, 1966.) The fact that, as the Epilogue outlines, traditional institutions and attitudes continued to flourish despite the drastic measures instituted by Mao in 1966 to purify the nation, must have been a bitter blow. Mao Tse-tung's vision of a new China depended on a total change of men's hearts as well as a transformation of social, political and economic institutions. In this sense his vision was genuinely 'totalitarian'. The irony was that all the evidence pointed to a considerable boom in farming and industry while the population clung tightly to its cultural legacy. In economic terms, the Cultural Revolution led to a signal victory for Mao and his development strategy. But he wanted more than prosperity; his goal was not mere affluence but a reign of virtue. However, for the outside observer, an economic breakthrough by a nation as underdeveloped as China merits investigation whatever the ideological situation.

The practical application of Mao's economic policies created considerable controversy. Industrial support for agriculture caused a serious debate. Peking had to admit the justice of the main complaint which was that no money was to be made from assisting the farmers. The state deliberately depressed the prices of commodities supplied to the countryside, which hit producers' profits. Factories were allowed only the slimmest margin between manufacturing costs and returns from rural sales. After the nine consecutive bumper harvests China had won by the end of 1970, was it still desirable, some inquired, to give the peasants such a privileged position? The official answer was that low prices were designed to boost sales to villages, particularly of inputs for raising agricultural productivity. If factories were permitted to make 'normal' returns on goods sold to the countryside, the door would re-open to 'profits in command', and the less financially rewarding goods required by the peasants would not be forthcoming.

Low prices were imperative to permit agriculture to increase purchases of the supplies essential to encourage the use of new techniques, pesticides and machinery, Peking stated. Eventually, the large market and increased investment funds offered by a flourishing agriculture would repay industry for the current policy of trimming profit margins. Peking had also to take to task enterprises whose reluctance to assist agriculture was based on technological snobbery. This group argued farm implements were crude, and technical advances were not encouraged by manufacturing agricultural equipment, a point conceded by Peking's spokesman. However, farm machinery had to be adaptable to the varied conditions of different areas of China and built on rugged lines. Machines of this standard represented a challenge to the country's industry. Strong opposition to supporting agriculture came from industrial undertakings which preferred glamorous projects for which they could obtain state finance for new buildings and equipment. In other words, the search for personal fame and the interests of the individual economic unit had not been eradicated by the Cultural Revolution. (RF, 6/1970.)

The resistance to the new policy continued throughout 1970, with constant stress on the poor profits from helping agriculture. Part of the difficulty lay in the call for factories to switch staff from manufacturing to maintenance of machines. Time was lost, at the factory's expense, as workers were sent round the villages repairing equipment at seemingly nominal fees. (PD, 23 August, 1970.) Another problem was the conflict many believed to exist between the peasants' interests and the needs of the rest of society. Factory managements were heard to argue that farming was the responsibility of the peasantry, and while temporary assistance to the villages was reasonable, they did not see why they should make long-term sacrifices for the farmers. (Liaoning RS, 19 January, 1970; PD, 15 December, 1970.) Industrial workers suspected, too, that the aid demanded for agriculture was an indirect additional levy imposed by the state. Enterprises would be expected to meet their normal production quotas as well as catering for the peasants. (Kansu RS, 27 February, 1970.)

Spokesmen for a textile machinery plant asked how they were to meet ordinary manufacturing obligations and at the same time find resources to turn out farming equipment. In the sectors directly linked to agriculture (fertilisers, for example), the claim was made that factories were already working exclusively for the farmers, and no extra services could be expected from them for the peasants. In other industries, such as coalmining, cadres were puzzled as to what contribution they could make towards improved farming. From the handicraft industries (capable of producing simple tools) came complaints at giving the countryside priority on the principle that enterprises would make more money from urban consumers. Repeatedly the point was raised that the ratio of profits to costs in producing goods for agriculture made the rural market unattractive. To manufacture farm inputs was an unrewarding nuisance; 'we are quite busy promoting production and have no time to support agriculture' summed up a popular attitude among the factories.

Nevertheless, the government insisted on obedience to the new policy. Coalmining managements were compelled to spare technicians to work in the villages. Peking was combed for staff to man two hundred teams to go to the communes and demonstrate simple maintenance techniques and train rural technicians. (Kansu RS, 27 February, 1970; NCNA, 17 March, 1970; *New Anhwei Daily*, 6 November, 1970; Shansi RS, 5 December, 1970.) The Cultural Revolution had not changed the basic sentiments of industry about engaging only in those operations which showed a profit. But Mao's victory had given Peking the authority to insist factories came to the aid of farming whatever the effect on their balance sheets.

The policy of promoting small-scale plants in the rural areas also met with hostility. The public still preferred large, modern plants. The production potential of small enterprises was despised, despite arguments about the total resources of a vast number of humble plants adding up to a huge increase in the ability to satisfy the country's wants. Their primitive technology was looked upon with disdain, and people preferred the latest technology when investing in new factories. In addition, and this reason may have been the most compelling, many districts felt they lacked the surplus resources to develop a network of small plants. Peking claimed such undertakings were cheap to construct, came into production quickly and offered a speedy return on the capital sunk in them. But the central government was obliged at the same time to explain that ingenuity and self-reliance would have to make up for shortages of capital and skill. The authorities tried to ease the strains of rural industrialisation, and Peking stated that discarded equipment from large factories should be renovated for use by small industrial units. (RF, 6/1970.) Considerable efforts were made to force large factories to support small undertakings. In Liaoning province, for instance, by-products from a chemical works were used to help start small electronic factories. (NCNA, 23 September, 1970.) In Honan province, technical service teams from a bearings factory were sent into the country to help eleven counties and municipalities establish their own manufacturing concerns. (RS, 1 December, 1970.) In Kwangsi region, a factory's personnel was asked to manufacture radio equipment. The workers apparently preferred to continue with their usual jobs, which was making ropes. However, after training provided for twenty-four of the labour force in a modern radio plant, the government directive was obeyed. (RS, 18 October, 1970.)

In other cases, groups of factories co-operated to turn out complete sets of equipment for new small enterprises. (NCNA, 3 June, 1970.) The sacrifices demanded of well-established undertakings to help newborn concerns could be enormous. One oilfield lost half its drilling, transport and maintenance equipment in 1970 when forced to assist the construction of new petroleum facilities. (*ibid.*, 17 October, 1970.) The workers in one steel plant objected at first when asked to contribute to developments in other parts of the country by surrendering some of its meagre and not very modern equipment. Despite initial complaints that the enterprise could not afford such generosity, sufficient machinery and technicians were released to set up a fully-equipped new plant. (PD, 20 January, 1971.)

Sometimes, oddly enough, when operators of small-scale units proposed seeking help from the cities, they were rebuked for not overcoming their own difficulties. (Kwangsi RS, 5 October, 1970.) This phenomenon might have been the result of the authorities' realisation that only by trying to solve their own difficulties would former peasants learn how to manage industry. Or China may have grasped that its modern industry had only a limited amount of equipment to offer new factories without harming existing production capacity. The government may also have realised that a relatively small number of personnel from city enterprises could be spared to train rural recruits to industrial life without draining off too many key skilled workers, especially since the trainees would return to their own localities instead of repaying the costs of their apprenticeship by working in the urban factory.

The resistance to small enterprises did not weaken during 1970. The opposition insisted: 'These enterprises are not economical.' This charge was countered with the contention that modest undertakings enjoyed an invaluable freedom to experiment, to innovate and break away from the normal production conventions which often hindered progress. Nevertheless, a slight change of emphasis seemed to emerge during this debate, and the value of heavy industry and large units received marginally more recognition. (*Peking Review,* 48/1970.) An article in October 1970 revealed that Heilungkiang province, regarded by China's press as a pace-maker in rural industry, had closed some small plants because they were unsuited to local economic conditions. The same province reported that attempts to increase control over the economic activities of individual districts had run into criticism from those who dismissed national planning as hindering local initiative. (RF, 10/1970.) In 1971, Kwangtung province seems to have realised that the returns from small undertakings in some industries were uneconomical. The province reduced by fifty per cent both the number of small coal pits and the workers they employed, yet 'small mines' increased output over the 1970 total by forty per cent according to an official report. Nevertheless, the stress on small enterprises continued. In Kwangsi region, for example, Kwangtung's neighbour, a district reported a substantial increase in small enterprises in this industry. (Canton RS, 24 December, 1971; Kwangsi RS, 20 December, 1971.)

Peking clearly faced an enormous challenge in dealing with semi-independent, local industrial systems. Unless the state contributed to the construction of rural factories, these units were the property of the communes or counties which developed them. One account of how a Kiangsi provincial authority went about setting up its own industry showed the complex factors involved. Very cannily, the officials first consulted the masses who blessed the idea of establishing an industrial complex which made it difficult for any superior authority to object. Iron and steel works were set up at county level; coalmines and small hydro-electric plants were operated by the communes. The county carefully reported that over eighty per cent of the labour employed by industry was working 'concurrently' in agriculture. This announcement prevented any outside intervention on the grounds that farming was being starved of labour for the benefit of the factories. Except for the iron, steel and chemical works, for which the county obtained state assistance, all the factories were completely self-financed and outside Peking's direct control. As the county authorities pointedly concluded in their report: 'There has been no state industry created at all in the last two years because the new factories were financed entirely by the masses.' (Kiangsi RS, 28 August, 1970.) In Fukien province, another county was not so lucky. A broadcast at the end of 1970 stated factories established 'without official permission' had been shut because they had taken too many workers away from agriculture. (RS, 16 November, 1970.)

Frequent claims were made about the creative freedom of small plants and their dramatic technical achievements. These are not so impressive when the case of the repair shop which began making cars — first fifty, then five hundred and then a thousand a year — is examined closely. (RF, 4/1970; KMD, 21 November, 1970.) These vehicles were virtually hand built. For China to begin by producing expensive, 'custom-made' cars before switching to mass production (repeating the history of the motor industry in the West) was a dubious luxury when skilled manpower, machinery, capital and materials were so scarce. Cost accounting could not be completely ignored, as Peking repeatedly reminded the nation, and a proper regard for efficiency and profits was essential. (PD, 2 March, 14 April, 29 November, 1970.) But the point was difficult to convey since districts had been specifically commanded to set up their own industrial bases in 1969 and use local initiative in developing factories, more or less regardless of the returns from any alternative investment opportunities. Peking's comments indicated that after the Cultural Revolution, many people believed 'profits' was an obscene expression, and cadres avoided strict financial control of an enterprise's activities for fear of bitter condemnation from the ultra-radicals.

In giving local authorities the liberty to develop their own economies, Peking had hoped they would stick to the principle of 'taking the whole nation as a chessboard' and pay strict attention to national needs. (*New Anhwei Daily,* 27 July, 1970.) This hope was apparently not realised. By autumn 1970, Peking was talking of the 'new system of the four controls — unified control of planning, investment, materials and the carrying-out of construction by [state] capital construction departments.' (PD, 17 October, 1970.) Previously, the guidelines for industrial activities had been 'quantity, value of output, quality, profit, production costs and labour productivity', all of which related to a factory's individual performance and not to co-ordinated planning. (Kiangsu RS, 20 July, 1970.)

By the end of 1970, the state was wrestling to obtain more direct power over the economy. Peking was preparing for the start of the fourth five-year plan on 1 January, 1971. Co-ordinated production at all levels was essential for the success of a balanced and integrated programme for development during the next plan period. Pleas for attention to national needs continued, with constant emphasis on fulfilling state targets before satisfying local demand. (*Hsinhua Daily,* 30 November, 1970.) Seemingly appeals to idealism were not enough. Only direct regulation could guarantee the central government had first claim on output capacity at local levels. Mao himself had failed to clarify the rules for balancing central control against local autonomy. His approach, as previously discussed, had been highly flexible. The balance would shift between the centre and individual districts as conditions changed.

The state had good reason in 1970 for seeking stronger controls, because rural industrial systems were competing directly with large factories for supplies and markets. (RF, 6/1970.) Peking had to step in to mediate this sort of dispute. The state also had to obtain access to more funds to pay for the new five-year plan. Some ninety per cent of the national budget in 1970 still came from the profits of state enterprises, and the proportion of total profits skimmed off by the government appeared very low compared to the funds left with the local authorities. (*ibid.,* 2/1970.) In a Kiangsi county, for instance, in 1969 the state received Yuan 200,000 from industrial profits while the commune and production brigades retained Yuan 900,000 for their own investments. (RS, 28 August, 1970.) This example demonstrated the operation of the principle that factories run by communes and their subsidiary organisations were the property of their members. Financial surpluses only went into the national exchequer when the state was a 'shareholder' in an enterprise.

Another problem was that misrepresentation, fraud and false reports had yet to be eradicated. Some cadres lied about production results to put up a good front. (NCNA, 3 November, 1969.) Balance sheets were doctored because enterprises suspected the state would only grant a proportion of their requests for capital and equipment. The higher the demands made on the central government's resources, the more leeway would be left for surrendering to Peking's calls for 'frugality' without harming the unit's real plans for expansion. (RF, 2/1970.) In Shanghai, campaigns to economise on funds and materials met with the response: 'It is for the collective anyway. What does it matter if we waste a little?' (*Liberation Daily,* 1 March, 1970.)

The government's worries involved not just the local factories indirectly controlled (if at all) by Peking but also the state sector. The central government confessed state-owned and supervised factories, 'the economic lifeline of the state', were under dangerously loose management. Decentralisation of authority opened loopholes for 'corruption and sabotage'. (PD, 11 March, 1970.) A typical attitude in a large state factory was: 'We have lots of things in a big plant. To throw away a little is nothing.' Government scrutiny of requisitions from factories seems to have been perfunctory. Enterprises claimed: 'We always get what we want.' Investigation of one factory over a two-year period reportedly produced enough machines and materials to equip thirty small factories and meet the requirements of fifty communes and production brigades (*ibid.*, 19 April, 1970.) These surplus stocks not only froze development resources but also allowed evasion of economic regulations. Undertakings bartered commodities and machinery, presumably to make up for defects in the national distribution system. Such practices inevitably weakened Peking's power to direct the economy, although, of course, they allowed enterprises to continue normal working when threatened by the planners' grosser miscalculations.

The sums involved in padding inventories were immense. A vehicle engine plant in Sian, under military supervision and run by one of Mao's new revolutionary committees, was asked to review its stocks. It confessed to a surplus worth Yuan 50,000. A second check discovered Yuan 360,000 worth of surplus materials. As a result of tighter controls, production costs fell by nine per cent while profits in 1970 were said to be over two hundred per cent higher than the total profits declared between 1964 and 1969. (Shensi RS, 18 April, 1971.) In the spring of 1971, Peking mounted a massive drive to end these abuses, discovering, for example, a factory in Nanning with Yuan 300,000 worth of idle equipment and materials. (Kwangsi RS, 14 April, 1971.)

The factories were not wholly to blame for this situation. They were pressed continually to complete targets ahead of schedule. Officials, conscious of the long working life of modern plants, wanted to obtain equipment sufficiently advanced to remain efficient far into the future. The temptation was strong to solve these problems by spending money lavishly. (RF, 2/1970.) The drive to push output to record levels also came into the picture, leading to 'the phenomena of blindly chasing quantity, only seeking to meet production quotas and neglecting quality'. To oppose these trends — dangerously reminiscent of the 1958 Great Leap Forward — the slogan was proposed: 'On schedule, fine quality, high output, high efficiency and low consumption of materials.' (Shansi RS, 10 October, 1970; Canton RS, 11 October, 1970.)

A permanent solution for the conflict between central and local government interests seems to have been impossible. Fukien province continued to speak of the need to develop an independent industrial system. (*Fukien Daily,* 15 January, 1971.) Kwangsi region praised a county for its efforts to achieve industrial self-sufficiency but gave it extra marks for respecting the ideal of 'the whole country a chessboard'. (RS, 20 February, 1971.) In Hunan province, the conflict of interests came through strongly in a statement by a senior communist official rejecting 'dictatorship by regulations and systems' (excessive state control) while demanding obedience to the authority both of the party and the national government, again using the chessboard analogy. (RS, 1 March, 1971.) Yunnan province quoted Mao's command that localities be allowed to run their own economic affairs but added: 'We must give priority to the needs of the party and the state, strengthen our grasp of the overall situation and embrace the idea of the whole country as a chessboard. We must resolutely carry out state plans. The activism of the localities can only be brought into play under the unified national plan. We must put the state first and the localities second.' (RS, 28 March, 1971.) In fact by the summer of 1970, state control had increased substantially. Former radicals, who had stormed so many government offices during the Cultural Revolution, found themselves at the mercy of the officials they had reviled in the political tempest which hit China in 1966. Thus Yao Wen-yuan, despite his senior party status, his national standing as one of China's most radical Maoists and his rank as number two in the Shanghai municipal and party administrations, confessed to undergraduates in his home city that he could not intervene to win the co-operation of central government departments in carrying out university reforms. (NCNA, 24 July, 1970.)

The difficulty with the chessboard concept, so frequently quoted to encourage co-ordination, is that pieces are valued according to their 'imperial' ranks. Furthermore, some hand controlled by a superior intellect has to descend upon the board to move even the loftiest piece and keep the game in motion — all of which is contrary to Mao's philosophy. Peking needed the sort of control which would reduce the districts to the status of bishops if not mere pawns by the end of 1970. Yet Mao Tse-tung had not regarded pawns as inanimate objects but foot-soldiers with minds of their own and the ability to win battles. But what was the central government to do when it wanted to play a particular gambit and found that its chess-pieces had strolled from square to square as they pleased?

The issues raised by the opponents of Mao's development policies were both economic and political, which made a satisfactory response from Peking all the more difficult. The role of profits as the basis for economic advance was not denied by the government. (KMD, 31 March, 1970.) Opposition to the official policy of reduced profit margins on goods sold to the agricultural sector was based principally on the conviction that the villages could afford to carry a bigger share of the development burden. By reducing industry's profits from trade with the peasants, less funds for investment were available to the central government. But the real problem was much wider, involving acute ideological dilemmas: the incorporation of agriculture into the rest of the socialist economy by nationalising the communes. Initial moves in this direction in southern China were squashed on the grounds that the time was still not ripe for such a shattering transformation of rural society. (Canton RS, 2 January, 1971.)

Similarly, the state had sound economic reasons in seeking greater control of the rural factory complexes started since 1969, and generally tighter industrial regulation from the centre. Serious abuses and a lack of co-ordination were wasting funds needed for China's growth. In seeking to direct the rural manufacturing enterprises, the main emphasis was on persuasion, the 'chessboard' campaign. Nobody denied the value of local initiative in fostering new factories financed, supplied and managed by the peasants and their organisations. But the state alone was in a position to set national targets. Clashes between the state's evaluation of the overall situation and local economic ambitions were unavoidable.

Mao had not professed to have found the formulas either for settling price policies or for resolving conflicts over the decentralisation of industrial management. He wanted each locality to have a voice in controlling its own development. Yet he understood the importance of unified plans. A simple remedy for these conflicts would have been to concentrate power in the hands of the national bureaucracy. After the Cultural Revolution, such a step was unthinkable, even if it had made good economic sense to try to control the details of such an enormous nation from Peking. H.B. Acton's pessimism about the prospects of finding a tolerable balance between genuine popular control and overall state regulation of economic affairs was not echoed by most Chinese under Mao. (*The Morals of Markets*, 84.) They had not despaired of finding the answer, although the search for a solution was tortuous and confusing.

The price and planning issues which arose in 1970 illustrated the weak link in Mao's economic strategy. Its strengths were more apparent when attention shifted from the national level to individual enterprises. The greatest benefit from giving the counties and communes their head was their investment, mostly in industry, of the large balances they had accumulated as a result of the good harvests since 1962 and the restrictions on consumption during the Cultural Revolution when industrial production slumped and transport was disrupted. The mobilisation of rural savings in particular achieved a long-standing ambition of the government. (Audrey Donnithorne, *China's Economic System,* 89.) The existence of a large cache of spare funds was borne out by the amounts officials were able to lay their hands on to buy off trouble through higher wages when attacked by Red Guards and 'revolutionary rebels' during 1967. The public's savings appear to have risen significantly during the post-1966 troubles. (*China's Renminbi: One of the Few Most Stable Currencies in the World,* 19-20. However, a somewhat different impression is given by NCNA, 27 December, 1971.) By encouraging local authorities to construct their own factories, irrigation schemes and hydro-electric projects, these private and commune funds were placed at the service of the country's development.

In Honan province, chemical fertiliser, farm machinery, textile, iron, steel, coal and cement undertakings were built with funds 'in general raised by the administrative region and the county concerned or jointly by several counties'. In Kiangsi province, a county organised its people to build equipment for an iron and steel plant out of waste and old materials. A county-run coalmine set up eight factories turning out a range of products from machines to explosives. On Hainan island, a modern steel plant was erected by persuading thirty-four industrial units to mobilise three thousand of their workers for the job. A coalmine produced the convertor; a hand-tractor factory and a porcelain plant combined to make the refractory materials. Anxious to build an industrial complex, one group of peasants said: 'We'll not bother the state for funds.' They dug into the commune's savings and raised more money through their spare-time activities. In Sian, aided by large enterprises, a thousand small factories were established in the city during the first half of 1970. No money was sought from the state for any of these projects, and difficulties were overcome through joint action by several enterprises. One example of co-operation in Sian was the group of seventeen factories, each with less than a hundred employees, which combined to manufacture three-wheeled cars.

In Shantung province, plans for a small steel plant encountered difficulties because of the lack of capital. 'The people of the district curtailed all expenses not devoted to production and appropriated funds from the district budget supplemented by funds from various counties and municipalities [within the district].' They constructed all but eighteen of the one hundred and thirty-one machines needed for the factory. In a southern province, 'people's war' was launched to open small coalmines, many of which were developed without any official help. In Shanghai, a former nail factory made its own equipment to get into the machine-tools business without seeking government finance. A single county built over a hundred small hydro-electric stations, raising ninety per cent of the capital from its communes and production brigades. Another county in southern China drew up a water-conservancy and electric-generating plan calling for an investment of Yuan 10 million. The state refused to allocate even a tenth of this sum, so the county withdrew its application for government support and went ahead with the scheme using local finance.

One county formerly sought cash from official sources for sinking wells. A resolution in favour of 'self-reliance' passed at a mass meeting resulted in eight hundred new wells without any aid from the state. During a mechanisation drive in Hupeh province, a debate broke out over seeking government subsidies, with one group stating: 'Mechanisation calls for huge investments and can only be undertaken by the state.' Eventually the peasants agreed to buy their own machines, which they could well afford after a steady rise in their earnings from such activities as livestock, cotton, grain and oil processing. One rural fertiliser factory bought used parts from other concerns to construct its own equipment. Between 1963 and 1969, a single county established a large number of factories whose accumulated profits ran to several million Yuan. It spent Yuan 800,000 on new irrigation facilities and Yuan 1.2 million on light railways. The county financed all industrial ventures from its own savings. A significant development in this district was a changeover from primitive production techniques to foreign technology. (NCNA, 10 November, 1969, 27 February, 19 March, 20 October, 1970, 17 February 1971; Shensi RS, 22 June, 30 August, 1970; Canton RS, 16 December, 1969, 6 January, 11 November, 1970; Hainan RS, 14 November, 1970; Shantung RS, 14 April, 1970; RF, 10/1969; PD, 15 December, 1969; KMD, 21 January, 1971.)

This combination of self-reliance and joint assaults on new

projects paid off handsomely for the local population and, less lavishly, for the government. One obstacle to modernising agriculture is the investment required for more irrigation and extra fertilisers essential in employing modern high-yield seeds. Machines too cost money. Calls from Mao Tse-tung for China to adopt more scientific farming methods increased the financial pressure on the rural population. In Hunan province, a county reported its struggle to become entirely independent of outside funds for agricultural development. By 1969, only half its communes had reached this happy position. Local industry's contribution in such a situation could be enormous. A Shansi county had a long tradition of smelting iron. Through expanding this industry, it made an income of Yuan 700,000 in 1970, and was able to purchase tractors, threshing machines, pumps and a large quantity of chemical fertiliser. Another county netted Yuan 3 million from the production of 415,000 tons of iron ore. It used its profits to buy thirty-six tractors, forty-three diesel engines and almost two hundred threshing machines and water pumps at a total cost of Yuan 600,000. A third county, this time in Anhwei province, made a profit from mining in 1970 of Yuan 3.4 million, of which Yuan 1.6 million was allocated to farming projects. Thus rural industrial development underwrote a high proportion of the cost of transforming China's farming. (Hunan RS, 4 March, 1970; Shansi RS, 30 March, 1971; Hupeh RS, 31 March, 1971; NCNA, 26 February, 1971.)

The benefits to the state were significant, even though most of the profits stayed in the countryside where they were made. Self-reliance drastically reduced the strain on the national purse. One area of Kwangtung province constructed a water-control and hydro-electric system which would have cost the state almost Yuan 8 million. The local people raised eighty per cent of the cash needed through their own efforts, 'which greatly reduced the burden on the state'. The return to the national exchequer on a paper mill in which the state had a financial stake was four times the total capital provided from official sources between 1966 and 1970. In Kiangsu province, the iron and steel industry previously relied on coke brought in by the national distribution network from other provinces. In 1970, it became virtually self-sufficient in this commodity with a consequent saving in transport costs.

One municipality under pressure to aid agriculture managed to meet its state output targets in 1970 while supplying considerable amounts of equipment to the countryside. A rural nitrogenous fertiliser factory reported it had handed over to the government in profits some Yuan 1.5 million from 1968 to 1970, indicating that when the government could obtain a claim on the earnings of local industries, dividends were handsome. Between 1953 and 1963, one commune spent almost Yuan 1 million in state funds on creating four hundred and thirty acres of terraced fields. In 1970, it managed to construct two hundred and ninety more acres without any state assistance. An agricultural machinery plant thought initially of obtaining Yuan 300,000 from official sources, changed its mind, raised the capital itself and built three hundred-ton punching machines it had planned to import. (Kwangsi RS, 28 September, 1970; Shensi RS, 20 February, 1971; Hunan RS, 11 January, 1971; Kiangsu RS, 28 December, 1970; Canton RS, 17 November, 1970, 26 February, 1971; NCNA, 5 December, 1969, 20 September, 1970.)

The state gained in other ways. China was perpetually short of resources for industrial development. Occasional glimpses emerged of fierce competition for access to national resources. 'At the beginning of the year [1970], when the state allocated funds, materials and equipment, some cadres one-sidedly emphasised the claims of light industry. They wanted to compete with heavy industry for capital, supplies and machinery. Others one-sidedly held that light industry was not a key point and was of no importance.' The argument was solved by light industry's representatives agreeing to drop their fight with the heavy sector, while their counterparts in heavy industry accepted that the light sector must be helped. Thus heavy industry got state help for its expansion, and light industry got what support the heavy sector could spare. (Canton RS, 17 November, 1970.) The impression given by this passage is that considerable wheeling and dealing took place between rival departments when plans were drawn up, and a trade-off in mutual co-operation was the usual settlement. Such a compromise, in a sense, would have fitted the spirit of the 1969 economic programme and its stress on co-ordination.

The authorities, by allowing local organisations to mastermind their own expansion and production, cleverly shifted responsibility down the official ladder for solving bottlenecks and shortages. Hunan province broadcast a very blunt set of prescriptions for overcoming production problems. When short of equipment, 'we should repair old machines and make use of rejects'. If raw materials were lacking, the factory should obtain its own alternative supplies. Should labour prove scarce, the transfer of a factory's staff from less vital departments and the mobilisation of its officials for manual work were the correct solutions. If capital should be unavailable, the factory ought to start its own investment fund. In addition, careful planning would usually allow a drastic reduction in capital requirements. The province was told of plans to expand one factory at a cost of Yuan 1.2 million. The workers investigated the project and completed the job for a mere Yuan 50,000. (Hunan RS, 11 May, 1970.)

The new economic order showed little sympathy for those who could not stand on their own feet. In one enterprise, for instance, a department was asked for a substantial rise in production without being provided with additional floor space. The answer: build a new floor in the gap between the machines and the ceiling. (PD, 11 March, 1970.) The state planning commission informed the nation that because of increasing demand for equipment to install in new enterprises and to replace obsolete machines, China could not hope to supply all that was required. The country should forget the old convention that factories did not build their own machinery. Innovation and renovation would have to be the slogans of many undertakings looking for equipment to expand their productive capacity. (Peking RS, 9 September, 1970.)

A later call from the commission for increased industrial productivity urged close scrutiny of designs for new industrial facilities. Often fifteen to twenty per cent, it claimed, could be trimmed off the original estimate of the investment required. Many factories could exploit materials lying idle in their stockrooms. Considerable savings could be made by using waste products. The commission quoted a Peking distillery which formerly produced only wine. By processing its waste by-products, the factory had started to manufacture pharmaceuticals, insecticides, as well as machinery and supplies for the electronics industry. Technical innovation, in particular, by calling upon the creative talent of the masses, could improve the efficiency of existing machines and the quality of their products. The commission cited a factory which had previously manufactured diesel engines according to a foreign design. The factory decided to develop a Chinese-type engine and successfully made a diesel motor which weighed less than half the old model and increased power output by three hundred per cent. (RF, 2/1971.) China was seeking, it seems, to repeat a pattern common in European and American industry where, John Jewkes has shown, a high proportion of modern technological advances has been produced either by individuals or in small enterprises. (*The Sources of Invention*, 161.)

Peking refused to accept any limit on the ability to find new methods of exploiting the potential of existing plant and supplies. Those who claimed that by dint of practising frugality over many years, all possible economies had been exhausted, found themselves condemned very bitterly. The case of a Chungking factory was drawn to their attention. Formerly, the enterprise had used metal-cutting techniques leading to considerable waste. The workers built a high-frequency rolling machine which cut down consumption of raw materials by twenty-five per cent. Conservatives who refused to make use of new materials because 'the old raw and semi-processed materials are reliable and we can be sure of the quality of products made with them' were sternly reprimanded. (RF, 9/1970.) Apart from shortages caused by factories which indulged in such improper conduct as overstocking materials and machinery, other economic 'gaps' were depicted as a sign of progress. Because the economy was progressing so quickly, strains and a lack of balance developed in certain sectors, making it hard to meet demand from industries which were advancing rapidly. The wrong attitude was to expect the government to come to the rescue or to seek permission to import scarce items. One machine-building plant when short of steel took this erroneous line: 'We shall do what is in accordance with the aid we receive.' The factory failed to meet its targets. Another enterprise in the same situation adopted the right course of action: its workers went out to track down every scrap of waste steel and find every possible substitute for steel in the manufacturing process. In short, the basic test of correct management was whether a factory regarded itself as shackled by the economic plan or challenged to improve its own performance by mistakes in the planners' forecasts which emerged as the nation bustled towards prosperity. (PD, 24 June, 1970.)

While China was told to learn all it could from foreign nations, 'even the finest foreign products can be regarded only as a standard of comparison to be transformed in the light of the actual conditions of our country'. This statement was aimed at officials who believed only large-scale and foreign-designed products represented advanced technological standards. In practice, it was claimed, small enterprises could work even better than some big undertakings. One large factory, asked to manufacture a high-grade alloy, replied it would need Yuan 6.5 million worth of capital and three years to start production. The project was handed over to six small workshops which trial-produced the alloy after four days and nights of research and began full-scale output within three months — all at a cost of under Yuan 1 million.

(RF, 4/1970.) Even labour was to be regarded as a scarce commodity. A linoleum factory told to increase output by thirty per cent requested an increase of almost two hundred workers. After investigation (by the masses, naturally), a hundred workers were transferred from the factory to other industrial establishments, and the target for the year was met with three months to spare. (PD, 16 January, 1971.)

Such reports often sound incredible. But Oskar Lange, the famous Polish communist economist, pointed out in 1938: 'The real danger of socialism is that of a bureaucratisation of economic life.' (*On the Economic Theory of Socialism,* 109.) He denied this implied managers in a capitalist corporation would perform any better than the official in a state-owned enterprise. The Chinese, however, believed the official was a constant and grave source of waste unless firmly supervised by the masses. A flood of instances of misused resources because of bureaucratic stupidity appeared in the Chinese press. In a lathe works, the casting and processing shop could not match the speed of the assembly department, and the flow of finished parts was erratic. To the masses' great irritation, the cadres cut down the assembly workers' quota instead of trying to solve the bottleneck in the casting and processing department. (PD, 4 September, 1970.) In another case, an official adopted foreign production standards and came up with a scheme in which the state would have to invest Yuan 800,000. The workers revised the plan, cutting the capital required to only twenty per cent of the original estimate. (*ibid.,* 19 April, 1970.) Such mistakes were usually interpreted as evidence that Liu Shao-chi's 'poison' was still at work in the bureaucracy. How far in fact officials came under fire not only for genuine errors but also because of suspicions about Liu Shao-chi's influence on them it is hard to say. Certainly, however, part of the cadre problem must have reflected the faulty recruitment policies Mao espoused immediately after coming to power in his struggle to keep the country going. Ezra Vogel shows how many of the communist groups which had caused serious trouble at the birth of the People's Republic were responsible for a variety of dubious activities after 1966. Seemingly, the bureaucracy never managed to shake off the bad habits the communists picked up from officials of the previous régime in the years immediately after 1949. (*Canton Under Communism,* Chapters 2 and 8.)

By controlling the bureaucrat who had a reputation to make for himself as the manager of the largest and most modern enterprise possible and compelling the factory labour force to accept responsibility for solving difficulties caused by faulty state planning and general shortages, Peking believed minimum outlay by the central government would still maintain a very high rate of development. In this context, Mao's slogan during the Cultural Revolution 'The working class is the leading class. Its leading role . . . in all fields of work should be brought into play' took on a positive meaning directly related to economic progress.

Mao Tse-tung's theory that development should move by stages from small-scale to large undertakings has already been discussed. The way the principle was subsequently developed by Premier Chou En-lai as a call for factories to be built on modest proportions initially, with a view to expansion when circumstances permitted, has been analysed in some detail. This concept of industrial growth saw a considerable flowering in 1970. Canton reported a wave of enthusiasm for electronics. Among the enterprises which moved into this field were workshops previously engaged in making table-tennis balls, mosquito repellents and paper bags. One new electronics concern in the city sent its workers off to learn from Shanghai before embarking on the manufacture of 'single-crystal silicon' products. A former tinsmiths' and blacksmiths' co-operative began producing X-ray machines. In Kwangsi region, a farm tool factory transformed itself into a plant producing a wide range of advanced agricultural machinery. Even where an enterprise did not change to new products, increases in both scale and efficiency were publicised. A cement factory begun by thirty workers in 1958 had handed over by 1970 just over Yuan 1 million in profits to the government, and its range of activities had increased substantially in the manufacture of cement products. Production costs had been slashed by sixty per cent since its first period of operations. A plant which once made motor vehicle accessories turned to manufacturing its own brand of trucks. (Canton RS, 15 May, 9 July, 1970; Kwangsi RS, 6 July, 1970; Hunan RS, 25 August, 1970; NCNA, 20 February, 23 August, 1970.)

When Mao's idea of transforming small enterprises into large factories first took concrete form through Chou's incorporation of the principle into national policy, co-operation between large and small undertakings was stressed. Many of the small factories set up in 1970 were in fact branches of larger concerns. In Hunan province, the process was described as 'a hen laying an egg'. The phrase was applied to an electricity supply company which set up three subsidiaries generating power and manufacturing electric motors. On Hainan island, sixty per cent of the new small industrial complexes planned during 1970 were branches of existing concerns, designed to meet the needs of their parent companies. In Kiangsi province, large undertakings in the light industry sector did not establish subsidiaries but apparently reproduced themselves by splitting up into two or three completely new enterprises. The famous Maanshan iron and steel works in Anhwei province built twenty branch workshops during 1970, producing two hundred different items which, according to the official account, ranged from caustic soda to batteries. A major effort was made to get large coalmines to play an active part in sinking new, small-scale pits. (Hunan RS, 25 January, 1971; Canton RS, 2 November, 1970; Anhwei RS, 14 November, 1970; NCNA, 23 August, 1970; PD, 4 January, 1971.)

The success reported from so many branches of light industry and the large sums of money claimed in profits by small factories in the countryside are not easy for the outsider to accept at face value. When analysed in the context of a continuous drive to spread talent, capital, equipment and experience beyond existing industrial areas and long-established factories, both through co-operative ventures and the establishment of subsidiaries, the capacity to set up new plants on the scale reported in China during 1970 begins to sound more credible. Behind industry's upsurge was an insistence by the central authorities that firms worked together to ensure no possible avenue of increased production went unnoticed. No factor of production – human labour, waste gases or obsolete machinery – should be left unemployed since a partnership between the enthusiastic small concern and the experienced large undertaking ought to be able to turn them into new assets for China's growth. Perhaps most important of all was Peking's attempt to reduce, through 'emulation' campaigns and pressure on scientists to popularise their discoveries (RF, 2/1971; PD, 19 March, 1971), the time-lag between the development of new technical knowledge and its general application – a problem which Edwin Mansfield has shown to be a serious weakness in Western industry. (*The Economics of Technological Change,* 131-33.)

Agriculture proved the most intractable sector of the economy. The villages had been less affected by the Cultural Revolution than the cities. In any case, as already argued, the pace at which the traditional life of an agricultural community can be drastically changed is relatively slow, even when modern cultivation techniques are adopted. The man toiling on the land remains master of the production process; the machine he uses does not dominate the pattern of his work as it would in a factory. In the villages throughout 1970, a sharp and protracted conflict took place between the more conservative elements and doctrinaire radicals determined to force through a social and economic revolution. Economic logic was not the exclusive property of either camp; the good sense expressed by each side varied according to the issue under dispute. Conservatism was most dangerous among the leadership. A high proportion of the rural cadres, judging from the thousands of words lavished on their denunciation, felt production had reached a plateau and scope for further expansion was very limited. The belated accomplishment of the national development programme for agriculture, published in draft form in 1956 and to be fulfilled by 1967 (CC, 119), became the goal in 1970. However, when a district had reached the programme's standards for its region, the temptation was to argue enough had been achieved. Such views were sneered at by the authorities as betraying a disinclination to work hard. Model farming communities, especially Tachai, were publicised on a massive scale to demonstrate the capacity to overcome all obstacles to ever-higher yields through unflinching self-sacrifice inspired by Mao Tse-tung's philosophy.

Peking was realistic enough to admit, even while condemning the theory 'production has reached its maximum', that after so many good harvests, the task of pushing output to new heights had become steadily more difficult. After the Cultural Revolution, the fear of displaying interest in production was widespread lest this be taken as evidence of a desire to put 'profits in command'. Peking's line was that officials criticised in the Cultural Revolution for neglecting politics and concentrating on production had been treated as they deserved. But a swing to the other extreme — 'it is safe to grasp revolution but dangerous to grasp production' — was equally mistaken. Behind the reluctance to scale new harvest peaks lay a genuine economic factor which was labour shortage. The masses had their local factories to run, plus an increasing burden of work in the fields. Water conservation projects, pig-breeding, construction and repair of farm machinery and the new, labour-intensive, scientific farming methods gobbled up the work hours which could be squeezed out of the villages. The solution proposed was to reduce the numbers engaged in non-productive occupations, mobilise women to work in the fields and overhaul the work-point system for reckoning farm wages. (Chekiang RS, 22 February, 1970; *Kirin Daily*, 27 January, 1970; *Chinghai Daily*, 12 March, 1970; RF, 3/1970; Heilungkiang RS, 19 June, 22 September, 1970.)

Rural cadres were under constant fire from their superiors. 'They stick to the old ways and are satisfied with things as they are. They fail to see that the masses, armed with Mao Tse-tung Thought, have limitless wisdom and strength ... The leadership at all levels must abandon such bad work habits as "too much leadership by principles", an excessive number of vaguely-defined instructions, the lack of depth in their work and the absence of clear ideas in their minds and speech. They must plunge themselves into the real situation and get out among the masses. When faced with a problem they must consult the masses and carry out a proper study of the situation.' (Hupeh RS, 4 August, 1970.) Another description of cadres' attitudes indicated they were astonishingly casual in their approach: 'When work progresses a little in our areas, we wag our tails ... Those whose work is mediocre console themselves that though not as good as those with better records, they are not as bad as areas with poorer harvests. Those who enjoy good natural conditions are content to coast along with the minimum effort. Backward areas are satisfied at having made some progress and are happy to remain backward ... The mentality of "lazybones" and shirkers is a key reason why work in our areas has not improved.' The cadres were urged to abandon the mentality of 'relying on heaven, earth and the state'. (Shansi RS, 31 October, 1970.) Some cadres became complacent and tended to slacken their efforts when harvest prospects looked promising. Officials were reminded repeatedly to arrange the agricultural activities of their districts rationally, go to the fields, take personal charge of the work and cut down on unnecessary meetings. (Chinghai RS, 7 July, 1970; Hupeh RS, 23 April, 1970.)

The pressure to raise cultivation standards was unremitting. Considerable flexibility was allowed to local leaders in deciding which problem should take first priority: irrigation, land reclamation, improved seeds or multiple cropping. Each district was supposed to concentrate on whatever local feature constituted the biggest hindrance to further growth. At each of the peak farming seasons, what amounted to military campaigns were launched to mobilise every possible source of assistance for the peasants. Spare labour and machinery were drafted to the farms; trade, transport and industrial concerns were ordered to devote their entire attention to serving the peasants' needs. No sooner was one 'double-crash' movement completed than another began. Summer harvesting, for example, was followed by an immediate start on preparations for the winter rice crop. The top leadership begged unceasingly for better management in the fields — to which seventy per cent of farm efficiency was attributed — 'to preserve soil moisture carefully, irrigate fields rationally, apply extra fertilisers at the right time . . . to ensure seedlings mature properly and to exhaust all possible ways of maintaining the right soil temperature to stimulate the early ripening of the crops'. (Fukien RS, 20 February, 1970; Sinkiang RS, 11 June, 1970; *Hunan Daily,* 9 July, 1970; Kiangsu RS, 7 November, 1970; Heilungkiang RS, 24 May, 1970; Hunan RS, 14 May, 1970.)

Peking declared: 'The fundamental road for agriculture is mechanisation.' (KMD, 9 October, 1970.) This slogan produced grave problems when accompanied by the insistence that: 'Mechanisation of agriculture should rely primarily on the strength of the collective' — communes should pay for their own equipment. (NCNA, 21 August, 1970.) But even saving more money to purchase machines was not enough. One commune, for instance, was praised for realising the heavy equipment bought from state-owned factories had to be supplemented by its own efforts to develop machinery suited to local conditions. (PD, 23 September, 1970.) Opposition to spending commune capital on farm implements could be fierce. One commune reluctantly agreed to buy a tractor, though the members resented the drain on their savings, felt doubtful about its maintenance and suspected its working life would be short. The debate continued after the tractor's arrival. In the end, the commune's senior cadre decided to get rid of it.

Another commune managed to persuade its peasants of the value of mechanisation, but the sacrifice this policy called for was considerable. The proportion of commune earnings set aside for investment had to be raised from eleven to sixteen per cent of total income. In other words, the peasants were obliged to increase the tax on themselves by almost fifty per cent to modernise their farm. In Hunan province, a commune reported an acrimonious debate over whether to distribute the cash earned from such activities as stock-rearing to its members 'to stimulate their enthusiasm' or spend the money on machinery. A national symposium on rice-transplanting machines found some delegates insisting: 'Conditions are not ready for carrying out agricultural mechanisation.' Peking eventually admitted official support was necessary to make a success of the mechanisation drive. But this help was to be confined to ordering the state sector of the economy to assist the peasants' own struggles to obtain machines, particularly through aiding the development of rural factories to manufacture farm equipment. (PD, 23 March, 23 September, 1970; NCNA, 21 August, 15 October, 1970; Canton RS, 23 February, 1970; *Hunan Daily,* 24 July, 1970.)

The government was determined to promote mechanisation what-ever the obstacles. Machines, it believed, would bring about a radical transformation in the 'small-peasant' outlook typical of China's rural population. Machines raised labour productivity and allowed more time to be devoted to forestry, livestock, fishing and the production of other non-staple commodities. (PD, 7 August, 1970.) The major advantage of machines, apparently, was their ability to overcome the effects of the manpower shortage in the countryside which was hindering the adoption of scientific techniques to raise yields. When the potential of modern, powered implements was explained to one village, the peasants volunteered to use their personal savings to buy machines which would increase output and allow development of profitable side-line activities. Mechanical rice transplanters were a popular example of the gains offered by mechanisation. These machines reduced the average trans-planting period of fifteen to twenty days to a mere six or seven days. The saving in man-hours allowed more careful and intensive work on the rice crop and released labour for other jobs. (KMD, 25 September, 1970.)

In late 1970, a new and far more serious issue began to create trouble for Peking. The peasants had been urged to increase their investment funds as much as possible, not only through cultivating the fields but by expanding side-line occupations and industries suited to their area. (RF, 3/1970.) As autumn approached, the radicals began to attack the existing commune system. Apparently, they wanted to adopt large-scale farm management, with the commune as the main unit of day-to-day administration, for agricultural (and industrial) operations, instead of the smaller production team or production brigade (generally equivalent to a village). The radicals also wanted, it seems, to abolish the right of production teams, brigades and the communes to retain title to their own property. Furthermore, relating wages to the individual's work rather than to his needs and the peasants' right to make money in their spare time were attacked by these 'ultra-leftists'. Acceptance of their proposals would have taken China back to the Great Leap Forward, and the authorities quickly condemned these suggestions. (Shensi RS, 9 September, 1970.) Mao Tse-tung's cautious approach to changing the face of the countryside remained in force, temporarily at any rate. But obviously, the date for the nationalisation of the communes would have to be fixed eventually. Peking apparently felt it politic not to raise this issue in 1970 and only reacted when the radicals tried to force its hand.

During the winter, criticism of the remaining elements of private ownership and enterprise in the villages was maintained by the radicals. In Shantung province, for example, they appear to have embarrassed the provincial leadership considerably. A statement was broadcast insisting cultivation of crops must take priority over all other activities even in villages where natural conditions were so poor that adequate incomes could be earned only through side-line activities. However, the province was informed that if labour were assigned by the commune or brigade to subsidiary occupations without harming grain production, the local economy would be strengthened. The province thus established an uneasy balance, with the radicals exerting strong pressure. The failure to tackle the 'ultra-leftists' aggressively led to the abolition of some private plots, a move which had to be reversed once the authorities realised its implications. (RS, 9 September, 1970, 5 March, 1971.) In Shansi province, the controversy flared into the open during the campaign to step up pigbreeding. The authorities had to intervene to condemn those who said keeping pigs would encourage a revival of rural capitalism. Production brigades which tried to limit to two the number of pigs any family could own were denounced. Shansi's provinical administration had seen which line was politically correct and ordered: 'Continue to encourage peasants to breed pigs and reward those who do well.' (RS, 12 October, 23 December, 1970.)

The provinces could guess quite easily how Peking wanted them to react even before the *People's Daily* joined in on 18 February, 1971 with an edict in the name of Mao Tse-tung that no alteration in the basic commune system was permissible. Already in December of 1970, the ministry of agriculture and forestry had explained the state was not prepared to take over the rural sector's burdens. 'State support for agriculture is basically different from the notion "the state should finance the peasants' agricultural operations". The purpose of state support is to give bigger play to the revolutionary spirit of self-reliance and hard struggle of the poor and lower-middle peasants to speed up agricultural development . . . As some poor and lower-middle peasants have said, "The more we rely on outside help, the lazier we will become".' (PD, 13 December, 1970.) Kwangtung province shortly afterwards felt bold enough to declare bluntly that the communes would not be 'revolutionised' and that current policies governing their operations had Mao's blessing. (RS, 2 January, 1971.)

The dilemma for Peking was simple. While a number of areas (Kwangtung province and much of Kwangsi region, for instance) had advanced sufficiently to qualify for nationalisation — 'ownership by the whole people' instead of collective ownership of commune property — under the criteria laid down in the national development programme, China was not ready financially to take such a drastic step. (NCNA, 24 July, 1971; Kwangsi RS, 23 November, 1970; *National Programme for Agricultural Development, 1956-1967,* 45.) The harsh truth was that collective ownership and freedom to engage in spare-time and side-line activities strengthened the profitability of the communes and allowed them to acquire their own funds for mechanisation. (PD, 25 March, 1971.) Even after Peking's February declaration of support for the communes as currently organised, confusion still prevailed among rural cadres. Especially powerful were the voices demanding an end to all compromise with socialist principles and to the pampering of peasant desires to own some form of property. In Yunnan province, local officials argued, incorrectly, that spare-time jobs would lead the peasants to neglect their commune duties. In Shansi province, by contrast, cadres were found stating that since they had pushed grain production up to Peking's targets, their constituents should concentrate on growing 'industrial crops to increase income'. This attitude was attacked, as the government was not prepared to tolerate any relegation of food output to second place. In another province, cadres went to the opposite extreme, concentrating entirely on grain and ignoring the legitimate opportunities which existed for making extra income on the side.

Fukien province illustrated best the confusion and complexity of the situation. The province had to denounce the high priority which side-line production occupied in the local economy. Many villages would make no attempt to improve production unless paid extra for their effort. But, stated one commune administration, material rewards had not succeeded in changing backward areas into advanced farming units. Apparently, the peasants still preferred to do the minimum in the fields and to spend their time on other jobs, which always seemed to offer bigger earnings. In addition, the province faced a serious labour shortage which appears to have been the result of the peasants' drift away from farming to other occupations. A senior provincial official told the Fukienese leadership they must develop not only agriculture but also light industry, handicrafts and trade; they could not regard the paddy fields as their only responsibility. But the province's cadres were caught whichever way they jumped, as he made plain. Diversification of the rural economy tempted villagers to neglect food crops for more profitable work but, of course, concentration on grain alone was

227

contrary to official policy. As a final complication, this official warned of a black market which had sprung up in the rice business. The moral seems to be that the peasants' spare-time jobs were not the real danger to revolutionary zeal to produce bigger crops. The obstacle to agricultural development lay in the peasants' preference for putting personal and local interests first. Hence the constant stress on making Mao's ideals a living guide to action in the countryside. As the Epilogue will show, the debate over nationalisation of the peasants' assets, rural mechanisation and the road to a complete socialist revolution in the villages was not halted until the emergence of a temporary compromise in agricultural policy in late 1971. (Yunnan RS, 13 April 1971; Shensi RS, 8 April, 1971; Fukien RS, 21, 23 & 24 March, 1971; RF, 9/1969.)

The peasants proved difficult to convince of the benefits of the new-fangled techniques urged upon them in the name of science. In poor areas, destitution so stunted the villagers' imaginations that they could not comprehend the notion of material progress. One production brigade remarked: 'We were born to live on dried potatoes. How can we dream of feeding on rice?' (PD, 18 November, 1970.) The more prosperous argued: 'We are quite satisfied because we already have enough to eat and wear.' (Shensi RS, 9 September, 1970.) Some cadres set their faces against improvements in agricultural performance because 'conditions are poor, difficulties are numerous'. (KMD, 6 April, 1970.) Another source of opposition to an agricultural revolution was the fear that 'a leap forward might lead to reckless actions'. (Anhwei RS, 10 August, 1970.) Clearly, the events of 1958 and the hunger after the Great Leap Forward's collapse had not been forgotten in the villages. Kiangsi province had some local leaders who were apparently incapable of learning new farming methods and refused to abandon traditional techniques. (RS, 4 September, 1970.)

Reluctance to undertake the extra work required to change from single to double cropping also emerged: 'To produce more late rice than early rice means more work and smaller results ... Since we have already achieved a bumper harvest of early rice, we can now rest.' (Fukien RS, 24 August, 1970.) Affection for the old farming routines was strong, and traditional patterns of cultivation were buttressed by the peasants' belief that in the last resort, sun and rain, not human sweat and night-soil, decided the fate of the harvest. 'The output of late rice depends entirely on heaven. Good results do not depend on our own efforts.' (Hunan RS, 20 August, 1970.) The peasants disliked discarding their ancient almanac which determined the auspicious days for every activity from ploughing to burying the dead. This book was based in fact on a close observation of the cycle of variations in the seasons' patterns. A new calendar had to be imposed on the peasants because the modern seeds demanded different growing schedules. In Kirin province, people were criticised for failing to realise the importance of starting to transplant rice early. They argued in their ignorance of modern hybrid seeds: 'It is safe to transplant them at a later date . . . There is plenty of time even if transplanting is not finished before the summer.' (RS, 28 May, 1970.)

The peasants felt the new techniques were risky, asserting in Liaoning province: 'It is safe to stick to the old methods.' (RS 13 April, 1970.) In Heilungkiang province, country people maintained scientific farming was positively dangerous. (RS, 15 March, 1970.) The word went round in Shansi province that 'deep-ploughing is harmful'. (RS, 10 October, 1970.) The rural population sometimes found the new seeds produced unpalatable grains: 'When the commune popularised the planting of a high-yield sorghum . . . some people spread the rumour that "combat-revisionism" no. 10 sorghum . . . was no good for eating.' (KMD, 23 April, 1970.) The peasants' anxieties were not completely without foundation. A detailed account was published of the painful and obviously expensive struggle to plant millet more efficiently in northern China. The article showed that scientific farming made enormous demands on the local leaders' ability to defeat ignorance, conservatism, complacency, apart from coping with bad weather and their own lack of education.

In one of the most desolate areas of northwestern China, a commune found the courage to try a new variety of broad bean recommended as yielding thirty per cent more than the normal strains. The peasants made the mistake of accepting this advice without reservation. A large tract was sown with the modern seed. To the commune's horror, the harvest was smaller than normal. Instead of returning permanently to the tested methods of the past, the commune experimented with the new variety on a small plot and discovered it required an entirely different weeding technique. The message emphasised by Peking in confessing such costly failures was that 'politics in command' was the only recipe for success. This slogan took on a real significance when it encouraged the peasants to ponder Mao's teachings on careful investigation before action, modifying theory in the light of local conditions and experiments by the masses before full-scale adoption of new methods. When applied in this manner, the study of

Mao's philosophy became something more than mere political indoctrination. His essays called on the ordinary people to use their native wit to question not only tradition but modern science as well. The spirit of inquiry, of accepting nothing at face value, is perhaps the biggest advance towards a modern economy. (NCNA, 23, 25 & 29 November, 1970.)

The millions of young people sent down to the countryside showed themselves of special value in easing the transition to new production routines — unlike most of their predecessors before the Cultural Revolution. Hunan villagers, for instance, used to believe: 'Those sent to the countryside for production were either people not working properly and hanging about or people who had made mistakes.' (*Chung-kuo Ching-nien Pao,* 17 April, 1962.) Special efforts were made to ensure young people settled down in the villages and to allay their parents' anxieties. (Tsingtao RS, 12 February, 1971.) In addition, officials transferred to rural duties were frequently given special responsibility for the welfare of the young intellectuals who probably found it easier to get along with these educated cadres than the ordinary semi-literate village leaders. (NCNA, 11 May, 1970.) Nevertheless, in some instances, the intellectuals from the cities were still regarded as a nuisance by the villagers who doubted if they could earn their keep in the fields. Sometimes, too, the peasants looked on the youngsters as no more than additional labour and neglected their other talents. (NCNA, 29 August, 1970; KMD, 29 September, 1970.) But when allowed to put their superior education to work, the young intellectuals took on a host of tasks which must have revolutionised many rural communities. In Hupeh province, they took part in scientific research and served as accountants, store-keepers, clerks, agrotechnicians, teachers and medical auxiliaries. Their good standing in this part of China was demonstrated by the selection of eighty of them to join various branches of the local administration, from production brigades right up to the provincial government. (NCNA, 29 March, 1970.) A similar pattern was observed in Kwangtung province where young intellectuals were recruited as cadres. (Canton RS, 5 June, 1970.) In one commune, the educated youths sent to work in the countryside found solutions for serious obstacles to higher cotton output. By 1970, these young people had raised cotton yields by five hundred per cent compared with 1965. (KMD, 28 September, 1970.) In Yunnan province, one of China's most backward regions, the intellectuals mastered local minority peoples' languages, set about teaching them simple medicine and scientific farming and ran night schools of all kinds. (*Yunnan Daily*, 23 September, 1970.) Students sent to a mountain area were at first repelled by their inability to wash their hands clean of the smell of dung. Eventually they learned to live like the peasants, designed and helped to build a hydro-electric station and worked with the villagers to overcome the adverse effects of the local climate on rice yields. (RF, 8/1970.)

On balance, developments after October 1969 indicated the basic validity of Mao Tse-tung's economic principles. Yet serious obstacles to sustained growth survived the Cultural Revolution's violent onslaught against those attitudes and practices among the population (and the cadres in particular) which Mao viewed as impediments to China's modernisation. His development strategy also proved incomplete. Its biggest defect was the failure to resolve the conflict between national and local interests which intensified as economic authority was turned over to the basic levels of the administration. But Mao could probably have claimed that had the nation followed the unselfish ideals he recommended, clashes between the central government and semi-independent district economies would have been avoided. This point underlines Mao's belief that if only the mind could purge itself of fear and greed, life would be more hopeful, more prosperous and in less need of official control. This principle did not help the central administration, which had good reason to ask for greater power in administering the economy. Unfortunately, Mao had never elaborated what a government should do while waiting for its people to adopt the correct outlook on life.

But the actual operations of industry and agriculture showed considerable promise of low-cost economic development. Responsibility was given to the masses in the cities and villages, and Peking left them to solve their own difficulties. The result was an upsurge of voluntary investment by the population of time, energy and money in projects which accelerated economic advance. Peking's determination not merely to exploit the obvious methods of increasing output but to search relentlessly for even the most trivial contributions to national output was a sign of China's continuing poverty. But it was also a symbol of the refusal by Mao's administration to accept any but the highest possible rate of development. What had seemed empty slogans about emulation, innovation, self-reliance and the masses when freshly minted in the Cultural Revolution took on a significance from 1969 which made sound sense.

231

Again the only real difficulty lay in people's ideas. The policies of the workers being left to fend for themselves, the officials and technicians being forced to adopt new techniques for guiding organisations towards prosperity, and the peasants being asked to pay hard cash for sacrificing tradition, were being stretched to what seemed close to the limits of human tolerance. The feverish pursuit of progress called for a continuous surge of energy from the entire population in order to overcome the shortages and bottlenecks which appeared as industrial and agricultural expansion increased the country's demand for materials, machinery and capital.

During the West's industrial revolution the captain of industry, ruthless in his quest to build a bigger and richer business empire, also drove himself beyond the endurance of most normal men. Under capitalism, the ambitions of the mill-owner or iron-master could be served by mindless 'hands' thankful to have found work and not be broken on the wheel of progress through total destitution. Stalin used fear to fix his people's minds on the fulfilment of his economic dreams. Mao chose in the Cultural Revolution to give the economy to the people. It is just possible that an entire nation can find enough consolation for the nerve-wracking ordeal of continually striving to push output to new records from the thought that they are building a new world. Capitalists, after all, had goaded themselves to undertake new risks and greater responsibilities by the promise of riches, power and comfort if they won their battles to build industrial empires.

A remarkable feature of the first period after the proclamation of a Maoist development programme in 1969 was the way Mao Tse-tung's practical proposals for progress bore fruit so quickly. The rapid creation of small subsidiaries by large enterprises, the progress from primitive workshops to advanced manufacturing, the birth of a huge network of rural industries confirmed the solid basis for Mao's confidence in his own strategy for economic growth. Workers could learn modern techniques through self-help; villages ran their own factories with small doses of advice from outside; intellectuals were able to bring new skills into a closed peasant world. Mao had waited a long time for an opportunity to put his theories to the test. When his chance came, the dividends were attractive. His mixture of caution, shrewdness and utopianism appeared to be the right catalyst for the economic transformation of a nation, instinctively and through experience, cynical about the performance of politicians and suspicious of the intentions of governments.

Epilogue

As a blueprint for prosperity, Mao Tse-tung's theories were, he believed, only as effective as their ability to inspire his people. The threat to the success of his economic doctrines came from the deep-rooted social and cultural instincts of the Chinese. The Cultural Revolution was supposed to make the nation's soul as 'white' as poverty had made the economy 'blank', so that Mao could draw 'beautiful pictures' on China's mind and spur the country to fight more urgently for a better world. The Cultural Revolution did not create this 'purity'. Particularly galling must have been the survival of old social patterns which had been denounced for two decades by the communist government and for half a century by Mao himself. The stubborn loyalty with which China preserved its ancient customs testified to the resilience of its culture and to the awesome challenge Mao had accepted in seeking to abolish 'feudalism'.

Tradition's strength flowed first from the family, an institution which could hardly be eliminated overnight, if ever. The clan system also preserved the past. Clans could not be eradicated without uprooting the 500 million peasants and resettling them at random across the country. This undertaking even Mao never contemplated. The family was described in 1970 as an 'air-raid shelter' for self-interest, revisionism and feudalism. (*Kiangsi Daily*, 25 February, 1970.) Customs which symbolised family and clan ties refused to die. The argument was heard: 'It is human nature to arrange banquets and give away presents for festivals, marriages and funerals.' (PD, 2 February, 1970.) Marriage was particularly difficult to reform. Apparently, the ordinary Chinese under Mao still believed, as his forefathers had, that marriage could not be celebrated without some display. The reasons for the exchange of dowries and the feasting which have accompanied Chinese weddings are firstly, that marriages were arranged by parents through formal bargains involving an exchange of property, and secondly, that marriage was formalised by a social not religious ceremony (though ancestor worship had a place in the nuptial rites). To marry without presenting bride and groom to relatives and friends at a banquet was, and seemingly remained, akin to 'living in sin'.

One ardent local communist, to his wife's delight, received a betrothal gift from a prospective son-in-law. The reasons for refusing the present were partly Maoist contempt for feudalism but partly practical: 'When our son-in-law's elder brother married, he was extravagant and wasted a large sum on presents and banquets under the influence of the old ideology, culture, customs and habits. Subsequently, he had great difficulty in making ends meet.' In other words, the wedding costs had been beyond the young man's means, and he had got into debt. (*ibid.*, 22 January, 1970.) In Hupeh province, one commune seems to have tried to organise mass 'proletarian' weddings, possibly because individual couples would not have dared to defy tradition on their own. The pressure to observe old customs in this area was strong, with youngsters advised: 'Marriage is a big event in a man's life and calls for a big splash.' (RS, 12 January, 1971.) In another district, as soon as harvesting was over, people 'worked out privately how much extra grain should be allotted to them and thought about . . . getting married and giving birthday banquets'. (*Hunan Daily,* 5 August, 1970.) Marriage 'deals' of the traditional kind between families were reported in Shantung, indicating young people still accepted mates found by their parents. (RS, 18 January, 1971.)

The clans' authority persisted. They still kept records of the history of their member families, and clan relationships were seen by Peking as a threat to the party's authority. (RF, 2/1970.) Clan feuds had not been wiped out, reading between the lines of one cryptic account from Liaoning province. (NCNA, 15 January, 1971.) The clan was a fortress behind whose walls any member could claim sanctuary. Thus the *People's Daily* seemed to feel a considerable coup had been won when a group of trained cadres managed to win a village's confidence, persuaded it to break with clan ethics and hand over a 'class enemy who was hiding very deeply'. (2 June, 1970.) The cadres' understanding of clan solidarity was very evident. One group of officials sent down to the countryside confessed: 'We were worried that family relationships in the countryside were very complicated and that many people would be upset if we pointed out the faults of anyone in their ranks.' (PD, 7 April, 1970.)

The chances of the old culture surviving indefinitely seemed high.

In the evening, the peasants gathered in one village (and this example could be applied to both urban and rural areas) to listen to stories from Chinese classical history, to talk about the old days, to discuss food and drink and to keep alive ancient superstitions. (*Fukien Daily*, 12 August, 1970.) Despite China's space satellites, ordinary people apparently continued to find deep satisfaction in tales of ancient dynasties, discussions of local customs and in looking nostalgically over their shoulders to times gone by — just as the Chinese have done for centuries. The influence of tradition was such that 'some comrades are afraid that if they change customs, they will be divorced from the masses'. (RF, 2/1971.)

Mao Tse-tung failed to avert another danger to his ideas which was the cynicism with which cadres regarded political study. In the final analysis, every government, however firm its popular base, must rely on a political apparatus to explain its ideals and programmes to the public. In China, no real distinction could be drawn between party members and government officials after the Cultural Revolution when it came to propagating the thoughts of Mao Tse-tung. The public was often described as bored with politics. One commune declared of Mao's works: 'Discussion is of no importance as we have already studied and applied them.' (NCNA, 18 August, 1970.) Party members expressed the same sentiment: 'We have already taken part in study classes on the new party constitution and in the party rebuilding campaign; and we have learned enough.' Some officials said: 'We cannot demand so much from rural party members whose educational standards are low.' In another instance, the party had not even bothered to arrange classes for members.(Chekiang RS, 3 June, 28 August, 1970.) Honan province complained of cadres who displayed no enthusiasm for reading Mao and said only a minority of officials appreciated the importance of putting Mao's principles in command of all their activities. (RS, 7 October, 1970.) In Kiangsi province, members of the party were reported to have only a hazy understanding of Mao's fundamental concept of class struggle. (RS, 18 June, 1970.)

The most colourful comment on political study came from a Wuhan conference attended by several of the city's leaders: 'We have got through the production barrier. We are still rough old fellows whether we study or not.' (Hupeh RS, 10 October, 1970.) Urged late in 1970 to get down to serious reading of Mao's philosophy and the marxist classics, one response was: 'Philosophy is mysterious . . . This study has nothing to do with me.' (*Shansi Daily*, 21 October, 1970.)

Another objection to political courses came from veterans who stated they had nothing more to learn after twenty or thirty years of making revolution. New cadres felt their working-class backgrounds exempted them from the duty to remould their thinking through Mao classes. (Honan RS, 2 November, 1970; Heilungkiang RS, 5 October, 1970.) Even political campaigns were felt to be a waste of energy. 'Revolutionary mass criticism' was dismissed in one Shanghai factory as 'the same old thing'. (RF, 10/1970.) Senior cadres felt the criticism campaigns, stressed so strongly by Mao, were not their concern but the business of the masses and minor officials. (Fukien RS, 29 April, 1970.)

Ominous signs appeared of a return to old mandarin habits. Bureaucrats requested well-equipped offices and spacious living quarters. They resented rebukes from their seniors; refused to co-operate with their colleagues; and treated their subordinates harshly. Cadres attacked during the Cultural Revolution felt the time had come to settle old scores. Others, however, felt the main thing was to safeguard their careers by picking easy jobs and avoiding mistakes. 'It is dangerous to be a cadre' was a remark heard all over the country from both old and new officials. In addition, serious differences in attitude were exhibited by officials who had survived the Cultural Revolution and men who joined the bureaucracy after 1966. China did not lack individuals all too willing to flatter cadres and play upon their liking for the good things of life. None of this augured well for the prospects of producing fit heirs to Mao throughout the administration who would jealously protect his doctrines. (Anhwei RS, 18 February, 1970; PD, 27 October, 1969; 6 November, 1970; Chekiang RS, 25 September, 1970; Hupeh RS, 15 April, 1970; Kiangsu RS, 20 June, 1970; KMD, 5 March, 1970.)

The third peril to the long-term survival of Mao's ideals as an effective influence in Chinese economic life was peasant selfishness. Peking stated in 1969: 'Production teams reaping a good harvest should give their members a little more grain than is distributed to members of teams which produce poor harvests.' (RF, 12/1969.) Statements published during 1970 laid down a similar principle (derived from Mao): an annual improvement in peasant incomes should take place each year. But the peasants preferred to take matters into their own hands rather than trust to the generosity of the state. Throughout the year, peasants in Hupeh province (among many others) were criticised for their 'greed': 'After a bumper harvest in the county, a few people, seriously influenced by capitalist thinking, argued they should save less

236

and eat more, share out more and hand over less to the government.'
(Hupeh RS, 20 June, 7 September, 1970.) 'Eat all, divide all and
consume all' was a favourite folk-saying. (*Kwangsi Daily*, 13 July,
1970.)

While evidence indicated some areas handed over so much to state
procurement agencies that not enough food was left for communal
reserves and the peasants' own needs, the main tendency was to let as
little grain (and other crops) as possible leave the villages for the official
granaries. (Fukien RS, 4 July, 1970; Kirin RS, 15 October, 1970.) This
situation meant that while the peasants received industrial products at
the cheapest possible price, the countryside handed over the minimum
amount to assist China's development. The central and provincial
authorities tried to correct this selfish behaviour by regular campaigns
to instil Maoist ideals into the rural mind. But the peasants generally
seemed deaf to appeals from the government for more consideration of
the national interest.

One paradoxical aspect of the communist struggle against 'feudalism' is that it may have been an unnecessary effort. The Japanese,
whose industrial revolution, it has been argued, closely paralleled Mao's
model for China, have successfully created a modern community of
remarkable efficiency. But they have retained many elements from
their traditional society. (Robert J. Ballon, ed., *The Japanese Employee,* Chapters Two and Three.) Mao, while advocating a distinctively
Chinese solution to the country's problems seems to have been
convinced that the 'feudal', mandarin and self-seeking traits of
traditional society needed complete eradication. As a result Mao
Tse-tung, in declaring that man and his innate virtue were the key to
the creation of a modern, just and prosperous society, had no option
but to contend with three sets of 'saboteurs' who were chipping away
at the very foundations of his strategy for creating China's splendid
future. The elimination of these 'subversive' elements – the 'feudalist',
the uninspired bureaucrat and the greedy peasant – would be achieved,
the Maoist had to believe, by political education. But the waves of
revolutionary 'class struggle' seemed to wash over these three rocks. If
they were eroding, the process was pitifully slow. These groups, in a
sense, held the future of Mao's philosophy in their hands. Without some
technique for wearing them down rapidly, these were the groups which
must in the long term undermine Maoism as an economic system. Given
the acknowledged survival of powerful traditional 'guilds' in Shanghai
at least as late as 1967, it could not be assumed that industrialisation

would lessen China's longing to safeguard its cultural heritage and the more important 'feudal' customs.

As with any nation, to rely so heavily on newspapers and radio broadcasts to analyse the most basic aspirations of the population is a dangerous procedure. Chinese communists are insistent in private discussions that, in reality, the Cultural Revolution has swept away the strength of traditional family attitudes, transformed the narrow mentality of the bulk of the country people and injected a new spirit of service and dedication into the bureaucracy. These sources claim their personal observations of Chinese life after the Cultural Revolution convince them that the 'feudal' forces and general selfishness which hindered progress before 1966 have been eliminated except in the most remote and backward areas of the nation. These communists, with their special access to information on developments inside China, explain press and radio denunciations of family behaviour, erring cadres and greedy peasants as part of a bid to eradicate the last remaining traces of these old faults. The reports carried in the official news media, they state, represent only isolated instances of mistakes in outlook and ideology and cannot be taken as representative of conditions in general.

This view deserves respect. Perhaps these Chinese communists are correct in their sanguine confidence that Mao had overcome the real source of resistance to his philosophy. Certainly with modernisation and education, the nation's traditional attitudes will undergo change as their relevance to the new style of living and working diminishes. Possibly Maoism represents the outlook which the future China will adopt as the basis of its culture. However, Mao always claimed that tradition was a considerable obstacle to the success of his plans for the people, and the volume of reports from all over the country on the continuing influence of heretical ideas testifies strongly to the continued existence of deep-rooted 'feudal', 'selfish' and 'mandarin' habits as a firm barrier to Mao's total triumph. In addition, the weight of Chinese history and the demonstrations it provides of the population's ability to withstand official pressures are factors to be reckoned with.

In the end, of course, as Mao Tse-tung probably realised, his economic philosophy would have to be replaced by a new version of Maoism. Just as Marx, the father of communism, could not foresee (as Mao noted) the problems of imperialism, so Mao Tse-tung had created his ideology in the context of an impoverished China. Once prosperity comes, the nation will have to revise the structure Mao laid down for industry and agriculture, for his strategy, aimed at creating a modern state, was not deeply concerned with the ordering of a society which had found its way to affluence. The Chinese have often claimed the West is foolish to expect that as the country gets richer, its revolutionary fervour will diminish and that it will make the same compromises with marxist purity as the Russians.

This is a brave assertion. Human nature, given a glimpse of comfort, usually succumbs to temptation. Yet this may be too pessimistic a forecast. Martin Patchen's investigation of an American organisation (the Tennessee Valley Authority, whose functions are similar to the activities of a rural Chinese county) indicates a significant response from workers to participation in management, a challenge to their abilities, control over work methods – in short, to an American equivalent of Mao's principle, 'the masses in command'. (*Participation, Achievement and Involvement on the Job.*) Geoffrey K. Ingham's study of Britain's small factories (the basis of China's industrial transformation) shows workers willing to sacrifice high wages for other forms of satisfaction. (*Size of Industrial Organisation and Worker Behaviour,* 143.) If multipurpose bodies in the United States, handling both rural and industrial development, and British factories can use non-monetary incentives to keep their workers happy, why should China despair of doing likewise?

In case anyone felt that after the upheavals of 1966 and the subsequent anarchy, Mao Tse-tung and his supporters would never again dare to use such violence to stamp out all 'reactionary' and 'revisionist' ideas which might infect China in the future, the Chairman declared: 'The present great Cultural Revolution is only the first, and in the future there are bound to be others.' (PD, 23 May, 1967.) He was determined not to be obliterated from the country's memory by heresies old or new, and proved himself ready in autumn 1971 to chastise the highest in the land whom he suspected of seeking to sabotage his polices, and to embark on further refinements of his tactics to speed progress towards prosperity.

The pledge to struggle on for the political soul of the Chinese nation was no empty slogan. In late 1971, Mao's official heir, Vice Chairman of the Communist Party and Minister of Defence Lin Piao, was suddenly erased from the political scene together with a significant number of the national military establishment. At the end of September, Lin was still being cited as responsible for laying down national policy; on 3 October, one province referred to him as a 'glorious example'; on 8 October came the last public mention of Lin before he vanished from sight completely. (Anhwei RS, 28 September, 1971; Hupeh RS, 3 October, 1971; Kirin RS, 8 October, 1971.) While Lin's political demise was confirmed by senior Peking officials, they failed to reveal the reasons for his downfall. (*Le Monde,* 11 February, 1972.)

The power structure in the Chinese capital after this sudden eclipse of the man who had been nominated to follow Mao Tse-tung as leader of the country's communist party was obscure. Considerable confusion was created by the repeated echoes of the initial phase of the the first Cultural Revolution in 1966. At one point, a shadowy figure was under attack whose career bore a marked resemblance to that of Prime Minister Chou En-lai. (PD, 24 October, 1971). Mao himself, one area hinted, had been downgraded in the minds of some comrades. (Szechwan RS, 14 October, 1971.) However, Chou survived the immediate upheaval. Although implied criticism of Mao's record in the political, economic and military fields had been refuted vigorously in the editorial celebrating the golden jubilee of the communist party on 1 July, a reissue of the basic text of the editorial in October indicated Mao's position was once again secure by deleting those passages which had defended his leadership. (NCNA, 30 June, 1971; *China Pictorial,* 10/1971.)

The charges against Lin were made by innuendo. His power as a military commander was weakened by the application in 1971 of article 5 of the communist party constitution promulgated in April 1969 which laid down that all branches of the government and national life must be subject to party control. As one province revealed, once the party structure had been rebuilt – and China's party-rebuilding at provincial level was completed in August 1971 – the army became subordinate to the civilian party committees. (Hunan RS, 16 October, 1971.) This principle was emphasised at national level at the end of November. (NCNA, 30 November, 1971.) The quality of the army in the purely military sphere was already under question before Lin's disappearance, and allegations later appeared of outright neglect of military training. (PD, 6 September, 1971, for example, and RF, 1/1972.) This switch away from stress on the political role of the armed forces appeared to be an attempt to buy the loyalty of the troops who were anxious to return to military life and to leave politics to the civilians. (Kweichow RS, 14 November, 1971.)

But the army was not permitted to take refuge in its billets as the storm toppled its highest commanders. The soldiers found themselves attacked for mistakes in policy during the Cultural Revolution. (Shensi RS, 21 October, 1971.) Hints appeared of serious indiscipline in the armed forces, and a campaign was launched to remind the nation of the need for total obedience by the troops to the central authorities and for unity between the army and the people. (PD, 7 November, 1971.) Szechwan province warned of the dangers of 'warlord' ideas within the army, an inevitable peril when so much political power had been placed in the hands of those who wielded the gun. (RS, 26 December, 1971.)

But the soldiers were so much a part of national life by this time that potential supporters of Lin Piao could not be neutralised by ordering the soldiers back to barracks. (See Ralph L. Powell, *Asian Survey*, June 1970, August 1971; Jurgen Domes, *Current Scene*, 7 February, 1971.) The 158 senior members of the country's major party committees included ninety army commanders, and soldiers were prominent throughout the lower echelons of the economic and political administration. The armed forces could not be treated with the contumely which marked the onslaught on Liu Shao-chi's power base in the civilian communist party during the Red Guard upheavals of 1966. The population continued to be fed with reminders of the duty to learn from the army, and soldiers were still hailed as courageous servants of the people. (*Yunnan Daily*, 16 January, 1972; Shensi RS, 15 November, 1971.)

Although the effort to bring the army under the absolute control of the party was clearly necessary in engineering the downfall of Lin Piao, criticisms of the soldiers' work lead straight into the main burden of the case against the minister of defence. The army had been handed responsibility for rearing 'millions of successors to the proletarian revolutionary cause', and Lin had spelt out the armed forces' role in superintending the political education of the country during the Cultural Revolution. (*Liberation Army Daily*, 1 August, 1966; ID, 49.) The gravest accusations against Lin concerned the errors made in the reconstruction of the communist party destroyed in the years 1966 to 1969.

Lin was accused of tampering deliberately with the criteria which Mao had set forth on the subject of party building. This charge was in some ways unfair. Lin had put forward additional tests for the ideal cadre but only as an aside in the midst of a long commentary on Mao's own teachings on the subject, though Lin's gloss on Mao often seemed subsequently to receive more attention than Mao's own criteria. (PD, 2 January, 1967; RF, 12/1971.) Lin's 'distortion' of Mao's theories on party building was alleged to have created cliques within the party, to have weakened party unity and lowered standards for party membership. (Kweichow RS, 27 November, 1971.) The *Red Flag* journal in November 1971 disclosed serious alarm in the government about the threat of a collapse of the party into rival factions.

Other charges against Lin included: an attempt to propagate the theory 'heroes make history'; the notion that Mao's genius, not his links with the people and their revolution, was the most important factor in Mao's development of communist ideology. This idea was interpreted as a plot to separate Mao from the masses. Lin was alleged to have induced the public to learn reams of Mao quotations in order to vulgarise Maoism. Lin also seems to have been held guilty of trying to stop any further development by Mao of his philosophy. If true, this bid would have enhanced Lin's power as official commentator on a fixed set of doctrines, with Mao relegated to the background because no more ideological contributions would be required from him. (ID, 240; Szechwan RS, 11 Januarry, 1972; *Szechwan Daily,* 6 January, 1972; Kweichow RS, 8 January, 1972; PD, 28 January, 1972; KMD, 22 January, 1972.)

Ironically, Lin Piao was ousted for much the same mistakes as Liu Shao-chi whom he had replaced as successor to Mao Tse-tung. Lin, like Liu, had failed to produce for Mao a body of communists whom he could trust to implement his ideas for the transformation of China. But the irony was double-edged. The abuse hurled at Lin (though without naming him outright) was derived from Liu Shao-chi's writings. The 'heroes', claiming to be 'one hundred per cent Bolsheviks', the 'sham marxists' in the party became standard denunciations of Lin and his supporters. These same crimes had been prime targets for Liu's wrath when still responsible for cleansing the Chinese communist movement. (Canton RS, 21 January, 1972; Boyd Compton, *Mao's China,* 123, 199, 260.)

For a time China seemed on the verge of yet another Cultural Revolution. An article in the *People's Daily* on 20 October, 1971, referred ominously to 'arrows in the back', implying bitter struggles in progress in the Peking hierarchy. A major article denounced any compromise with the class enemy. (RF, 11/1971.) Another commentary concluded: 'We believe that revolution can change everything.' China was told: 'Our comrades must grasp that they cannot evade class struggle . . . In the face of the continuous attempt by the class enemy to apply idealism in engaging in conspiracies against the party . . . every single revolutionary should arise and utter his condemnation of idealism.' (*ibid.*)

'Idealism' here meant 'ultra-leftism' which involved 'pursuing empty politics, preaching the theory "that the spirit can achieve everything", setting politics against production and technique'. 'Idealism' was viewed as a bid to 'spread anarchism and the ultra-leftist trend and issue blind commands, having no respect for science and the objective laws of production'. (Hainan RS, 22 & 24 November, 1971.) Although erring elements were ousted in some areas, a full-blown Cultural Revolution failed to emerge. (Shansi RS, 25 October, 1971; *Yunnan Daily*, 2 December, 1971.)

The reasons for deciding against a new upsurge by the whole country against Mao's foes were obscure. Perhaps with China's hopes of establishing a new reputation for moderation as it entered into an era of diplomatic triumphs – membership of the United Nations in November 1971 and President Richard Nixon's visit to Peking the following February – the central authorities felt that a rebirth of the Red Guards would be dangerous. The years 1966 and 1967, after all, had badly tarnished the Chinese international image when the revolutionaries turned their zeal upon the Chinese foreign ministry and diplomatic missions in Peking.

Possibly more important was the conclusion which seemed to be reached that Lin was basically motivated by a form of ambition which would not have endangered Mao until after his death. The country was told in the most authoritative manner possible: 'Hidden anti-party and anti-socialist counter-revolutionaries are very few in number. The overwhelming majority of good people who committed mistakes in political line are able to return to the correct line through criticism and self-criticism.' China was also reminded of Mao's observation that, in many cases, erring cadres 'violate party discipline through not knowing what it is' and were led astray by plotters. (NCNA, 30 November, 1971.) Lin was thus seen as lacking popular support. The greatest worry was the prospect that Lin Piao would denounce Mao after his death as 'Khruschev viciously denounced Stalin following Stalin's death' although he had 'pretentiously praised Stalin as the close friend and comrade-in-arms of the great Lenin, the greatest genius, teacher and leader of mankind ... when Stalin was alive.' (Ninghsia RS, 5 November, 1971.)

The failure of Lin to rebuild the communist party along Maoist lines was linked to debates over economic development. An anarchic party with members of low calibre meant a lack of effective leadership to tackle the continuing weaknesses of the civil service, to deal with 'feudalism' and to revolutionise the minds of the peasants. Economic policy was complicated throughout 1971 because of these three stubborn obstacles, as Peking viewed them.

The fundamental problem was the countryside. In 1970, an unpublicised inter-provincial conference on agriculture had been convened which resulted in a call to imitate the model farming community of Tachai. The public campaign began with a major article on Tachai in the *People's Daily* on 23 September, 1970. (Chinghai RS, 10 February, 1972.) The Cultural Revolution had not touched the bulk of the peasants until late 1968 and even then was strictly limited in its impact. Richard Baum suggests that the attempt to bring the Cultural Revolution to the villages led to serious resentment among rural cadres and sufficient dissension in the countryside to warrant treating the peasants with considerable discretion. (Thomas W. Robinson, ed., *The Cultural Revolution in China*, 367, 453, 475-76.) The Tachai campaign was supposed to help transform peasant conservatism into a desire for progress and complete the Cultural Revolution in the villages.

For the ordinary rural cadre, the call to imitate Tachai posed acute embarrassments. The essence of the Tachai system was the payment of wages according to the political consciousness of the peasant, his public-spiritedness and his actual output, all three factors to be assessed by open debate among his fellow-villagers. (Ryoichi Mikitani, *Keizai Hyoron*, April 1967.) As already noted, out of fear of being criticised for 'conservatism', cadres allowed basic party policies on agriculture to be changed. Attempts were made by radical groups to 'skip a stage in the development of revolution' by abolishing payment by results and by forbidding all forms of private enterprise.

By late 1971, a majority of provinces revealed that local administrations were pushing back the radicals despite claims that 'as a result of the Cultural Revolution the ideological consciousness of the peasants was rising ceaselessly' so that farming could be done for love of revolution rather than reward. One report stated: 'An erroneous feeling prevails among some people unwilling to correct their mistakes in going too far in implementing policies. They regard the correction of such mistakes as "a retreat" and claim that since this is the road they will take eventually, there is no need for them to correct these mistakes ... It should be pointed out that what the party calls for to be accomplished tomorrow should not be done today.'

The radicals were accused of upsetting the peasants who

complained: 'Those who have worked more do not get more. Those who have laboured less are not paid less.' Villages sometimes found their economic autonomy abolished. The peasants' reaction was to share out immediately communal savings among themselves before they were absorbed into a larger farming unit. A number of reports from the countryside indicated that the abolition of payment according to work and a ban on private plots and private enterprise in the villages reduced the volume of output as rural morale sagged. (Hainan RS, 6 February, 1972; Heilungkiang RS, 30 October, 1971; Hupeh RS, 22 January, 1972; *Inner Mongolia Daily,* 29 December, 1971; Shansi RS, 31 January, 1972.)

Although the need to reward the peasants for their labours was recognised, the villages would have to be weaned at some stage from their traditional concern with private gain if China was to achieve full communism. The question of how and when to 'rupture' the concept of private property (including the desire for material incentives in return for work) was a running debate in the latter half of 1971. The weight of opinion as summed up in the official press was for great caution in trying to alter rural thinking. While admitting that changes were necessary in the way economic life was organised, the prevailing view was that sweeping reforms were untimely, (RF, 5, 7-8/1971; PD, 23 July, 30 November 1971.) 'The spontaneous tendency towards capitalism' was denounced, and individual interests were to be subordinated to the welfare of the group and the nation. But a clear warning was given that no interference with peasant management of their own affairs and their enjoyment of spare-time production for personal profit would be tolerated. (RF, 12/1971.)

This situation amounted to a compromise over the advance towards completing China's socialist revolution. Some way of indirectly attacking the traditional peasant mentality had to be found. The solution was very pragmatic. F.G. Bailey has observed that ideological appeals have little influence on peasants' attitudes. To alter their preference for the established patterns of agriculture and of country life, a mixture of 'carrot and stick' has to be employed to change the political and economic environment which makes the peasant value the practices handed down from one generation to the next. (*Peasants and Peasant Society,* 317-19.) The answer to China's rural conservatism was found in mechanisation of farming, a task which Mao had stated should be completed between 1975 and 1980. (Kiangsi RS, 18 December, 1971.)

Machinery would solve the shortage of farm labour, raise agricultural productivity and, by encouraging the manufacture (and presumably control) of heavy equipment by the counties and communes, pave the way for a transfer of agricultural management from the peasants in their villages to the larger, more anonymous commune or even county administrations. (PD, 9 & 17 September, 1971.) This transfer would be the final stage of the transition to direct state control of the farming sector. The new policy was adopted at a national conference on agricultural mechanisation held sometime around September, before Lin Pao's downfall and apparently meeting with his support. (Hopei RS, 3 September, 1971; Yunnan RS, 24 October, 1971; Hunan RS, 1 November, 1971; Inner Mongolia RS, 11 December, 1971.) The new mechanisation drive provoked immediate resistance in many areas. The chief complaint sprang from the peasants' reluctance to pay for the manufacture of their own equipment and also their apparent suspicion that the counties and communes were undermining the position of the villages. (PD, 15 September, 1971.)

To implement the mechanisation programme, apply the Tachai system without reducing peasants' incentives and mobilise their capacity to finance rural modernisation called for local leadership of high quality. Almost every major article on rural policies emphasised the importance of strengthening the rural bureaucracy. (RF, 12/1971, 1/1972; *Hopei Daily,* 13 November, 1971.) The leadership which had emerged in the power struggles of the Cultural Revolution had been warned nearly two years earlier that its survival would depend on successful performance rather than on Maoist credentials. (PD, 9 June, 1969.)

The dissatisfaction felt with Lin Piao's reconstruction of the communist party, the backbone of Chinese political authority, indicates why his removal was essential on economic grounds, quite apart from his personal ambitions. The calibre of cadre essential for implementing the new rural policies offers an explanation of why he was so quickly removed from office after the national conference on agricultural mechanisation. With the attacks on Lin Piao's strategy for creating a new communist party came a wave of announcements that ninety per cent or more of the pre-1966 officials had been reinstated. (KMD, 21 January, 1972; Szechwan RS, 11 February, 1972; Shensi RS, 9 February, 1972.) The cadres who had been running the peasant world before the Cultural Revolution had the advantages of long, practical experience, relative moderation and, seemingly, a distaste for radical experiments unpopular with the peasants. One cadre was even hailed for refusing to be intimidated when accused of being a 'rightist'. This was a sign of extent to which the pendulum had swung against the more extreme Maoists. (KMD, 25 January, 1972.)

The central government hoped that mechanisation would break through the legacy of traditional farming and the rural outlook it had produced. But 'feudalism' seemed to need a more frontal assault. References to traditional practices which sabotaged the revolution came into prominence once more. (RF, 11/1971; PD, 21 & 26 December, 1971; New Anhwei Daily, 6 January, 1972.) Yet even in this campaign, some effort was made not to upset the peasants. (Hunan RS, 25 January, 1972.)

The rehabilitation of old cadres, the toleration of rural desires for material rewards and the relative restraint towards peasant culture left the seeds of a new conflict. The clock appeared to have been turned back to the era before the Cultural Revolution. A striking instance of this return to the past came from Hunan which stated bluntly that until mechanisation was completed, the country could not afford to reform the existing semi-socialist situation in the countryside. Hunan also claimed that a period of relatively stable policies was necessary, which jarred with the Maoist concept of constant revolutionary struggle. (RF, 13/1971.)

A strong body of opinion must have been opposed to the Hunan line. Many believed demands for postponing socialist revolution until production was on a firm footing to be a doctrine of the heretic Liu Shao-chi. (Wen-hui Pao, 11 December, 1969; RF, 3/1970; Anhwei RS, 11 August, 1971.) Furthermore, the Tachai model was explained specifically as a major step towards eradicating all traces of rural capitalism. (RF, 11/1971.) A change in the economic organisation in the direction of complete socialism remained in the forefront of Peking's mind even while compromise rural policies were adopted to revolutionise the peasantry through an indirect and gradual process. (NCNA, 31 December, 1971.) The programme outlined for China's farmers in late 1971 was no more than a temporary expedient which could provoke bitter political quarrels in the future. The potential for further conflicts was apparent even though those in favour of caution were allowed to cite Mao in their support.

The proposal to mechanise agriculture was accompanied by a debate over industrial priorities. The two questions were related, partly because those responsible for the country's factories still felt 'supporting agriculture is a losing business'. (Kwangsi RS, 28 December, 1971.) This assertion contained some truth since the prices (and thus the profits) obtained for machinery, fuel and chemicals used by the peasants were reduced substantially in the latter half of 1971. At the same time, peasants were given higher prices for their industrial crops. (NCNA, 27 December, 1971.) These changes were an inducement to the villages to use larger inputs of machines, fertilisers and insecticides, thus subsidising the modernisation of agriculture at industry's expense. To ensure the benefits of these price changes were not frittered away on consumption but remained available to finance development, a campaign was launched to increase bank savings and to ensure an adequate proportion of total profits, whether farm or factory, was set aside for investment. (RF, 1/1972; NCNA, 24 February, 1972; *Chekiang Daily,* 21 January, 1972.)

The other element in the industrial debate was related to the old argument over the relative priorities of the light and heavy sectors. Mao's preference for the light sector won the day. (PD, 6 November, 1971.) However, a new factor was the revelation of demands by the armed forces for a greater priority for such defence industries as electronics. Some evidence hinted that the army was not entirely in favour of the rural mechanisation programme since the soldiers would have preferred to see the nation concentrate on the most modern methods of manufacture available instead of decentralising production into relatively primitive industrial bases in the countryside. (KMD, 13 December 1971.)

Whatever the merits of the army's line in the context of national defence needs, the refusal to adopt techniques merely because they were the most up-to-date China could obtain made economic sense. A study of Pakistan, for example, has demonstrated that even its textile industry has been more lavish in its use of equipment than the advanced economy of Japan, without any justification in terms of Pakistan's development requirements. (E.A.G. Robinson and Michael Kidron, eds, *Economic Development in South Asia,* 207.) Peking was avoiding the trap of buying the latest factory plant regardless of whether it suited the country's current level of development. Nevertheless, since the debate was related in part to national defence, this pragmatic approach to modern techniques could not be viewed as permanent policy. Any increase in Sino-Soviet tension, for instance, could shift the balance in the soldiers' favour.

The downfall of Lin Piao did not weaken the basic Maoist thrust of Chinese economic policy: farm mechanisation; priority for light industry; and a check on the heavy sector's demands. Lin's disgrace nevertheless coincided with changes of emphasis in the country's development programme which in turn seemed likely to lead to fresh ideological conflicts and future charges of betrayal of true Maoism.

The economic approach adopted in late 1971 was concerned with using modern methods for production wherever they made economic sense. But those in direct charge of economic affairs displayed an apparent decline in concern for the total transformation of both the human and material setting in which production takes place, a revolution indispensable for full economic development and a vital Maoist tenet. To give peasants more machines and to proceed step by step with the evolution of a comprehensive industrial sector without overthrowing the mental and social barriers to progress could leave China in the same position compared to Japan as Thailand is today. For no guarantee exists that modern equipment by itself inspires an ambition to break away from old values to develop an economy to its maximum potential regardless of the traditions which have to be jettisoned in the process. (Norman Jacobs, *Modernization without Development*, 9-11.) This sort of consideration may have played a part in the argument. Mao Tse-tung's entire philosophy was opposed to policies which would leave his country in this sort of economic backwater.

Any national leader who could topple within six years first his head of state and then his official heir could hardly let the Chinese people rest for long from political struggle and ideological purification when 1971 had seen 'political charlatans' unmasked at the heart of the central government and a continued distaste for unselfish behaviour among the masses and their local leaders. While Mao Tse-tung lived, another upheaval similar to the Cultural Revolution was only a matter of time to seek his ultimate goal of touching 'people to their very souls'. Only then could unity be forged among the 750 million Chinese to enable them to pursue single-mindedly Mao's vision of prosperity with justice. And in the meantime, the promise made in his 1931 poem remained a half-fulfilled dream:

'Great gusts of wind and dust choked half the world.
Workers and peasants in their millions were wakened up,
Acting with one mind.'

Select Biblography

Only those works used directly in the preparation of this book or cited in the text are listed here. Studies on the system of government in China and the progress of the economy used purely for background have been excluded. Articles referred to in this book have not been included in the bibliography for reasons of space. Wherever possible, the most accessible or permanent source of reference materials has been used: MacFarquhar's *China Under Mao*, for example, rather than the original articles in the *China Quarterly* which his compilation contains.

Acton, H.B. *The Morals of Markets: An Ethical Exploration*. London: Longman, 1971.

Adelman, Irma. *Theories of Economic Growth and Development*. Stanford University Press, 1965.

The Agrarian Reform Law of the People's Republic of China: and Other Relevant Documents. Peking: Foreign Languages Press, 1959.

Allen, G.C. and Donnithorne, Audrey G. *Western Enterprise in Far Eastern Economic Development: China and Japan*. London: George Allen & Unwin, 1962.

Anschel, Kurt R., Brannon, Russell H. and Smith, Eldon D. (eds.) *Agricultural Co-operatives and Markets in Developing Countries*. New York: Frederick A. Praeger, 1969.

Aron, Raymond. *Main Currents in Sociological Thought 1: Montesquieu, Comte, Marx, Tocqueville, The Sociologists and the Revolution of 1848*. London: Penguin, 1969.

Aron, Raymond. *Main Currents in Sociological Thought 2: Durkheim, Pareto, Weber*, London: Penguin, 1970.

Balazs, Etienne. *Chinese Civilization and Bureaucracy: Variations on a Theme*. New Haven: Yale University Press, 1968.

Ballon, Robert J. (ed.) *The Japanese Employee*. Tokyo: Sophia University, 1969.

Baran, Paul A. and Sweezy, Paul M. *Monopoly Capital: An Essay on the American Economic and Social Order*. London: Penguin, 1968.

Belshaw, Cyril S. *The Conditions of Social Performance: An Exploratory Theory*. London: Routledge & Kegan Paul, 1969.

Beteille, André. *(ed.) Social Inequality: Selected Readings*. London: Penguin, 1969.

Betrayal of Proletarian Dictatorship is the Heart of the Book on "Self Cultivation". Peking: Foreign Languages Press, 1967.

Bhagwati, Jagdish and Eckaus, Richard S. (eds.) *Foreign Aid: Selected Readings*. London: Penguin, 1970.

Bienen, Henry. *Violence and Social Change: A Review of Current Literature*. The University of Chicago Press, 1968.

Bodde, Derek. *China's Cultural Tradition: What and Whither*. New York: Holt, Rinehart and Winston, 1957.

Boserup, Ester. *The Conditions of Agricultural Growth: The Economics of Agrarian Change under Population Pressure*. London: George Allen & Unwin, 1965.

Brown, Lester R. *Seeds of Change: The Green Revolution and Development in the 1970s*. London: Pall Mall Press, 1970.

Bruton, Henry J. *Principles of Development Economics*. Englewood Cliffs: Prentice-Hall, 1965.

The Case of Peng Teh-huai, 1959-1968. Hong Kong: Union Research Institute, 1968.

Chen Po-ta, *Mao Tse-tung on the Chinese Revolution*. Peking: Foreign Languages Press, 1963.

Chen Po-ta, *Notes on Mao Tse-tung's "Report of an Investigation into the Peasant Movement in Hunan"*. Peking: Foreign Languages Press, 1954.

Ch'en, Jerome. *Mao and the Chinese Revolution*. New York: Oxford University Press, 1967.

Ch'en, Jerome. (ed.) *Mao Papers: Anthology and Bibliography*. London: Oxford University Press, 1970.

SELECT BIBLIOGRAPHY

Chin, Steve S.K. and King, Frank H.H. (eds.) *Selected Seminar Papers on Contemporary China, I.* University of Hong Kong, 1971.

China's Renminbi: One of the Few Most Stable Currencies in the World. Peking: Foreign Languages Press, 1969.

The Chinese Communes: A Documentary Review and Analysis of the 'Great Leap Forward'. London: Soviet Survey.

Clark, Colin and Haswell, Margaret. *The Economics of Subsistence Agriculture.* London: Macmillan, 1964.

Cohen, Arthur A. *The Communism of Mao Tse-tung.* The University of Chicago Press, 1968.

Compton, Boyd. *Mao's China: Party Reform Documents, 1942-44.* Seattle: University of Washington Press, 1966.

Crick, Bernard. *In Defence of Politics.* London: Penguin, 1964.

Developing Rural India: Plan and Practice. New York: Cornell University Press, 1968.

Development of the Emerging Countries: An Agenda for Research. Washington, D.C.: The Brookings Institution, 1965.

Donnithorne, Audrey. *China's Economic System.* London: George Allen & Unwin, 1967.

Dore, R.P. *Land Reform in Japan.* London: Oxford University Press, 1966.

Downs, Anthony. *An Economic Theory of Democracy.* New York: Harper & Row, 1957.

Due, John F. *Intermediate Economic Analysis.* Homewood: Richard D. Irwin, 1958.

Duncan, Hugh Dalziel. *Communication and Social Order.* London: Oxford University Press, 1968.

Duverger, Maurice, *The Idea of Politics: The Uses of Power in Society.* London: Methuen, 1966.

Federalism and Economic Growth in Underdeveloped Countries. London: George Allen & Unwin, 1961.

Fehl, Noah Edward. *Rites and Propriety in Literature and Life: A Perspective for a Cultural History of Ancient China.* The Chinese University of Hong Kong, 1971.

Fitzgerald, C.P. *The Birth of Communist China.* London: Penguin, 1970.

Fox, Karl A. and Johnson, D. Gale. (eds.) *Readings in the Economics of Agriculture.* London: George Allen & Unwin, 1970.

George, Alexander L. *The Chinese Communist Army in Action: The Korean War and Its Aftermath.* New York: Columbia University Press, 1969.

Ginsberg, Morris. *Essays in Sociology and Social Philosophy.* London: Penguin, 1968.

Goodwin, R.M. *Elementary Economics from the Higher Standpoint.* Cambridge University Press, 1970.

Great Victory for Chairman Mao's Revolutionary Line. Peking: Foreign Languages Press, 1967.

Hadley, Eleanor M. *Antitrust in Japan.* Princeton University Press, 1970.

Heilbroner, Robert L. (ed.) *Economic Means and Social Ends: Essays in Political Economics.* Englewood Cliffs: Prentice-Hall, 1969.

Hirschman, Albert O. *The Strategy of Economic Development.* New Haven: Yale University Press, 1965.

The Historical Experience of the Dictatorship of the Proletariat. Peking: Foreign Languages Press, 1961.

Hoselitz, Bert F. *Sociological Aspects of Economic Growth.* London: The Free Press of Glencoe, 1964.

Howe, Christopher. *Employment and Economic Growth in Urban China 1949-1957.* Cambridge University Press, 1971.

Hsiung, James Chieh. *Ideology and Practice: The Evolution of Chinese Communism.* New York: Praeger Publishers, 1970.

Hsueh Mu-chiao, Su Hsing and Lin Tse-li. *The Socialist Transformation of the National Economy in China.* Peking: Foreign Languages Press, 1960.

Hyppolite, Jean. *Studies on Marx and Hegel.* London: Heinemann, 1969.

Hucker, Charles O. *The Traditional Chinese State in Ming Times (1368-1644).* Tucson: The University of Arizona Press, 1970.

253

Ingham, Geoffrey K. *Size of Industrial Organization and Worker Behaviour*. Cambridge University Press, 1970.

Isaacs, Harold R. *The Tragedy of the Chinese Revolution*. Stanford University Press, 1962.

Jacobs, Norman. *Modernization without Development: Thailand as an Asian Case Study*. New York: Praeger Publishers, 1971.

Jahoda, Gustav. *The Psychology of Superstition*. London: Penguin, 1970.

Jewkes, John, Sawers, David and Stillerman, Richard. *The Sources of Invention*. London: Macmillan, 1969.

Johnson, Harry G. *Essays in Monetary Economics*. London: George Allen & Unwin, 1967.

Jones, E.L. and Woolf, S.J. (eds.) *Agrarian Change and Economic Development: The Historical Problems*. London: Methuen, 1969.

Jones, Philip P. and Poleman, Thomas T. *Communes and the Agricultural Crisis in Communist China*. Stanford: Food Research Institute, 1962.

Kang Chao. *Agricultural Production in Communist China, 1949-1965*. Madison: The University of Wisconsin Press, 1970.

Keizer, Willem. *The Soviet Quest for Economic Rationality: The Conflict of Economic and Political Aims in the Soviet Economy, 1953-1968*. Rotterdam University Press, 1971.

Kindleberger, Charles P. *Economic Development*. New York: The McGraw-Hill Book Company, 1958.

Klein, Lawrence and Ohkawa, Kazushi. (eds.) *Economic Growth: The Japanese Experience Since the Meiji Era*. Homewood: Richard D. Irwin, 1968.

Lamfalussy, A. *Investment and Growth in Mature Economies: The Case of Belgium*. London: Macmillan, 1961.

Landes, David S. *The Unbound Prometheus: Technological Change and Industrial Development in Western Europe from 1750 to the Present*. Cambridge University Press, 1969.

Lange, Oskar and Taylor, Fred M. *On the Economic Theory of Socialism*. New York: McGraw-Hill Book Company, 1965.

Latey, Maurice. *Tyranny: A Study in the Abuse of Power*. London: Macmillan, 1969.

Leibenstein, Harvey. *Economic Backwardness and Economic Growth: Studies in the Theory of Economic Development*. New York: John Wiley & Sons, 1963.

Levenson, Joseph R. *Liang Ch'i-Ch'ao and the Mind of Modern China*. Berkeley: University of California Press, 1970.

Lewis, John Wilson. *Leadership in Communist China*. Ithaca: Cornell University Press, 1966.

Lewis, John Wilson. (ed.) *Party Leadership and Revolutionary Power in China*. Cambridge University Press, 1970.

Lewis, W. Arthur. *The Principles of Economic Planning*. London: Unwin University Books, 1965.

Lewis, W. Arthur. *The Theory of Economic Growth*. London: George Allen & Unwin, 1960.

Leys, Collin. (ed.) *Politics and Change in Developing Countries: Studies in the Theory and Practice of Development*. Cambridge University Press, 1969.

Li Yu-ning. *The Introduction of Socialism into China*. New York: Columbia University Press, 1971.

Lifton, Robert Jay. *Revolutionary Immortality: Mao Tse-tung and the Chinese Cultural Revolution*. London: Weidenfeld & Nicolson, 1969.

Lifton, Robert J. *Thought Reform and the Psychology of Totalism: A Study of 'Brainwashing' in China*. London: Penguin, 1967.

Little, I.M.D. *A Critique of Welfare Economics*. Oxford: The Clarendon Press, 1958.

Liu, James T.C. and Tu, Wei-ming. (eds.) *Traditional China*. Englewood Cliffs: Prentice-Hall, 1970.

Lowe, Adolph. *On Economic Knowledge: Toward a Science of Political Economics*. New York: Harper & Row, 1965.

Lowenthal, Richard. (ed.) *Issues in the Future of Asia: Communist and Non-Communist Alternatives*. London: Frederick A. Praeger, 1969.

MacFarquhar, Roderick. (ed.) *China Under Mao: Politics Takes*

Command: A Selection of Articles from the China Quarterly. Cambridge: The M.I.T. Press, 1966.

Maddison, Angus. *Economic Progress and Policy in Developing Countries.* London: George Allen & Unwin, 1970.

Mansfield, Edwin. *The Economics of Technological Change.* London: Longman, 1969.

Marris, Robin. *The Economic Theory of 'Managerial' Capitalism.* London: Macmillan, 1964.

Marshall, Alfred. *Elements of Economics of Industry: Being the First Volume of Elements of Economics.* London: Macmillan, 1909.

McClelland, David C. and Winter, David G. *Motivating Economic Achievement.* New York: The Free Press, 1969.

Meier, Gerald M. and Baldwin, Robert E. *Economic Development: Theory, History, Policy.* New York: John Wiley & Sons, 1964.

Montgomery, John D. and Stiffin, William J. (eds.) *Approaches to Development: Politics, Administration and Change.* New York: McGraw-Hill Book Company, 1966.

Moodie, Graeme C. and Studdert-Kennedy, Gerald. *Opinions, Publics and Pressure Groups: An Essay on Vox Populi and Representative Government.* London: George Allen & Unwin, 1970.

Moore, Barrington, Jr. *Social Origins of Dictatorship and Democracy: Lord and Peasant in the Making of the Modern World.* London: Penguin, 1969.

Moore, Charles A. (ed.) *The Chinese Mind: Essentials of Chinese Philosophy and Culture.* Honolulu: East-West Center Press, 1967.

Myint, H. *Economic Theory and the Underdeveloped Countries.* New York: Oxford University Press, 1971.

Myrdal, Gunnar. *Asian Drama: An Inquiry into the Poverty of Nations.* Vols. I, II and III. New York: Pantheon, 1968.

Myrdal, Gunnar. *Economic Theory and Underdeveloped Regions.* London: Methuen, 1963.

National Programme for Agricultural Development, 1956-1967. Peking: Foreign Languages Press, 1960.

Niu Chung-huang. *China Will Overtake Britain.* Peking: Foreign Languages Press, 1958.

Nove, Alec. *The Soviet Economy: An Introduction*. London: George Allen & Unwin, 1968.

On Khrushchov's Phoney Communism and Its Historical Lessons for the World. Peking: Foreign Languages Press, 1964.

Parthasarathy, Gogula. *Agricultural Development and Small Farmers: A Study of Andhra Pradesh*. Delhi: Vikas Publications, 1971.

Patchen, Martin. *Participation, Achievement and Involvement on the Job*. Englewood Cliffs: Prentice-Hall, 1970.

Perkins, Dwight H. *Market Control and Planning in Communist China*. Cambridge: Harvard University Press, 1966.

Pigou, A.C.*The Economics of Welfare*. London: Macmillan, 1960.

Pollard, Sidney. *The Genesis of Modern Management: A Study of the Industrial Revolution in Great Britain*. London: Penguin, 1968.

Proposals of the Eighth National Congress of the Communist Party of China for the Second Five-year Plan for Development of the National Economy (1958-1962). Peking: Foreign Languages Press, 1956.

Prybyla, Jan S. *The Political Economy of Communist China*. Scranton: International Textbook Company, 1970.

Pye, Lucian W. *The Spirit of Chinese Politics: A Psychocultural Study of the Authority Crisis in Political Development*. Cambridge: The M.I.T. Press, 1968.

Pye, Lucian W. (ed.) *Communications and Political Development*. Princeton University Press, 1967.

Robinson, E.A.G. and Kidron, Michael. (eds.) *Economic Development in South Asia*. London: Macmillan, 1970.

Robinson, Joan. *Economic Philosophy*. London: Penguin, 1964.

Robinson, Joan. *Freedom & Necessity: An Introduction to the Study of Society*. London: George Allen & Unwin, 1970.

Robinson, Thomas W. (ed.) *The Cultural Revolution in China*. Berkeley: University of California Press, 1971.

Rosovsky, Henry. (ed.)*Industrialization in Two Systems: Essays in Honor of Alexander Gerschenkron*. New York: John Wiley & Sons, 1966.

Salter, W.E.G. *Productivity and Technical Change.* Cambridge University Press, 1969.

Schickele, Rainer. *Agrarian Revolution and Economic Progress: A Primer for Development.* New York: Frederick A. Praeger, 1968.

Schram, Stuart. *Political Leaders of the Twentieth Century: Mao Tse-tung.* London: Penguin, 1970.

Schram, Stuart. *The Political Thought of Mao Tse-tung.* London: Penguin, 1969.

Scitovsky, Tibor. *Welfare and Competition: The Economics of a Fully Employed Economy.* London: Unwin University Books, 1963.

Second Session of the Eighth National Congress of the Communist Party of China. Peking: Foreign Languages Press, 1958.

Seven Letters Exchanged Between the Central Committees of the Communist Party of China and the Communist Party of the Soviet Union. Peking: Foreign Languages Press, 1964.

Sen, A.K. *Choice of Techniques: An Aspect of the Theory of Planned Economic Development.* Oxford: Basil Blackwell, 1968.

Sen, Amartya. (ed.) *Growth Economics: Selected Readings.* London: Penguin, 1970.

Shaffer, Harry G. and Prybyla, Jan S. (eds.) *From Underdevelopment to Affluence: Western, Soviet, and Chinese Views.* New York: Appleton-Century-Crofts, 1968.

Shand, R.T. (ed.) *Agricultural Development in Asia.* Canberra: Australian National University Press, 1969.

Sharin, Teodor. (ed.) *Peasants and Peasant Societies: Selected Readings.* London: Penguin, 1971.

Smith, Peter B. (ed.) *Group Processes: Selected Readings.* London: Penguin, 1970.

Snow, Edgar. *Red China Today: The Other Side of the River.* London: Penguin, 1970.

Socialist Industrialization and Agricultural Collectivization in China. Peking: Foreign Languages Press, 1964.

Sources of Chinese Tradition. Vol. I. New York: Columbia University Press, 1966.

Spiegelglas, Stephen and Welsh, Charles J. (eds.) *Economic Development: Challenge and Promise*. Englewood Cliffs: Prentice-Hall, 1970.

Strauss, Erich. *Soviet Agriculture in Perspective: A Study of its Successes and Failures*. London: George Allen & Unwin, 1969.

The Struggle Between the Two Roads in China's Countryside. Peking: Foreign Languages Press, 1968.

Surveys of Economic Theory: Growth and Development. Vol. II. London: Macmillan, 1965.

Takahashi, Kamekichi. *The Rise and Development of Japan's Modern Economy: The Basis for "Miraculous" Growth*. Tokyo: The Jiji Press, 1969.

Take the Road of Integrating with the Workers, Peasants and Soldiers. Peking: Foreign Languages Press, 1970.

Teng Hsiao-ping. *Report on the Rectification Campaign*. Peking: Foreign Languages Press, 1957.

Thompson, E.P. *The Making of the English Working Class*. London: Penguin, 1968.

Townsend, James R. *Political Participation in Communist China*. Berkeley: University of California Press, 1969.

Treadgold, Donald W. (ed.) *Soviet and Chinese Communism: Similarities and Differences*. Seattle: University of Washington Press, 1968.

Tung Ta-lin. *Agricultural Co-operation in China*. Peking: Foreign Languages Press, 1959.

Valsan, E.H. *Community Development Programs and Rural Local Government: Comparative Case Studies of India and the Philippines*. New York: Praeger Publishers, 1970.

Warr, Peter B. (ed.) *Thought and Personality: Selected Readings*. London: Penguin, 1970.

Vogel, Ezra F. *Canton Under Communism: Programs and Politics in a Provincial Capital, 1949-1968*. Cambridge: Harvard University Press, 1969.

Wilczynski, J. *The Economics of Socialism: Principles Governing the Operation of the Centrally Planned Economies in the USSR and Eastern Europe under the New. System*. London: George Allen & Unwin, 1970.

SELECT BIBLIOGRAPHY

Wiles, P.J.D. *Communist International Economics*. Oxford: Basil Blackwell, 1968.

Wilson, Dick. *Asia Awakes: A Continent in Transition*. London: Weidenfeld & Nicolson, 1970.

Wirth, Louis. *On Cities and Social Life: Selected Papers*. The University of Chicago Press, 1964.

Wriggins, W. Howard. *The Ruler's Imperative: Strategies for Political Survival in Asia and Africa*. New York: Columbia University Press, 1969.

Wu Yu-chang. *The Revolution of 1911*. Peking: Foreign Languages Press, 1962.

Yao Wen-yuan. *Comments on Tao Chu's Two Books*. Peking: Foreign Languages Press, 1968.

Zagoria, Donald S. *The Sino-Soviet Conflict, 1956-1961*. Princeton University Press, 1962.

Zinkin, Maurice. *Development for Free Asia*. London: Chatto & Windus, 1963.

Subject Index

261

Author Index

AUTHOR INDEX